COMPETING VOICES FROM THE MEXICAN REVOLUTION

FIGHTING WORDS

COMPETING VOICES FROM THE MEXICAN REVOLUTION

Chris Frazer

GREENWOOD PRESS
An Imprint of ABC-CLIO, LLC

A B C C L I O

Santa Barbara, California • Denver, Colorado • Oxford, England

Library of Congress Cataloging-in-Publication Data

Competing voices from the Mexican Revolution : fighting words /
  [edited by] Chris Frazer.
     p. cm. — (Fighting words)
  Includes bibliographical references and index.
     ISBN 978-1-84645-037-2 (hard copy : alk. paper) — 978-0-313-38513-1 (ebook)
  1. Mexico—History—Revolution, 1910-1920—Sources. I. Frazer, Chris, 1959–
F1234.C734 2009
972.08′16—dc22   2009036457

14 13 12 11 10   1 2 3 4 5

This book is also available on the World Wide Web as an eBook.
Visit www.abc-clio.com for details.

Greenwood Press
An Imprint of ABC-CLIO, LLC

ABC-CLIO, LLC
130 Cremona Drive, P.O. Box 1911
Santa Barbara, California 93116-1911

This book is printed on acid-free paper ∞

Manufactured in the United States of America

CONTENTS

SERIES FOREWORD

Fighting Words is a unique new series aimed at a broad audience, from college-level professors and undergraduates to high-school teachers, students, and the general reader. Each volume in this series focuses on a unique historical controversy, told through firsthand accounts from the diverse perspectives of both the victors and the vanquished. The series is designed to introduce readers to a broad range of competing narratives about the past, giving voices to those often left silent in the secondary literature.

Each volume offers competing perspectives through relatively short primary documents, such as newspaper articles, contemporary chronicles, excerpts from participants' letters or memoirs, as well as other carefully selected sources; brief introductions provide the necessary background information and context to help guide readers through the disparate accounts. Where necessary, key documents are reproduced in their entirety. However, most of the documents are brief in nature, and sharp in content, which will help to promote general classroom discussion and debate. The inclusion of vivid and colorful accounts from the participants themselves, combined with other primary sources from all sides, gives the series an exciting and engaging flavor.

The *Fighting Words* series is designed to promote meaningful discussion and debate about the past. Furthermore, the volumes in this series encourage readers to think critically about the evidence that historians use, or ignore, to reconstruct an understanding of that past. Each volume will challenge accepted assumptions about the topics covered, and readers will question the nature of primary sources, the motivations, the agendas and perspectives of the authors, and the silences inherent in all of the sources. Ultimately, readers will be left to ponder the question, whose history is this?

J. Michael Francis

ABOUT THE SERIES EDITOR

Dr. J. Michael Francis received his PhD in 1998 from the University of Cambridge, where he specialized in colonial Latin American history. Since then, he has taught at the University of North Florida, where he is an associate professor of history. He has written numerous articles on the history of early-colonial New Granada (Colombia). In 2006, he edited a three-volume reference work called *Iberia and the Americas: Culture, Politics, and History* (ABC-CLIO). His most recent book, *Invading Colombia: Spanish Accounts of the Gonzalo Jiménez de Quesada Expedition of Conquest*, was published in 2007 by Penn State University Press.

Dr. Francis serves as book review editor for the journal *Ethnohistory* and series co-editor for *Latin American Originals* (Penn State University Press). He also sits on the advisory board of the University Press of Florida. In 2007, Dr. Francis was appointed as a research associate at the American Museum of Natural History in New York. At present, he is completing a new manuscript entitled *Politics, Murder, and Martyrdom in Spanish Florida: Don Juan and the Guale Uprising of 1597*, which will be published in 2009 by the American Museum of Natural History Press.

ABOUT THE AUTHOR

Dr. Chris Frazer is an associate professor at St. Francis Xavier University, in Antigonish, Nova Scotia, Canada. Dr. Frazer teaches and researches Latin American history, with a focus on modern Mexico and Cuba. Dr. Frazer is the author of *Bandit Nation: A History of Outlaws and Cultural Struggle in Mexico, 1810–1920*.

ACKNOWLEDGMENTS

A project like this collection does not happen without a host of helping and able hands. Here, I would like to thank a few who have been indispensable in bringing this work to completion. At the top of the list are my wife, Mena Enxuga, and our daughters, Rachelle and Daniella, who patiently endured my moments of distraction but always encouraged my efforts. I am also grateful to the editor of the *Fighting Words* series, J. Michael Francis, associate professor at the University of North Florida, for pitching this project to me a few short years ago. At the time it seemed a bit daunting but also a lot of fun, and I am glad to have accepted. This project allowed me to return to the Mexican Revolution in its broad sweep, and to bring a fresh set of eyes to the primary sources of this pivotal historical event. My sincere thanks go to Simon Mason, the former Senior Acquisitions Editor for Greenwood World Publishing who gave the original green light on this volume, and to Mariah Gumpert who inherited this project as the Acquisitions Editor for ABC-CLIO when it purchased Greenwood. Making this project happen also required support and encouragement from my colleagues at St. Francis Xavier University, and most importantly my department chair at the time, Dr. Nancy Forestell. I must also acknowledge the financial support I received from the St. FX University Council on Research, which allowed me to visit archives and libraries in Mexico City and the United States. In Mexico City, I benefited from the hospitality and friendship of the *Casa de los Amigos*, a Quaker guest house, and its staff and guests. They have become a second home for me, and I always anticipate my visits to *la ciudad* for this reason alone. I must also express my deep appreciation and respect for the archivists and librarians at the *Archivo General de la Nación* in Mexico City, the Nettie Lee Benson Latin American Collection at the University of Texas at Austin, and the librarians at Brown University and Harvard University. Finally, I must say a word about the translations. Many of the documents in this collection have not previously appeared in English translation from the Spanish original; except where indicated, all translations are my own, and I am alone responsible for any inaccuracies or errors.

INTRODUCTION

The Mexican Revolution was a landmark in Latin American, and even world, history, and it was certainly the defining historical event for Mexico in the twentieth century. The military phase of the Revolution lasted from 1910 to 1920, while the institutional phase—that of state-building—lasted to 1940, including the most radical period of construction and land reform. Until it was displaced as the model in 1959 by the Cuban Revolution, the Mexican Revolution persisted as a template for revolutionary Latin American nationalists who hoped to pry their region loose from the grip of North American and European neocolonialism. Within Mexico itself, the Revolution gave rise to a new state and a new ruling class, refashioned the terms of national identity, created a new roster of national heroes linked to the revolutionary struggle, and in the Constitution of 1917, forged the social and political rights to which Mexicans feel entitled today. In the twenty-first century, the Revolution remains a touchstone for Mexicans as they struggle to democratize and redefine their nation in the context of globalization and neoliberalism. There is probably no better expression of this enduring legacy than the confrontation that unfolded in 1994, when Mayan peasants in the southern state of Chiapas rebelled against the government of outgoing president Carlos Salinas de Gortari, which had introduced a neoliberal reform and signed the North American Free Trade Agreement (NAFTA) with the United States and Canada. Among other things, the NAFTA led to the removal of sections in the Constitution that had guaranteed land reform to peasant communities. The rebels called themselves the *Ejército Zapatista de Liberación Nacional* (EZLN), or the Zapatista Army of National Liberation, a reference to the most revered figure of the Mexican Revolution, Emiliano Zapata, whose principal goal in fighting the Revolution had been the redistribution of land to the peasants.

For nearly 100 years, the Revolution has influenced what it means to be Mexican, and it continues to cast a long shadow over contemporary struggles in Mexico. For most of this period, the dominant political reality in Mexico was the pervasive influence of the *Partido Revolucionario Institucional* (PRI), or Institutional Revolutionary Party, which established a de facto monopoly over state power from 1929, until Vicente Fox and the conservative *Partido Acción Nacional* (PAN, National Action Party) defeated PRI in the presidential elections of 2000.[1] During these decades, the PRI's legitimacy and longevity depended on a vast network of patronage, on its control of state institutions and enterprises, and by its (public and official) rhetorical identification with the Revolution. However, the radical momentum of the Revolution crested with the presidency of Lázaro Cárdenas in 1934–1940, with the implementation of a sweeping land reform, labor militancy, and the nationalization of key industries like the oil fields and the railroads. Thereafter, the PRI and Mexican presidents became increasingly conservative, and a widening gap opened between the Party's revolutionary rhetoric and political practice. By the mid-1960s, many Mexicans, and especially intellectuals, students, and political activists, began to ask if the Revolution and promises were dead. Their desire to reassess the Revolution, and the postrevolutionary history of Mexico, accelerated after 1968 when the regime of President Gustavo Díaz Ordaz sanctioned a massacre of university students who were protesting in Tlatelolco to demand greater democracy and social justice —in essence, insisting that the state fulfill the mandate of the Revolution. Events over the next 25 years saw Mexico lurch through a dirty war that PRI waged against left-wing political opponents in the 1970s, economic growth and collapse in the 1980s, and a shift toward neoliberalism in PRI policies. All of this began to unravel a constructed social consensus in Mexico that had been based on the PRI's mythical representation of the Revolution as a "monolithic popular revolution, seamless and uniform." [2] This precipitated an erosion of confidence in the PRI's revolutionary credentials, dividing the Party between a conservative faction that was dedicated to neoliberalism and a more radical faction that continued to identify with a radical nationalist vision derived from the Revolution. By the 1990s, the divide became official with the formation of a new leftist *Partido Revolucionario Democratico* (PRD, the Revolutionary Democratic Party). The split, combined with popular opposition to PRI neoliberalism, provided an opening for the ascent of the PAN to the presidency.

Meanwhile, the desire of intellectuals and activists, in Mexico and abroad, to reinterpret the Revolution continued to grow, so that the Revolution of 1910 became the dominant topic of Mexican historiography dealing with the national period (that is to say, the historical period after Mexico achieved independence). In the last three decades of the twentieth century, historians effectively debunked the old PRI orthodoxy as a political myth of post-1920 state-building. However, this has not led to a new historical consensus about the Mexican Revolution. A few have even cast doubt over whether the Revolution merits being called a revolution, arguing that the upheavals of 1910–1920 were more akin to an extremely violent and destructive rebellion that did little more than bring to power a new generation of disgruntled middle-class nationalists. However, most historians still see the Revolution as fundamentally transformative and agree, at a minimum, that it "led to the destruction of old social, political, and economic patterns in favour of newer ones." [3] All the same, historians continue to debate the origins, trajectory, nature, and outcome of the Mexican Revolution. In broad strokes, the main interpretive differences are two: those who recognize that the Revolution was complex and heterogeneous, but who see it as fundamentally popular and agrarian, and who locate the roots of the revolution in the social crisis imposed on lower-class Mexicans—mainly the peasantry—by the impact of economic growth in Mexico's export sectors (raw materials and agricultural products); and revisionists who downplay the role of the peasant classes, and emphasize the role of the middle classes and elite dissidents who demanded political and nationalist reforms that would lead to a more inclusive and democratic society.[4] Also at issue is whether or not it is still valid to demonize the Porfirian era, as the old PRI mythology had done, and to what extent post-1920 state-building created a refurbished model of the Porfirian state.

The best history writing attempts to handle evidence objectively and to interpret it fairly and accurately. However, history writing is never a neutral affair. This book, which consists of edited, translated, and abridged primary sources, does not pretend to solve the historiographic debates mentioned above. Nor does it attempt to offer a comprehensive survey of the Revolution and its controversies. However, it is necessary to acknowledge that it has been influenced in the selection, handling, and organization of sources by the "school" of interpretation that sees the Revolution as fundamentally popular and agrarian. In the end, though, this book invites students and other readers to draw their own conclusions about the origins and nature of the Revolution. The principal purpose of this collection is to help the reader unpack and understand the frequently perplexing conflicts, and shifting alliances, and issues that characterized the struggles waged by the different classes, social groups, military forces, and political interests that had a vital stake in the outcome of the Mexican Revolution.

In this volume, the reader will encounter a wide range of documents and sources that seek to illuminate the diversity and clash of opinions at various moments during the course of the Revolution. As much as possible, it has avoided reliance on the seemingly endless stream of manifestos and political plans that emanated from the various factions at each juncture of the Revolution. Exceptions have been made for a handful of plans that we may regard as foundational documents—for example, the Plan of San Luis Potosí issued by Francisco Madero, or the Plan of Ayala issued by Emiliano Zapata. For the most part, the plans and manifestos issued during the Revolution make for dull reading and, as the Revolution proceeded—in particular during the civil war that the revolutionary factions waged from 1914 to 1920—such documents tended to adopt formulaic qualities that offer little to illuminate the real differences that existed between contending forces and players. On the other hand, this collection emphasizes excerpts from memoirs, polemical tracts, literary works, diplomatic and political correspondence, and newspaper articles. Readers will encounter the views of key players in the Revolution, including some of the best-known personalities—Mexicans like Porfirio Díaz, Francisco Madero, Emiliano Zapata, Ricardo Flores Magón, and Francisco "Pancho" Villa, to name but a few—as well as other important figures, like Justo Sierra, Francisco Bulnes, Alvaro Obregón, Victoriano Huerta, Heriberto Frías, and Venustiano Carranza. Beyond these, an effort has been made to incorporate the views of more minor Mexican figures who identified with one faction or another. This collection also considers issues of international diplomacy, with special attention to views emanating from the United States. The Revolution attracted attention by most of the powers in the Americas and much of Europe (particularly Britain, France, Germany, and Spain), as well as Japan. However, practical constraints of time, space, and economy ruled out the inclusion of material articulating the perspective of foreign powers or their citizens other than the United States. Thus, readers will encounter the perceptions and arguments of high U.S. officials and diplomats, like U.S. President Woodrow Wilson, or the controversial U.S. Ambassador Henry Lane Wilson, as well as radical writers like John Reed and John Kenneth Turner. Finally, it should be noted that this collection has made a conscious effort to include sources that address both the views and the roles of women who participated in the Revolution, and has also done likewise with popular ballads (known as *corridos* in Mexico) in order to help capture the reactions and perspectives of lower-class Mexicans.

The immediate roots of the Mexican Revolution can be found in the Porfirian era, which was born when General Porfirio Díaz toppled President Sebastián Lerdo in the Revolution of Tuxtepec in 1876. At that time, Díaz accused the incumbent president of violating the constitution by seeking consecutive reelection. Díaz also condemned Lerdo for trampling on state and municipal autonomy, and undermining national sovereignty with generous concessions to U.S. railway promoters. Díaz served a term as president, stepped aside in 1880, and returned in 1884. He then amended the constitution to permit reelection and served seven consecutive terms, granting generous concessions to foreign investors, and eviscerating state and municipal autonomy until Francisco Madero led a revolt that toppled the Porfirian government in 1911, demanding respect for the principle of "no re-election." However, the grievances of Madero and his rebels were not only political. Underlying these were injustices that derived from the economic, social, and cultural changes that Mexicans experienced after Díaz came to power in 1876. The politics of the Porfirian state were authoritarian, for Díaz and his allies viewed the state as an instrument for imposing industrial capitalism and commercial agriculture on a rural population that was still tied to petty commodity production and subsistence farming. The government opened the floodgates to foreign investment from the United States and Europe—$1 billion between 1884 and 1900—and enriched the political and economic elites. Economic growth was based on raw material and agricultural exports. It featured the construction of a railroad network to move products northward and to coastal ports, the mining and the processing of silver and industrial metals in the northern states, the establishment of light manufacturing in central Mexico, oil production in the Gulf of Mexico, and enormous *haciendas* (ranches and estates) dedicated to cattle in the north, sugar and rice in the south, and *henequén* (or sisal) in the Yucatán. This process led to the privatization of public lands and the expropriation of properties belonging to peasants, for the expansion of commercial agriculture required additional land under production, and also cheap labor—as did the mines, railroads, and factories. The expropriation of peasants accomplished this by driving the rural population into the commercial economy as landless rural laborers or as factory hands. By 1910, the concentration of land was so complete that only two percent of the population owned land, while most of the rural population lived and worked on estates and haciendas.

The Porfirian elites relied on legal and extralegal means to achieve their ends, including the military and rural police—known as the *Rurales*. This was the reality of Porfirian order and progress. The favorite slogan of Díaz was, "Bread and the Club," which meant "bread for the army, bread for the bureaucrats, bread for the foreigners, and even bread for the Church—and the club for the common people of Mexico and those who differed with him." [1] Expropriations often occurred through fraud, manipulation, and force, but the elites also used legal means. The first was the 1856 Lerdo Law, which abolished corporate landholding. Originally aimed at the Catholic Church, the law also extinguished communal landowning (the ejido system) by indigenous and other peasant communities. The second was the 1883 Law of Vacant Lands (terrenos baldías) that allowed land companies to acquire one-third of public lands they surveyed. Often these so-called vacant lands were home to communities that could not prove their legal title, and so were dispossessed.

One such slice of bread went to Finance Minister José Yves Limantour who owned vast tracts of "vacant land" in western Chihuahua, home to 200 mestizos (people of mixed indigenous and European descent) in the village of Tomóchic. Limantour leased concessions to foreign logging and mining firms. Tomóchic was one of several military colonies established in the eighteenth and nineteenth centuries to battle the Apaches. In exchange for military service, the colonists received individual and communal land titles. The end of the Apache wars and the onset of modernization made villages like Tomóchic redundant. The Díaz government reneged on the pact between the state and the colonies; it curbed their autonomy and ignored their land titles. Tomóchic eventually resisted. Led by Cruz Chávez in 1891, the village declared that it would recognize no authority except God and rose in rebellion. The government suppressed the uprising, but it required 1,200 federal troops, commanded by General Tomás Rangel, who killed nearly every resident in a battle that lasted two weeks. The rebellion was sparked by several related grievances: encroachments on crop lands and pasturage; impositions by the local *jefe político* (political chief) who coerced their labor; the persistence of drought that imperilled food security; an economic recession that reduced access to jobs in local mines; and disrespect by state and Catholic officials for the religious cult that had developed around a miracle-working adolescent woman named Teresa Urrea, revered as the Saint of Cabora.

★ ★ ★

The Battle of Tomóchic [2]

Heriberto Frías, 1893

Heriberto Frías was born to a bourgeois family in Querétaro but was raised in Mexico City. He was a second lieutenant in the federal force that suppressed Tomóchic. The experience horrified Frías, who began to question the morality and legitimacy of the Díaz government. Frías wrote a fictional account of the battle, published anonymously in the newspaper *El Demócrata*, between 1893 and 1895, and then in book form in 1906. Dismissed from the military and jailed by the government, Frías later became a journalist and supported the revolution in 1910. In this except from his book, the reflections of Second Lieutenant Miguel Mercado, a stand-in for Frías, captures the ambiguities and cultural disconnect that he and many of his middle-class and bourgeois peers felt towards the Tomóchis—but also a sense of discomfort that something was not right with Porfirian society.

A renegade group had taken up arms against the government and they were making a defiant stand in the heart of the Sierra Madre mountains.

What kind of rebellion was this?

The rebels' cause seemed just, although their political objectives were unclear. Their bravery and gift for warfare, however, were legendary.

The Tomóchic fighters were demigods; they were brave, confident, and invincible. Their leader, Cruz Chávez, preached a strange religion, a non-clerical Catholicism of ignorant people lacking in culture.

The government and the clergy had abandoned these aloof and inscrutable people. Although these institutions supplied no services to the people, taxes rose with each passing day.

Second Lieutenant Mercado headed for the camp. Around a soothing fire, Miguel learned more about what he already knew: it had been atrocious and terrible in Tomóchic. It was the subject that everyone kept silent about.

The rebellion involved a handful of men. Although intelligent and strong, they were ignorant. These proud souls adhered to an odd religion that reached way beyond the bounds of convention to schism and lunacy. Then there was Teresa of Cabora, along with those who fanned the flames of her sainthood . . . only a few sparks could be gleaned from the outside: excesses perpetrated by local authorities, sinister bosses, and outrages committed by soldiers.

Once again, Miguel realized that it was thanks to the strong arm of General Díaz that the nation had stamped out the rebellion with one brutal blow. The proud, mystical war cry of Tomóchic, backed by audacity and a few Winchester rifles wielded skilfully in the depths of the mountains, had to be mercilessly smothered.

The second lieutenant tried to imagine the consequences of the Tomóchic contagion spreading. How much needless blood would be spilled then? How soon would the ambitious politicians, greedy and hypocritical, have exchanged the "chilapeno" hats they wore in the uprisings for the top hats worn at official banquets?

From Miguel Mercado's perspective, everything had been inexorably ordained. The Tomóchis had been heroic and had shown themselves worthy of a better destiny—but so too had the troops and the heroic officers. The small tactical errors, the pathetic vices and routines revealed the outmoded Mexican military at its worst. All of it was a symptom of an evil that resided deep within the army. It was a manifestation of a systemic illness that would inevitably yield to the times.

Corrido of Tomóchic[3]

Anonymous

Corridos are narrative ballads that originated in northern Mexico, especially along the frontier with the United States, and became a popular form of oral culture among workers and peasants across the country, most of whom were illiterate. Corridos provided them with news and opinions about contemporary and historical events. Although these ballads are not always reliable sources of historical detail, they are very important for the insights they offer into the attitudes of workers and peasants. This ballad appeared in the north not long after the battle of Tomóchic. It lacks the ambiguity that characterized the novel by Frías, and reflects the sympathy felt by rural residents for the grievances and the struggles of the Tomóchis.

Señores, keep in mind that I am going to sing
the Corrido of Tomóchic, and it's a popular song.

The government decided to finish the Tomóchis.
But day and night—it was a fight for the 11th and the Ninth Battalions.

Rangel took the summit with five hundred men
Oh! They were not well-prepared, and they soon met their match.

The Tomóchis starting shooting from the hill of the Cross;
those ragged Tomóchis were ready to fight.

Cruz Chávez told the soldiers: "It is not easy, baldies,[4]
whatever you think; we are ready for the 11th and Ninth Battalion."

The Tomóchis were brave; they knew how to die in the sun.
They defied deadly shrapnel, and defended their land and their homes.

Eight Tomóchis came out and formed pairs, two by two.
They shouted to the baldies: "Long live the power of God!"

How fine the soldiers looked, with a general at their side.
But Cruz Chávez cried out: "We'll die with the 11th and Ninth Battalion."

Love for Santa Teresita of Cabora, rang out in Cruz Chávez's voice.
But no baldies were inspired to fight and to die with honor.

A brave young Tomóchi cried out: "The holy Mother inspires me;
she is right here beside me as I fight Don Lorenzo Torres."

In Cabora is grace; in Tomóchic, power. But the arrogant Government
had no understanding, so it sent the 11th and Ninth Battalions.

Now the history has been written of this fierce, bloody war;
the baldies fell dead like flies defending their governor.

Women in the church tower were also sharpshooters;
they shed their own blood as they fought for their freedom.

But the Tomóchis were done for and the baldies died too.
Yet God's power lives on as the Supreme Good.

The Tomóchis were brave; they knew how to die in the sun.
They defied deadly shrapnel and defended their homes and their land.

The Planters of Morelos[5]

Rosa King

At the same time as the conflict in Tomóchic, a peon-turned-bandit in
the northern state of Durango was gaining his reputation as a local
Robin Hood. By his own account, Doroteo Arango became the outlaw
Francisco (Pancho) Villa after defending his sister from the abusive
hacendado (landowner) who employed him; Villa shot and wounded
the landowner and then headed for the hills. Meanwhile in the southern
state of Morelos, in 1892, a delegation from the village of Anenecuilco
met with President Díaz to protest the encroachment of a neighboring
hacienda onto their lands. Their pleas were refused and the delegates
were punished for their audacity; one of them, a young Emiliano
Zapata, was sentenced to serve in the army. In Morelos, as elsewhere,
hacendados and peasants inhabited separate worlds, linked only by the
nexus of exploitation. The cultural distance between them is illustrated
by the next selection, written by Rosa King, an English woman who
moved to Cuernavaca, Morelos, in 1907 to establish the Bella Vista
Hotel. As we will see, progress and improvement for the planters meant
the displacement and exploitation of peasants.

About this time Governor Alarcón died and Pablo Escandón was appointed
his successor. Pablo, like many Mexican gentlemen, had been educated in
England, and he often dropped in for tea. Like so many of his class, Pablo was
more at home in Europe than in Mexico; while he loved his own country he
found it a little barbarous. The broad new boulevards, parks, and magnificent

buildings that were being erected in Mexico City were a source of great satisfaction to him. "It is almost Paris!" he said.

"You think it has always been like this Señora King," he said. "But you are wrong. You cannot understand what barbarians we used to be, before Porfirito[6] civilized us. Consider our railroads and telegraphs, ports and industries, financed by the foreign capital he cunningly coaxed in. Today, we are cosmopolitan; our young men, educated abroad, are a credit to their country whilst they amuse themselves in London or Paris. And all the work of Porfirio Díaz!"

Dictator Díaz was a personal friend of Pablo's, and he loved to talk about him. "Thirty-five years in the saddle; no more squabbles and revolts; no foreign emperors [like Maximilian]; peace and prosperity all around . . . There is a man Señora King!"

Pablo's appointment had not been well received in Cuernavaca. The people of Morelos had asked President Díaz to appoint another more popular man. But the request was passed over. It was because of the increasing land disputes that the dictator wanted a man of his own class and clique. At the time, I was sorry that the people were not pulling with Pablo, who had a sincere interest in beautifying our town.

We would discuss this with great animation, for Cuernavaca was close to my heart. I liked the town as it was, but Don Pablo had sensible, practical ideas.

"Look down that street to the market," he'd say. "Fruit squashed all over the place. Dirt. Smells. It's a disgrace to our fair city. What would you say, Señora King, if we took it all away and put a little park there with nice neat walks and a fountain?"

"And the market?" I asked.

"Oh, we shall build a big clean building for that. A stone building, I think. I am going to get the hacendados together and talk to them about it."

"But what have the hacendados to do with the poor little Indian market?"

"Ah," said Pablo, wagging his head. "A market building costs money. And the hacendados have the money."

It was a fact. The hacendados had the money—all of it. Practically the entire state was owned by thirty-six of these great landholders.

Pablo got up. "And now," he said, "to get them together—if they're not all in Mexico City or Paris."

For the hacendados of Morelos were notoriously never at home. They thought of the land in terms of the golden stream that flowed into their laps. If they had lived on their haciendas [estates] they would have seen that the golden stream was tainted with the sweat and blood of their laborers. They might have come to know the smell of wet dark earth in the newly turned furrows and the pride in first fruits, and to understand the passion of the indio [Indian] for the milpa [cornfield] of his fathers.

As it was, the hacendados came down once or twice a year. After a few weeks, they would weary of simple diversions and be off to Mexico City or

Europe. Then, as the calls for money became more urgent, the manager would tighten up and the overseers would drive the peons (landless rural worker), with whips if necessary. I would see the poor wretches, their feet bare and hardened like stones, their backs bent under burdens too heavy for a horse or a mule, treated as people would not treat animals. They could not leave, because they were bound to the land like serfs, by their debt to the hacienda store.

The Strike Continues at Rio Blanco[7]

El País, January 1, 1907

Another source of conflict was the relationship between capital and labor in an industrial setting. In 1906, miners in Cananea, in the northern state of Sonora, went out on strike against the U.S.-owned Consolidated Copper Company. The miners wanted better pay and an end to discriminatory hiring that favored U.S. miners. The authorities used Rurales and Rangers from Arizona to crush the strike and hang the leaders; others went to jail and later joined the revolution. The repression inflamed nationalists who were incensed at the role of U.S. vigilantes during a conflict with a U.S.-owned company on Mexican soil. Another conflict erupted at textile mills in the central Mexican states of Veracruz, Puebla, and Tlaxcala in 1907. Workers at Río Blanco in Veracruz formed a union called the *Gran Círculo de Obreros Libre* (Grand Circle of Free Workers), which spread throughout the industry. Workers in Puebla went on strike, demanding an end to 12-hour days and higher wages; they petitioned Díaz to arbitrate when mill owners closed 96 factories and locked out 30,000 workers. Díaz decided in favor of the mill owners, and the Río Bravo workers went on strike. Company guards shot and killed one worker, and in the ensuing riot, workers burned down the company store. Later, the army and rural police fired into a protest march, killing 100 men, women, and children, wounding hundreds more. The army executed the union chairperson and secretary. The following selection comes from a pro-government newspaper, reporting the government arbitration, just prior to the riot and massacre.

Yesterday the ringleaders of the workers left the capital for Puebla. They had come to Mexico City to meet with Vice-President Ramón Corral, designated by General Díaz to study the matter and to make a recommendation for a prompt end of the strike.

It is not known what the President and Vice-President Ramón Corral decided, but likely they made it clear to the ringleaders that their demands are absurd, will lead to ruin and misery for the workers, and are only supported by a handful of union schemers.

According to information from some groups of workers in the capital, we know that the workers of Puebla will not give these infamous delegates a triumphal welcome, for it is rumoured that they have used strike funds to favour a few workers against the interests of the many.

Whether or not this is the case, it is true that the demands of the workers resulted in a justified defence by the mill owners to ensure that they are not foolishly despoiled of their rights—especially now, when we see the same kind of social movement [the labor and socialist movements] that is presently all the rage in Europe, but which represents nothing more than the ridiculous and isolated pretensions of a few individuals.

The industrialists, and the administrators and managers, of the mills that have shut down, had agreed that they would submit to the decision made on this delicate matter by General Díaz. They explained that they shut their facilities and suspended work because the workers have chosen the wrong path to resolve their grievances—and that the workers' demands are completely unreasonable.

The Strikes of Puebla and Orizaba[8]

Antonio Manero

Despite censorship, Rio Blanco evoked condemnation, even from some Porfirian politicians like Antonio Manero. Manero argued that the repression of workers worked against the regime by damaging its credibility. Manero justified the refusal of the mill owners to accede to the demands of the workers, and characterizes the latter as naïve, but he reserves his harshest criticism for the government.

In the State of Puebla and its environs, big factories manufactured yarn and cotton. The factory workers felt they were paid too little for their work. As a result they formed a powerful union and launched a struggle against the capitalists. They went on strike, sustained by a strike fund. But at that time, the cotton industry was in a serious recessionary crisis. All manufacturers had enormous quantities of finished goods that they could not sell, and thought it was impossible to meet the wage demands.

Since their demands were not met, the workers decided for a general strike in the mills in Puebla and Tlaxcala. Perhaps due to inexperience, the workers did not realize that the timing was wrong. The cotton industry was in a slump, and the manufacturers did not mind closing and locking out the workers for the season.

The consequences were dire for workers, for they were exhausting their resources and could not reach an agreement with the employers. The entire Republic watched this fight between labour and capital closely, including mill workers in Río Blanco who provided donations so that the workers in Puebla and Tlaxcala could continue their strike.

Recognizing that their situation was particularly difficult, the workers decided to ask the President if he would intervene to settle the conflict. They did the same with the governors of Puebla and Tlaxcala, and even with the Bishop of their diocese.

In the midst of this, the manufacturers of Río Blanco decided to close their factories to prevent workers from sending funds to the strikers in Puebla and Tlaxcala. Meanwhile the workers and the industrialists made their arguments to the President.

It must have been difficult for the arbitrator, for the arguments on each side were of undoubted weight. The issue to untangle was essentially economic: the workers argued that the wage was too small; the manufacturers argued that they would have to close the factories if they had to pay a higher wage.

The wages were modified by General Díaz, but this did not satisfy the workers in Río Blanco who were outraged by the closure of their mill. They returned to work, but inwardly boiling with passions that would blow up at the slightest spark.

The outrage was greatest in Río Blanco. Thus the unchecked fury of the workers exploded, not against their employers, but against the company store and its owner, towards whom the workers felt a deep resentment.

For this reason the federal government sent in the army, shot workers mercilessly and without cause, killing and wounding hapless victims whose only offence was a moment of misconduct. The number of those executed remains uncertain, but naturally the excessive rigour of the measure was an injustice, which profoundly affected the whole country.

Porfirio Díaz and the Social Evolution of Mexico[9]

Justo Sierra, 1902

After 1900 the Porfirian bourgeoisie and foreign investors were preoccupied with who might succeed Díaz, who turned 70 that year. The issue became acute as economic and social crises punctuated the first decade of Mexico's twentieth century. Anxiety over the presidential succession underlies this excerpt by Justo Sierra, published in 1902. He was Minister of Education in 1905–1911, one of two prominent *científicos* (scientists) in the Porfirian cabinet; the other was Limantour. Científicos were disciples of the French sociologist Auguste Comte— who advocated rule by technocratic elites until the masses were ready for democracy—and the scientific racism of English philosopher Herbert Spencer who argued that evolution had made some nations, races, and classes more suited to govern than others. Sierra rationalized Díaz's dictatorship as the apex of Mexican development in the nineteenth century. Sierra worried that constant reelection of Díaz would produce an "elective monarchy in Republican disguise," thereby crippling the development of a mature democracy, but he still welcomed the long period of stability as an essential foundation upon which to modernize Mexico.[10]

Something of a choleric unanimity returned the old caudillo of the Tuxtepec revolution to power in 1884. Events in the capital—political anarchy and financial distress—made peace unstable, threatening to revive the cycle of civil war. It seemed that the progress of the last eight years might be lost. Public opinion summoned President Díaz back to power. In 1884, Mexico's liabilities were overwhelming. The government had to restore its credit abroad in order to finance modernization. The key to this was settling the English debt, but this seemed impossible. The government had to rebuild a disorganized Treasury and partially suspend debt payments. It had to restore justice, impose respect for the law, and undo certain coalitions in local government, a clear sign of the morbid weakness afflicting central authority. Such were its *liabilities*. Among its *assets* the administration could count on the reputation of General Díaz. But he needed maximum authority in his hands—not only legal authority, but the *political authority* to lead legislatures and state governments. He needed *social authority* as the supreme arbiter of peace, an authority which flowed from trust in his ability to settle conflicts. And he needed *moral authority*, that indefinable power of someone with absolute clarity of virtues and a singular lack of vanity and pride.

The task of restoring order and confidence went ahead. The demand within in the country was clear, as it was among those who held Mexican debt securities abroad. They wanted assurances that General Díaz could remain in office and continue his work. This was done by amending the Constitution to allow indefinite re-election of the President.

This extinguished the agenda of Tuxtepec. Under the Jacobin guise of democratic principles, it had satisfied momentary passions, but disregarded the real needs of the Nation, and so the Plan of Tuxtepec died. But it also opened the door for foreign capital to exploit the riches of the country. This was the third major turning point in our history: the first was Independence, which gave life to our national personality; the second was the Reform, which gave life to our social personality; the third brought Peace, and gave life to our international personality. These are the three stages of our evolution. In moments of crisis, the people need leaders like Cromwell and Napoleon, as well as Washington, Lincoln, Bismark, Cavour and Juárez; it requires one man, one conscience, one will to unify moral forces, transmute them and drive them forward. This man was President Díaz.

Power was therefore a desideratum of the nation. This nation acclaims the man and has enhanced his power with extralegal entitlements. Díaz has not demanded them, nor does he shrink from wielding them. Is this dangerous? It is terribly dangerous, for it creates habits contrary to government itself, without which there can be great men, but not great peoples. Yet Mexico has confidence in the future. Everything will come in its time. Make no mistake!

Thus, without violating legality, President Díaz has received extraordinary powers. The people's subservience to the President can be called a social dictatorship, or a spontaneous Caesarism. The truth is that one cannot categorize this regime according to classic forms of despotism. It is a personal government that widens, defends and strengthens legal government. It is born of a national will to leave anarchy behind. So our government is authoritarian, because we have entrusted one man to keep peace and lead our economic transformation, to neutralize despotism in other branches of government, to extinguish cacicazgos [local despotism] and to disarm local tyrannies. To properly assess the all-embracing authority of Díaz, one should measure the difference between what was demanded of him and what he has achieved.

The political evolution of Mexico has been sacrificed. This is an unimpeachable fact: there is no political party, no organized group. A few have appeared but they have encountered apathy; they were therefore artificial. The day when a party appears and remains, our political evolution will resume its march, and the man will appear who is more necessary in a democracy than in an aristocracy. The function creates the organ.

But if we compare Mexico at independence with the present, we must agree that the transformation has been surprising. Its full value is evident to those who know the past and witnessed change: peace for ten to twenty years, the dream of a railroad system linking us with the outside world—an endless track of iron along which foreign capital fell like seeds, producing bountiful crops of wealth—the dream of a domestic industry capable of rapid growth. Everything has been done, everything moves, and everything is in place.

Yet we still need to attract immigrant European blood to mix with our indigenous groups, if we do not want to regress. We need to change the mentality of our indigenous people through education. This is an urgent task. Either that or death.

To make the Indian socially useful we must settle him on intensively cultivated land; to identify his spirit with ours through a common language, aspirations, loves and hatreds, mental abilities and moral judgement; to inspire him with the divine ideal of a homeland for all—to create a national soul. That is the program for national education: everything that strives for this is patriotic. Any barrier is a betrayal.

And so it remains to define our tasks: to educate is to strengthen, for freedom—the marrow of lions—is the heritage of the strong, whether individually or collectively. The weak have never been free. Thus, the entire social evolution of Mexico will be abortive and frustrated if we do not arrive at the ultimate end: Freedom.

President Díaz, Hero of the Americas[11]

James Creelman, 1908

In 1908 U.S. journalist James Creelman interviewed President Porfirio Díaz for *Pearson's Magazine*. The interview was to reassure U.S. politicians and investors that Mexico would be stable after the departure of Porfirio Díaz. But it exploded like a bomb in Mexico, for Díaz declared that the Mexican people were ready for democracy and he planned to step down in 1910. Díaz recanted when the looming vacancy precipitated a power struggle over succession among his supporters. He perceived danger in dividing the ruling class when opposition and unrest were mounting. Díaz doused the ambitions of insiders like governor of Nuevo León, General Bernardo Reyes, but could not curb the aspirations of elite dissident Francisco Madero of Coahuila who mounted a vigorous campaign for the presidency in 1910.

Aside from its political importance, the Creelman interview expressed the same científico values articulated by Sierra. It also illustrates the hero worship and personality cult that surrounded Porfirio Díaz. This was a deliberate effort to render Díaz a national patriarch and instill a culture of obedience and deference to authority.

There is not a more romantic or heroic figure in the world, nor one more intensely watched by the friends and foes of democracy, than the soldier-statesman Porfirio Díaz, whose iron rule has converted the warring, ignorant, superstitious and impoverished masses of Mexico into a strong, steady, peaceful, debt-paying and progressive nation.

For twenty-seven years he has governed the Mexican Republic with such power that national elections have become mere formalities. Yet to-day this astonishing man announces that he will retire from the Presidency at the end of his present term, so that he may see his successor peacefully established and that the people of Mexico may show the world that they can change presidents without weakness or war.

"It is a mistake to suppose that the future of democracy in Mexico has been endangered by the long continuance in office of one President," he said quietly. "I can say sincerely that office has not corrupted my ideals and that I believe democracy to be the one true, just principle of government, although in practice it is possible only to highly developed peoples.

"Here in Mexico we have had different conditions. I received this Government from a victorious army at a time when the people were divided and unprepared for the exercise of the extreme principles of democratic government.

"We preserved the republican and democratic form of government. Yet we adopted a patriarchal policy in the actual administration of the nation's affairs, guiding and restraining popular tendencies, with full faith that an enforced peace would allow education, industry and commerce to develop stability and unity in a naturally intelligent, gentle and affectionate people.

"I have waited patiently for the day when the people of the Mexican Republic would be prepared to change their government at every election without danger of armed revolutions and without injury to national credit or interference with national progress. I believe that day has come."

"General Díaz," I interrupted, "you have unprecedented experience in the history of republics. For thirty years the destinies of this nation have been in your hands, to mold them as you will; but men die, while nations must continue to live. Do you believe that Mexico can continue to exist in peace as a republic? Are you satisfied that its future is assured under free institutions?"

"The future of Mexico is assured," he said in a clear voice. "The principles of democracy have not been planted very deep in our people, I fear. But the nation has grown and it loves liberty. Our difficulty has been that people do not concern themselves enough about public matters for a democracy. The individual Mexican thinks much about his own rights and is always ready to assert them. But he does not think so much about the rights of others. He thinks of his privileges, but not of his duties.

"The Indians, who are more than half of our population, care little for politics. They are accustomed to look to those in authority for leadership instead of thinking for themselves."

"But you have no opposition party, Mr. President. How can free institutions flourish when there is no opposition to keep the majority, or governing party, in check?"

"I welcome an opposition party," he said. "If it appears, I regard it as a blessing, not as an evil. And if it can develop power, not to exploit but to govern, I will stand by it, support it, advise it and forget myself in the inauguration of complete democracy in the country.

"It is enough for me that I have seen Mexico rise among the peaceful and useful nations. I have no desire to continue in the Presidency. This nation is ready for her ultimate life of freedom.

"The railway has played a great part in the peace of Mexico," he continued. "When I became President there were two small lines. Now we have nineteen thousand miles of railways. Back then we had a slow and costly mail service and the mail coach would be stopped by highwaymen. Now we have a cheap, safe and rapid mail service. Telegraphing was difficult in those times. Today we have more than forty-five thousand miles of telegraph wires.

"We began by making robbery punishable by death and compelling the execution of offenders within hours after they were caught and condemned. When telegraph wires were cut, we punished the chief officer of the district if he did not catch the criminal; when the cutting occurred on a plantation, the proprietor who failed to prevent it was hanged to the nearest telegraph pole. These were military orders, remember.

"We were harsh, sometimes to the point of cruelty. But it was necessary to the life and progress of the nation. If there was cruelty, results have justified it.

"It was better that a little blood be shed so that much blood could be saved. The blood that was shed was bad; the blood that was saved was good."

"And which do you regard as the greatest force for peace, the army or the schoolhouse?" I asked.

"The schoolhouse. There can be no doubt. All citizens should receive the same training, so that their ideals may be harmonized and national unity intensified. When men read alike and think alike they are more likely to act alike."

"And you believe that the vast Indian population of Mexico is capable of high development?"

"I do. The Indians are gentle and grateful, except the Yaquis and some Mayas. They have the traditions of an ancient civilization. They are to be found among the lawyers, engineers, physicians, army officers and other professional men."

There are nineteen thousand miles of railways, nearly all with American managers, engineers and conductors. One has only to ride the Mexican Central or enjoy the deluxe trains of the National Line to realize the high transportation standards of the country. Two-thirds of the railways are owned by Americans, who have invested about $300,000,000 in them profitably.

More than $1,200,000,000 of foreign capital has been invested in Mexico since President Díaz put stability into the nation. Capital for railways, mines, factories and plantations has been pouring in at the rate of $200,000,000 a year. In six months the Government sold more than a million acres of land.

Americans and other foreigners interested in mines, real estate, factories, railways and other enterprises have assured me many times that, under Díaz, conditions for investment in Mexico are as reliable as the most highly developed European countries. The President declares that these conditions will continue after his death or retirement.

The cities shine with electric lights and are noisy with trolley cars; English is taught in public schools; the public treasury is full and the national debt decreasing; there are seventy thousand foreigners living prosperously in the

Republic—more Americans than Spaniards; public affairs have developed strong men.

It is the hour of growth, strength and peace which convinces Porfirio Díaz that he has finished his task. Such is Porfirio Díaz, foremost man of the American hemisphere. What he has done for a people disorganized and degraded by war, lawlessness and comic opera politics, is the great inspiration, the hope of the Latin-American republics.

The Porfirian Plunderbund[12]

John Kenneth Turner, 1910

An opposite view of Porfirio Díaz emerges in the following portrait by John Kenneth Turner, a left-wing journalist who sympathized with the radical politics of Ricardo Flores Magón and the Mexican Liberal Party. Turner traveled through Mexico in 1908–1909, disguised as a business-man, to investigate social and political conditions. As Mexico headed into revolution in 1910, Turner's findings were published in *Barbarous Mexico*, a sensational exposé of Porfirian corruption and exploitation. He condemned the Porfirian republic as an enormous fraud designed to exploit Mexicans to the sole benefit of the Mexican and foreign elites.

The slavery and peonage of Mexico, the poverty and illiteracy, the general prostration of the people, are due to what I call the "system" of General Porfirio Díaz.

Díaz is the central prop of slavery, but there are other props as well. For example, there is the collection of commercial interests which profit by the Díaz system of slavery and autocracy. Not the least among these commercial interests are American.

Mexico is spoken of throughout the world as a Republic and still pretends to be one. Mexico has a constitution. It provides for a national congress, state legislatures and municipal aldermen to make laws, federal, state and local judges to interpret them, and a president, governors and local executives to administer them. It provides for manhood suffrage, freedom of the press and speech, equality before the law, and other guarantees of life, liberty and the pursuit of happiness.

In defiance of the majority, General Díaz came to the presidency thirty-four years ago. In defiance of the majority he has remained there ever since. Using the army and the police, he controlled elections, the press and public speech and made popular government a farce. By distributing public offices among his generals and granting them free rein to plunder at will, he assured himself of continued army support. By making political deals with men high in the esteem of the Catholic Church he gained the silent support of priests and the Pope.

By promising full payment of all foreign debts and distributing favors among citizens of other countries, he made his peace with the world at large.

He installed his generals as state governors and organized a national plunderbund. Thus he assured himself of the loyalty of the generals and put them where he could most effectively use them to keep down the people. One variety of rich plums he handed out was in the form of charters giving governors the right to organize companies and build railroads, each charter carrying a huge railroad subsidy. In his first term in office Díaz passed sixty-one railroad subsidy acts aggregating $40,000,000 and all but two or three of these were in favour of governors.

The largest perquisite whereby Díaz enriched himself, his family and friends, his governors, his financial ring and his foreign favourites, was the confiscation of the lands of the common people—a confiscation which is going on to this day. Note that this land robbery was the first step of the Mexican people back to bondage as slaves and peons.

The lands of the Yaqui of Sonora were taken and given to political favourites of the ruler. The lands of the Maya of Yucatan, now enslaved by henequen planters, were taken in the same manner. The final act in this confiscation was accomplished in 1904 when the government set aside the last of their lands into a territory called Quintana Roo. This territory contains 43,000 square kilometres or 27,000 square miles which Díaz handed over to eight Mexican politicians.

In like manner practically all native people have been reduced to peonage, if not slavery. Smallholders of every tribe and nation have been expropriated until their number is almost down to zero. Their lands are in the hands of the government machine, or in the hands of foreigners.

This is why the typical Mexican farm is the million-acre farm, why it has been so easy for Americans like William Randolph Hearst, Harrison Gray Otis, E. H. Harriman, the Rockefellers, and the Guggenheims to obtain millions of Mexican acres. This is why members of the Díaz machine are millionaires in Mexican real estate.

Chief among the methods used in taking land away from the people was through a land registration law. This law permitted any person to claim lands if the possessor could not prove title. The result was a plundering. No sooner had it passed than the members of the government formed land companies to select the most desirable lands, register them, and evict the owners. This they did on a tremendous scale. Thus hundreds of thousands of small farmers lost their property. Thus small farmers are still losing their property.

Of course such bandit methods were certain to meet with resistance, and so we find numerous instances of soldiers being called out to enforce collection of taxes or the eviction of time-honored landholders.

Public action is never taken to improve the condition of common people. It is taken to make government more secure. Mexico is a land of special privileges, although special privileges are provided for in the name of the common people. An instance is the "Agricultural Bank," created in 1908. To read the press one would imagine that the government had launched a gigantic and benevolent scheme to re-establish expropriated people in agriculture. But nothing could be further from the truth, for the purpose is to help out the rich farmer. The bank has been lending money for two years, but so far not a single case has been recorded in which aid was given to a small farm.

The special financial privileges in the cities are no less remarkable. There is a financial ring consisting of the Díaz machine and its close associates, who pluck all the financial plums, who get the contracts, the franchises and the concessions, and whom foreign capital uses to secure a footing in the country.

American capital has a smoother time with Díaz than with its own government, which is fine from the point of view of American capital, but not so good from the point of view of the Mexican people. The certainty of foreign intervention in his favour has prevented the Mexican people from using arms to remove a ruler who imposed himself upon them by the use of arms.

Bear in mind that England is nearly as heavily invested in Mexico as the United States. While the USA has $900,000,000 in Mexico, England has $750,000,000. These figures by no means represent the degree of political influence exerted by these two countries. There the United States bests all other countries combined.

To sum up, Díaz has absorbed all of the powerful men and interests within his sphere and made them a part of his machine. And for this the people paid, not only with their lands, but with their flesh and blood. They paid in peonage and slavery. For this they forfeited liberty, democracy and the blessings of progress.

The Presidential Succession in 1910[13]

Francisco Madero, 1908

Francisco Madero was the son of a wealthy landowner and industrialist in the northern state of Coahuila. The Maderos were active in state politics and close to Yves Limantour, the finance minister for Díaz. Yet, the family was excluded from the inner circles of Porfirian politics, the result of Díaz's animus towards Madero's grandfather, Evaristo, who supported Lerdo against Díaz in 1876. Their exclusion exposed the family to economic policies that favored foreign interests to the detriment of entrepreneurs like themselves. The political and economic grievances of the Madero family influenced the attitude of Francisco; he credited Díaz with bringing peace and stability to Mexico, but argued for a more open and democratic system, and especially adherence to the principle of no reelection. In 1908, Madero published *The Presidential Succession in 1910*, critiquing Porfirian politics. In 1909 Madero formed the Anti-Reelectionist Party as the vehicle for his election bid under the slogan of "No Re-election; Effective Suffrage." At first, Díaz refused to take Madero seriously, but the challenger barnstormed Mexico during the election campaign in 1910, riding a wave of support from workers, peasants, middle-class nationalists, and dissident members of the elite who were disenchanted with Díaz. When the incumbent sensed a threat, he moved to preempt Madero. The regime banned the anti-reelectionist movement in June, and jailed Madero in the city of San Luis Potosí. To no one's surprise, the elections delivered an overwhelming vote for Porfirio Díaz on June 21, 1910. Upon his release, Madero fled to the United States where he began to plan a rebellion.

I will begin by studying the causes which have brought about our country's current regime of centralism and absolutism, so that we do not again fall into those errors that have brought such dire consequences. Those causes were not only the continuous revolutions, which always leave a sad inheritance to the people—military dictatorships, which have had different consequences depending on their nature. When centralism and absolutism are frank and audacious, they have no other effect than to mark a break in the democratic development of the people, after which comes a powerful reaction that restores freedom in all its splendour, and allows the people to exercise their rights once more. By contrast, when a dictatorship is established in content rather than form, and when it hypocritically appears to observe the laws and support the Constitution, then it undermines the basis of freedom. It oppresses citizens with a hand that gently caresses and subdues them with the promise of material goods. The example of the ruling classes spreads quickly, so that servility becomes the only way to satisfy the ambition for self-enrichment and material pleasure, an ambition that remains after it has destroyed the noble desire to work for progress and the glory of the motherland.

For these reasons, I assert that a political party constituted according to the aspirations of the nation and inspired by democratic principles, is certain to succeed eventually. Although this victory will be difficult while General Díaz is alive, it will not be if he disappears from the political scene, for then it will be the only well-organized party founded on firm principles.

I appeal to Mexicans to help form this party, which will save our institutions, our freedoms, and even our national integrity. My appeal is also directed toward the man who for over thirty years has been the arbiter of the destiny of our homeland.

I suppose that General Díaz, even though he has enjoyed every possible honour, has seen all his aspirations fulfilled, and has felt for so long the poisonous breath of flattery, will wish to hear the harsh voice of truth and not regard as enemies those who are man enough to show him the precipice on which the motherland stands—and also to show him the remedy.

I may appear presumptuous to think I know more than General Díaz. But based on his statements to Creelman, I am convinced that General Díaz sees this as clearly as I do. If he took up arms against Benito Juárez and Sebastián Lerdo, it was because he saw indefinite re-election as a threat to democratic institutions. This will continue to happen, until political parties are founded on principles that meet national—and not personal—aspirations.

The fact is that General Díaz has worked against his own principles. So it remains my contention that General Díaz is aware that his departure from the Presidency is good for the country. But there are powerful forces that hold him back: his long-standing habit of command; his habit of leading the nation according to his own will; and the pressures of innumerable men—the beneficiaries of all concessions, all lucrative contracts—who call themselves his friends in order [to] satisfy their arrogance and greed. They fear that a new government will deprive them of the favour they now enjoy and skilfully exploit.

These are the reasons why General Díaz wants to continue leading the country. In an interview published in nearly every newspaper, he responded to hints by a relative that he should accept another re-election. He said: "for my homeland and family, everything." As this version was not officially denied, we must believe it—and even more so than the interview with Creelman—for this sounds more like the language and politics of the General.

The Nation is accustomed to obeying orders from its current leader without discussing them. And the Nation, so accustomed, will encounter great difficulties shaking off its servility. Everything is a matter of custom. But they have deep roots in the national soil, and cannot be uprooted without deep changes, without huge efforts, without requiring the selfless cooperation of all good Mexicans.

Yet we do not lose hope. If the Nation moves into the next election campaign, if the supporters of democracy form a strong party, even General Díaz may undergo a change of mind. For the blunt words of a troubled homeland may move the caudillo of the French Intervention and stir a pure patriotism that sets aside small details and miseries that might divert him from his greatest service to his homeland: that of leaving it free to form a government according to its aspirations and needs.

There are other reasons that General Díaz must consider. Anyone who has ruled Mexico for thirty years and linked his entire life to its most important events, and who is close to eighty years, belongs more to history than to the present time. General Díaz should be concerned about his historical reputation, rather than satisfying the greed of those who praise him in pursuit of personal ambitions, who only think of themselves, and have no regard for the motherland or the prestige of his administration.

I esteem General Díaz, because he distinguished himself in defending the country and has wielded absolute power with moderation—a rare deed in recorded history. But this respect does not preclude me from speaking loud and clear. Precisely because I have such a high opinion of him, I believe he will respect my sincerity.

I am not guided by unworthy passions. The only sentiment that guides me is love for the fatherland. All the same, I cannot contain the bitter protests of my soul when describing our wounds; nor can I suppress my outrage when talking of the great infamies committed under this regime.

The Revolution Will Come[14]

Ricardo Flores Magón, 1910

The oddly misnamed Mexican Liberal Party was actually a party of anarchists and socialists, founded in 1905 by Ricardo Flores Magón and his brothers Enrique and Jesús. They had earlier established a newspaper in 1900, *Regeneración*, to promote their views. The brothers, especially Ricardo, faced severe repression. Ricardo and Enrique fled to the United States in 1904, while Jesús abandoned revolutionary politics in favor of Madero's reform movement. Ricardo and Enrique faced harassment and prison north of the border when Díaz asked the United States to enforce neutrality laws that prohibited Mexicans from fomenting revolution from U.S. soil. The Magóns persisted. Their followers, known as Magonistas, were involved with the strikes at Cananea and Río Blanco, as well as founding the *Casa del Obrero Mundial* [House of World Workers] union movement in 1911. The Magóns rejected Madero's strategy of replacing the president and called for the overthrow of the system by means of an armed insurrection. The Magonistas first attempted an uprising in 1908 and were preparing another in 1910 when Francisco Madero was contemplating his options from exile in San Antonio, Texas. The Magonistas issued the following manifesto on November 19, 1910, one day before Madero was to initiate his rebellion. The Magóns ultimately failed, but their ideas did influence subsequent revolutionaries like Emiliano Zapata.

The fruit, ripened by internal rebellion, is ready to fall—a bitter fruit for self-important people whose circumstances bring honours, riches and distinctions—pleasures based on the sorrow and slavery of humankind. But a sweet and pleasant fruit for those who have had their dignity trampled under the hooves of beasts who, in a night lasting thirty-four years, have robbed, violated, murdered, cheated, and committed treachery—hiding their crimes under the mantle of law.

Who is afraid of the Revolution? The same people who oppressed or exploited the popular masses. Those people who have, by acts of injustice and rapine, stirred the conscience of honourable men across the land.

The Revolution will come sooner or later. The symptoms of a formidable cataclysm leave no room to doubt that something is about to emerge, that something else is about to collapse. Finally, after thirty-four years of shame, the Mexican people are raising their heads. Finally, after a long night, they are going to destroy the black edifice that afflicts and suffocates us.

It is time to repeat what we said: we must ensure that this movement does not become a blind effort to free itself from an enormous burden; it must be one in which reason dominates instinct. Libertarians must ensure that this movement takes the path marked by science. If we do not, the emerging Revolution will do nothing more than replace one President with another, or one boss for another. We must bear in mind that the people need bread, shelter, and land to cultivate. We must bear in mind that no government can decree the abolition of misery. It is the people themselves —the hungry and disinherited—who can abolish misery by taking possession of the land. By natural right, the land cannot be the monopoly of a few, but is the property of all humankind. It is not possible to predict where the coming Revolution will lead, but we can help those who struggle in good faith to advance down this road as far as possible: if, when we pick up the Winchester we dedicate ourselves to redeeming the rights of the proletariat, not just to put another boss in power; if we enter the armed struggle to conquer economic liberty, without which no freedoms exist at all. If we make this our purpose, we will channel the coming Revolution onto a road worthy of this epoch. But if we desire an easy victory, if we seek a short contest by abandoning our radical tendencies—so incompatible with the bourgeois and conservative parties—then we will have done the work of bandits and killers for the blood spilt will simply strengthen the bourgeoisie. And after the victory, this caste will gain power and chain the proletariat with its own blood, its own sacrifice, and its own martyrdom.

This is why, proletarians, you must not be misled. The conservative and bourgeois parties speak about freedom, justice, law, and honourable government. They say that changing the men in power will bring freedom, justice, law and honourable government. Do not be deceived! What you need is the welfare of your families and their daily bread; no government can give you that. You must conquer these things by taking possession of the land, which is the original source of wealth. Understand, that no government will give you land because the laws defend the "rights" of the rich. You must take it yourselves, despite the law, despite the government, despite the alleged right of property. You must take it in the name of natural justice and the right [of] every human to live and develop his physical and intellectual abilities.

When you possess the land, you will have freedom and justice, for these are the result of economic independence—the ability to live without depending on a boss and to enjoy the products of your own labour.

So, take the land! The law says you must not, since it is private property. But the law was written by those keeping you in slavery. This is why it requires enforcement by the police, the jailer, the judge, the executioner, the soldier, and the official. The law was imposed upon us, and we must respond to arbitrary impositions with rebellion.

So, to the struggle! The Revolution, irresistible and overwhelming, will not tarry. If you want freedom, gather beneath Liberal Party's flag. But if you merely want the strange pleasure of shedding blood by "playing soldier," gather beneath other flags—the anti-reelectionists, for example. When you are finished "playing soldier," they will harness you to the yoke of the boss and the government. You will have enjoyed changing the old President, with whom you were disgusted, for a brand-new one, freshly made.

Comrades, I understand that you are ready to struggle, but you must fight for the benefit of the poor classes. Until now, all revolutions have profited the upper classes, but the interest of the rich is to keep the poor eternally poor; the poverty of the masses is the guarantee of their wealth. If no man was compelled by necessity to work for another man, the rich would be obliged to do something useful, to produce something useful in order to live. There would no longer be slaves to exploit.

Forward, comrades! Soon you will hear the first shots. Soon the oppressed will issue their cry of rebellion. Let no one fail to support this movement, launched with all the force of conviction, with the supreme demand: Land and Liberty!

CHAPTER TWO

MADERO'S REVOLUTION:
UNLEASHING THE TIGER

In October 1910, from his refuge in San Antonio, Texas, Francisco Madero denounced the electoral fraud that returned Porfirio Díaz to office, declared himself the Provisional President of Mexico, and called for an armed uprising in a manifesto called the Plan of San Luis Potosí, named for the city where Madero was imprisoned during the presidential election. Madero even set a precise time and date: November 20, 1910, at 6:00 PM. The rebellion nearly fizzled before it started. Two days before the appointed time, the federal army cornered one of Madero's supporters in Puebla, Aquiles Serdán, and killed him along with his family. Elsewhere in Mexico, not much happened—except in Chihuahua where memories of Tomóchic persisted alongside new anger focused on Luis Terrazas who controlled the state's politics and owned 50 haciendas with 7 million acres of land. In Chihuahua, Madero's main agent was a cattle merchant named Abraham González who recruited the two men who became responsible for the military success of the rebel forces: a mule skinner named Pascual Orozco—Madero's General-in-Chief—and a bandit named Francisco Villa. On paper, the Mexican military had a formidable 14,000 troops, but it was a parade army of conscripts commanded by aging divisional generals, all older than 70 years. In contrast, Orozco, Villa, and other insurgent military chiefs were highly motivated and their troops were steeped in the frontier traditions of guerrilla warfare. Early rebel victories gave the insurgency momentum, so that by January 1911 the rebellion was engulfing much of Mexico. Meanwhile, the Mexican Liberal Party (Partido Liberal Mexicano [PLM]) forces led by Ricardo Flores Magón invaded Baja California and controlled parts of that state. By March, the rebellion reached Morelos where Emiliano Zapata endorsed the Plan of San Luis Potosí and led a peasant army that gained control over the countryside there and in neighboring states.

In contrast to the Magonistas who restricted their appeal to workers and peasants, the power of Madero's revolution derived from the support it received from a broad range of classes who harbored grievances against the Porfirian regime. It attracted dissident members of the bourgeoisie, some nationalists, who resented exclusion from the inner circles of power as well as the preferential treatment that foreign capitalists enjoyed in Mexico; it attracted middle-class intellectuals and professionals who desired democratic reform; it attracted workers demanding union rights and better workplace conditions; and it attracted peasants who wanted to recover their land.

Madero may have also enjoyed tacit support from U.S. President William Taft, and explicit support from U.S. corporations in Mexico. Certainly the U.S. government did not hound Madero as it did the Magóns. When the revolution began to crest in March, Taft ordered 20,000 U.S. troops to the border. Mexicans read this as U.S. opposition to Díaz and it weakened his government. Historians still debate this interpretation. But there is no doubt that Washington was unhappy with Díaz's policy of countering the U.S. presence in Mexico's economy with inducements to investment from Europe. Nowhere was this more evident than in the oil fields at Tampico on the Gulf of Mexico where U.S.-owned Standard Oil and the Mexican Petroleum Company were locked in a fierce competition with British-owned El Aguila Company. Even before the revolution, Madero had retained a lawyer from Standard Oil to drum up U.S. support for the rebellion.

Whether or not President Taft intended to tip the balance in favor of either Díaz or Madero, it is clear that Washington was concerned that the rebellion might become unmanageable. Díaz and Madero also worried that the revolt might become a peasant war pushing for more radical demands. By April there were as many as 25,000 rebels under arms, many operating beyond the control of Madero.[1] On May 21 the Treaty of Ciudad Juárez marked the end for Díaz, and it was a notably conservative arrangement. As Alan Knight has noted, Madero repudiated the Plan of San Luis Potosí in order to reach an accommodation with the científicos.[2] The deal left the entire Porfirian state intact, minus the state governors and Porfirio Díaz who left Mexico for Paris on May 26. Replacing Díaz as interim president was the ex-foreign minister Francisco León de la Barra. Most remaining officials—politicians, bureaucrats, and judges—kept their posts. Madero also agreed to disband the revolutionary army and to keep in place the Rurales and the army. Elections for a new president and vice president were scheduled for October 1911. Meanwhile, Madero began to prepare his triumphant entry into Mexico City, but Díaz may have had the last word as he boarded the steamship *Ypiranga* for exile. The ousted dictator reportedly said: "Madero has unleashed a tiger; let us see if he can control it."

★ ★ ★

The Plan of San Luis Potosí [3]

Francisco Madero, October 1910

Francisco Madero summoned Mexicans to arms with the Plan of San Luis Potosí. The manifesto brims with indignation over the electoral fraud of 1910, but the plan was hardly radical, let alone revolutionary. It was political in the narrowest sense and did not offer an alternative to the Porfirian system other than to replace Díaz as president and to amend the constitution to prohibit reelection. Nor did the Plan address social concerns other than a promise to restore stolen lands to their rightful owners; even this reads as an afterthought—a bid for support from peasants. Conspicuously absent are proposals for workers, or even economic nationalists among the middle classes and bourgeoisie. To the contrary, Madero promised to uphold existing legislation and to respect agreements made between the Porfirian government and foreign governments and corporations. No doubt Madero had an eye towards Washington and the interests of U.S. corporations. As Paul Garner observed, the Plan reads like "a classic nineteenth century *pronunciamiento* (or pronouncement against the government) strikingly similar in structure and content to Porfirio Díaz's own Plan of Tuxtepec in 1876." [4] Yet Madero was not disingenuous when he called his movement revolutionary. He perceived of "revolution" through the patriarchal lens of elite political culture and the inherited traditions of nineteenth-century Mexico. In that tradition, revolution was nearly synonymous with rebellions or revolts that changed political leaders but rarely intended to alter economic or social relations. Thus, a rebellion or revolt—and even a cuartelazo or military coup—merited the title of a "revolution" when it unfolded under upper-class leaders; a rebellion of the lower classes, minus elite leadership, was barely one step above banditry.

In the constant struggle to see liberty and justice triumph, people are forced to make their greatest sacrifices at precise historical moments.

Our beloved country has reached one of those moments. An intolerable tyranny now oppresses us. In exchange for tyranny we are given peace, a shameful peace based on force, but not law. We do not have peace to improve the country and its prosperity, but to enrich a small group that abuses public office and unscrupulously exploits their access to lucrative concessions and contracts.

The legislature and judiciary are completely subordinated to the president; the division of powers, the sovereignty of states, the liberty of councils, and the rights of citizens exist only in writing; in fact, one can say that martial law is permanent. The administration of justice, instead of protecting the weak, legalizes plunder committed by the strong. Judges, rather than offering justice, are agents of the president whose interests they faithfully serve. The legislative chambers have no will but that of the dictator. The state governors are named by the dictator and, in turn, they impose municipal authorities.

From this it results that the whole machine obeys a single will—the caprice of General Porfirio Díaz who has shown that his principal motive is to stay in power at any cost.

For years, the Republic has been profoundly discontent. But General Díaz, with cunning and perseverance, has succeeded in annihilating all independent minds. As a result, it has not been possible to end his abuse of power.

The evil grows worse. Now the decided eagerness of General Díaz to impose a successor, in the person of Mr. Ramón Corral, has carried that evil to its limit and caused many Mexicans to throw themselves into a struggle to recover the rights and sovereignty of the people, and to re-establish them on a purely democratic basis.

The National Anti-reelectionist Party was organized to proclaim that "Effective Suffrage and No Re-Election" is the only principle that can save the Republic from the danger of a permanent dictatorship, everyday more onerous, despotic and immoral.

The Mexican people supported this party and responded to its call. They sent their representatives to a convention to nominate me and Dr. Francisco Vázquez Gómez for President and Vice-President. Our situation was extremely disadvantageous because our opponents controlled the instruments of the state and used them unscrupulously. But we believed it was our duty to serve the people, to accept the honour of being nominated.

Imitating the wise practices of republican countries, I toured the Republic issuing an appeal to my countrymen. These were truly triumphal marches; everywhere the people were electrified with the magic words, "Effective Suffrage and No Re-election." This was clear evidence of their unwavering resolve to win these principles. At last, the time came when General Díaz understood the true situation and realized that he could not fight me and win on the field of Democracy. He therefore sent me to prison before the elections, and committed the most shameless fraud by using violence and filling the prisons to exclude voters and candidates.

In Mexico, as a democratic republic, public power can have no origin other than the will of the people. For this reason, the Mexican people have protested the illegality of the last election. They have asked for its nullification by the Chamber of Deputies—even knowing beforehand that the chamber always obeys General Díaz, the exclusive source of their offices.

It is under these conditions that the sovereign people have energetically protested with demonstrations in different parts of the Republic; if the latter were not general throughout the territory it was due to terrible pressures exerted by a government that drowns any democratic protest in blood—as happened in Puebla, Vera Cruz, Tlaxcala, and elsewhere.

This violent and illegal system can no longer exist.

I realize that the people named me their candidate for the Presidency, not because they had an opportunity to discover my qualities as a statesman or a ruler, but the virility of a patriot determined to sacrifice for liberty and help free the people from the odious tyranny that oppresses them. From the moment I plunged into the democratic struggle I knew that General Díaz would not bow to the will of the nation. The noble Mexican people also knew what outrages awaited them. Despite this, the people have given liberty a large contingent of martyrs. With wonderful stoicism, they went to the polls and endured every sort of abuse.

This proved to the whole world that Mexicans are fit for democracy, that they thirst for liberty, that their present rulers do not measure up to their aspirations. Besides, the attitude of the people shows that they vigorously reject the government of General Díaz and that, if their electoral rights had been respected, I would have been elected President of the Republic.

Therefore, echoing the national will, I declare the recent election illegal. And, as the Republic is accordingly without rulers, I provisionally assume the Presidency until the people designate their rulers pursuant to the law. In order to attain this, it is necessary to eject from power, the audacious usurper whose present office comes from a scandalous and immoral fraud. With all honesty I declare it would be weakness and treason to the people, not to put myself at the front of fellow citizens who anxiously call on me to make General Díaz respect the national will, by force of arms.

The people have tolerated the current government despite its origins in violence and fraud. And it has a degree of legality in the eyes of foreign nations. However, its term expires at the end of this month. The new government, arising from fraud, must not take power. Otherwise it will face a nation protesting usurpation with weapons in hand. I have designated Sunday, November 20, from six p.m. onward, as the moment for all people in the Republic to raise their weapons in support of the following Plan:

We declare void the elections for President and Vice-President, the Supreme Court Judges, and Senators and Deputies.

We repudiate the government of General Díaz, and all authorities whose power should flow from a popular vote. They have not been legally elected by the people.

To avoid the disorders inherent in any revolution, we declare all laws enacted by the current administration are valid, except those contrary to the principles in this plan. Upon its victory the revolution will investigate all officials. In all cases, we will respect the commitments made by the Porfirian government to foreign states and corporations.

Many small landowners, mostly indigenous, have been dispossessed of their land through the abuse of the Law of Vacant Lands by the Ministry of Public Works, or by court rulings. Justice requires that lands be restored to former owners who were arbitrarily despoiled. We declare these acts subject to review and require that lands acquired in this immoral fashion be restored to their owners, with compensation. In cases where lands have passed to a third party, the original owners will be compensated by those who profited from the dispossession.

We declare that the supreme law of the Republic is the principle of "No Re-election" for President and Vice-President, Governors of States and Municipal Chairmen. The constitution will be revised accordingly.

I assume authority as Interim President with power to wage war on the usurper General Díaz. As soon as the capital city and more than half of the states are held by the forces of the people, the Interim President will convene general elections and will hand over power to the President-elect.

If authorities offer armed resistance, they will be compelled by force of arms to respect the popular will. The rules of war will be strictly enforced, with attention to bans on expanding bullets and shooting prisoners. It is the duty of each Mexican to respect the persons and interests of foreigners.

Authorities who resist will be imprisoned and tried when the revolution ends. When a city or town regains freedom, the Chief-in-arms will be the interim authority and will be confirmed in office or removed by the Interim President. One of the first steps of the interim government will be to release all political prisoners.

The Blast of the Bull's Horn[5]

Rosa King

In Morelos, peasant communities and their leaders, including Emiliano Zapata, endorsed the Plan of San Luis Potosí. There is no doubt they seconded Madero's call for political reforms and democratic rights. Zapata himself had suffered the sharp end of political repression as early as 1892 when authorities conscripted him into the army for protesting the expropriation of village's land by a neighboring hacienda. And as late as 1910, Zapata and others faced threats and intimidation for supporting the candidate of the Anti-Reelectionist Party for governor of Morelos. Still, the decisive factor in their decision to support Madero was the promise to restore lands. The voices of peasants like Zapata are muted in this excerpt from the memoirs of Rosa King, but it is still a compelling vignette of the reaction by Morelos Governor Pablo Escandón and three foreign residents—the English woman Rosa King and two U.S. citizens who sympathize with the plight of the peasants. King also effectively captures the essence of the conflict in Morelos: the struggle over land.

Occasionally, in my search for curios, I would come on something that harked back to the time when these Indians had been a free people and a nation controlling their valley. One of my most valued treasures was an old bull's horn, and one day a professor from one of the colleges in the Eastern United States spied this and picked it up with reverence.

"Do you know what this is?" he asked.

I said that I knew it was a very old ceremonial horn that had been used, as was also a drum made of a hollow log of some precious wood like mahogany, to call the tribes together in time of war.

"For any important assembly," corrected the professor, and added quietly, "I heard the blast of one of these not long ago."

"Good heavens!" I said, for I had not known any were still in use. An American youngster who had been examining the inlaid butt of an antiquated Spanish pistol turned frankly around to listen.

"I have come down to Mexico," said the professor, "to study early Spanish documents; not long ago I appealed to the patriarch of one of your neighboring Indian villages, whose name I have promised to keep secret, to let me look at the sixteenth-century parchments that prove the title of the village to its land; a title based, as you know, on the decree of Charles V, who was ashamed of the greed of his grandees and returned certain lands to the tribes for their use and that of their descendants. Only the patriarch, the *cacique*, knows where the documents are hidden, and he was most reluctant to bring them out lest some harm come to them. It seems the villages hereabout have been having trouble defending their lands from the hacendados, who want them for sugar cane."

"Yes, that is so," I nodded, "the governor has told me about it." Since I was a foreigner, and did not speak the language, Don Pablo Escandón, the Governor of Morelos, sometimes spoke more frankly to me than he might have otherwise. "The *hacendados* perpetually want more land for planting sugar cane, but since practically all the land in the state is already parceled out among them, there is nothing left but the scanty patches belonging to the Indian villages. When the hacendados try to buy these fields, the Indians refuse to sell. Money means little to them, but they know that so long as they have the milpa which fed their father and their father's father, they can grow what they need to eat."

"Very sensible of them, too," commented the professor.

"But the hacendados do not understand that point of view. When the time comes for planting, they want land in a hurry; so they seize the Indians' milpas by force and deposit the purchase money in the banks, to the Indians' account. They consider that this honourably ends the matter, but the Indians do not think so. They won't touch the money. They want their land."

"And they should have it," said the professor. "The patriarch eventually consented to call the people of his village together—they were called with a blast from just such a bull's horn as this, Mrs. King—and they gave him permission and authorization to show me the documents. I studied them carefully and the legality of the title is unquestionable."

"Perhaps," I said sadly, "but that doesn't seem to help the Indians. I believe they have even appealed to Don Porfirio, but they continue to lose their milpas. It seems a wicked thing to me, this taking the land by force from those who work it with their hands and love it. Some day, I think, there will be an upheaval here."

The younger American had been drinking in our conversation. Now he struck in earnestly, "It may come sooner than you think!" He was an eager, sensitive-looking boy. "Our newspapers have been carrying rumours of unrest in Mexico for the last year or two."

"Your newspapers!" I said, smiling a little. "Ours are written here on the spot, and they talk of nothing but peace and progress."

"The dictator muzzles them!" came back the boy. He put down the pistol and came closer. "No, really, Mrs. King, you have an election coming on, and Don Porfirio isn't going to have everything his own way this time. I studied Spanish at school, and as our train came down from the North I used to try to talk to the people. They're tired of Porfirio Díaz!"

"Of course people are tired of Porfirio Díaz, after thirty years," I said. "Many have been tired of him for quite a while. Why, only the other day, a gentleman for whom I have the greatest respect put up his hand here in my tearoom and solemnly swore that he would aid in his downfall! But such talk has been going on for years, and nothing ever comes of it."

The professor said kindly to the boy, "Don't take too seriously the campaign speeches of Madero, who has been set up as Díaz's opponent in the coming election. There has to be an opponent, to make the thing look right, but Madero is only a straw man for the dictator to knock down."

"Oh, I don't think so!" said the boy ingenuously. "Madero is different. I've been reading some pamphlets they gave me, and he tells the people all about the rights and liberties they ought to have, and how there should be justice for all and better living conditions for the working classes!"

The professor and I glanced at each other. Even the boy, I think, realized how the phrases sounded.

The professor was smiling. He had been standing in the doorway, still fingering the bull's horn, and now he said smoothly, "Conditions have been the same here for four hundred years. So long as the politicos [politicians] continue to hurl abuses at each other in perfect castellano [Spanish], we may conclude that all is well in your charming country, and you need have no fear Mrs. King. But," and he paused impressively, "when the blast of the bull's horn and the drum call of the hollow log sound again in the soul of the people, as they will one day, then there will be no peace and no safety. Then there will be a revolution!"

For weeks after, in Cuernavaca, we talked about the festivities celebrating the centennial of Mexico's independence. The newspapers filled our knowledge of the events we had not attended ourselves. My manager Willie Nevin was constantly pointing out that no nation could afford such spending, but it was Willie's fate to have his prescience of disaster ignored. I paid no attention to what he said even when the dictator put Madero, the candidate who was opposing him in the coming election, in jail for using accounts of the centennial extravagance to inflame the people against the party in power. Later, Mr. Madero was released.

Then came news that a Madero supporter, Aquiles Serdán of Puebla, had been killed with his wife, defending their home against government officers determined to search it. I was shocked, but did not realize the seriousness of the rioting that followed in Puebla.

That afternoon Don Pablo Escandón stopped in to see me. He was clearly upset. "But this is a revolt, Señora King! Imagine! And who do you suppose is mixed up in it? Our friend Señor Luis Cabrera."

I had a sudden remembrance of Señor Cabrera putting up his hand in my tearoom months before and swearing to aid in the downfall of Díaz.

"Oh, I knew all about that," I said, unimpressed.

"You did! What do you mean?" demanded Don Pablo, bristling. "I have a good mind to put you in jail for not having told me."

"You don't think it's really serious, do you?" I asked, with some surprise, and beginning to be a little alarmed.

"Oh, certainly not serious," said Don Pablo, laughing at my fears. "Our Porfirito with his army and his strength of character will make short work of the revolt."

A few weeks later Porfirio Díaz was fleeing for his life on the *Ipiranga* (a ship), the rich families running at his heels like turkeys; Francisco I. Madero was marching down from the north on Mexico City, joined by ragged thousands; and the peons of our own state, Morelos, were up in arms, led by Emiliano Zapata.

The blast of the bull's horn and the drum call of the hollow log had sounded in the soul of the people.

An Efficacious Remedy for Revolution and Banditry[6]

Porfirio Díaz, April 1, 1911

On April 1, 1911, Porfirio Díaz mounted the rostrum before the Congress of Mexico to deliver a speech promising reforms that were more specific and radical than Francisco Madero's Plan. Díaz pledged to adopt the principle of no reelection, to divide up the large estates and redistribute lands, to establish an independent judiciary, and to eliminate abuses by local officials. At issue was the remedy for ending the insurgency before it became too radical or prompted a military intervention by the United States. Certainly Díaz hoped the reforms would take the steam out of the insurgency; it is equally certain that his promises were insincere. But, this was not just a cynical effort to manipulate the masses. It was a gambit to push negotiations with Maderista leaders away from demands for Díaz's resignation and to co-opt them into the government. The two sides had been parleying in New York throughout March: Finance Minister José Yves Limantour and Mexico's Ambassador to Washington Francisco León de la Barra represented the regime while three represented the rebels, including Madero's father, Francisco Sr., his brother Gustavo, and his vice-presidential candidate in 1910, Francisco Vázquez Gómez. Díaz's speech offered bait for the Maderistas, the main one involving the potential dismissal of Vice President Ramón Corral; this implied replacing Corral with someone amenable to the rebels, possibly Francisco Madero himself.

Gentlemen of the Congress: a group who at the recent elections presented candidates for the presidency and vice presidency of the Republic, without having polled more than a small minority of the votes, not limiting their action to the legitimate exercise of popular suffrage, resorted to arms when the elections were over, disturbing the peace enjoyed for long years in this country. The leaders of the group sought, by activities conducted on foreign as well as on Mexican soil, to organize a revolutionary movement to break out on a prearranged date.

The protection afforded by the mountains, and effective cooperation in men and war supplies received from foreign parts as well as from Mexicans who have for years conspired against the present Government and against social order, explain how the revolt has extended throughout Chihuahua, and several points in Sonora and Durango, in spite of the efforts to limit it by the Federal Government and the States.

At the same time, unfortunately, numerous bands have sprung up without any political motive and, animated solely by a spirit of banditry which has begun to develop afresh, is spreading greater terror, perhaps, than that caused by the revolt.

In Baja California another movement began, caused by groups of communists, among them many American filibusters, with the fantastic project of forming a Socialist State. So unspeakable a purpose must provoke the greatest indignation, and I am sure that if necessary the Mexican people, always patriotic and jealous of their autonomy, will hasten to the defence of national territory.

Some time later there was an extraordinary concentration of American forces on the frontier. The Executive instructed his ambassador at Washington to request an explanation of the manoeuvre. The instructions crossed a message from President Taft in which he gave assurances that the concentration had no significance that might alarm us, friends of the United States. The withdrawal of ships which that Government mobilized, and the fact that the Army is about to conduct manoeuvres, are the best testimony to the sincerity of those assurances, which have been repeated on subsequent occasions.

Gentlemen of the Congress, it might be inferred that notwithstanding the revolt—started by a group of Mexicans who are labouring under lamentable misconceptions or have been grossly deceived—the country has kept on progressing economically and intellectually, but in truth such progress is now obstructed by the political situation which demands of the Government and of the sensible mass of the Nation, each in its own sphere, the greatest solicitude and the most strenuous efforts to apply some prompt and efficacious remedy. The Executive therefore thinks it fitting to make known the measures which he believes ought to be taken.

The recent change of government ministers aims at satisfying a general aspiration, which is that political personnel be renovated from time to time. If I have not hesitated to part with the services of capable, loyal and honest advisers, who for a length of time had given me their valued cooperation, my single aim has been to show that room should be made, from time to time, for new energies in the direction of public affairs.

Furthermore, measures will be taken that give heed to reasonable complaints made against some authorities, especially those in closest touch with the people. It is to be hoped that this policy will be seconded by the States, which are better able to remedy the evil in question.

The principle of no re-election for executive functionaries chosen by popular suffrage had not of late been broached in any legislative assembly, and for that reason the Executive had not thought to express an opinion. But seeing that the issue has recently been brought up in some state legislatures and has been discussed in the press, the executive manifests his hearty assent to the principle and declares that the administration will give its earnest support. Intimately bound up with the principle of no re-election is reform of electoral laws, for it is indispensable to insure the effective participation of those citizens who are considered capable of voting with a full consciousness of what they are doing.

In view of the unsatisfactory results of measures hitherto taken for the division of large rural estates on fair terms, the executive is determined to carry out this important project in the most efficient manner possible.

At different times endeavours have been made to reform the administration of justice, and these alone demonstrate the importance the executive attaches to this vital function. At the same time much remains to be done to correct defects which observation brings to light and public opinion points out. The various measures proposed will aim at insuring the independence of the judiciary by securing better personnel and lengthening their term of office.

In carrying out these reforms, the executive trusts that the legislative chambers will give him their support and bring their ripe experience to the consideration of these arduous problems. At the same time, the executive appeals earnestly to the patriotism and good judgment of the Mexican people, trusting they will prove equal to the task of extricating the Republic from the difficulties by which it is surrounded and maintaining unimpaired the ideals of progress and civilization which have won our country so high a place in the esteem and respect of other nations.

Open Letter to Madero: You Must Extinguish the Revolution[7]

Luis Cabrera, April 27, 1911

The Porfirian gambit nearly worked. An uneasy armistice in April found Madero and his forces encamped outside Ciudad Juárez, Chihuahua, still controlled by the federal army. Madero and his negotiators began hesitating in their demand that Díaz quit office; Madero toyed with simply accepting a private letter from Díaz promising to resign. This alarmed Luis Cabrera, a middle-class intellectual and key advisor to Madero. Like many of his generation and class, Cabrera shared the Porfirian commitment to modernization, but opposed policies that closed off political and economic opportunities to those outside the president's inner circle. Cabrera feared that Díaz was maneuvering an end to the revolution to the disadvantage of the rebels. April 27, Cabrera published an open letter to Madero urging him to remain firm in demanding that Díaz must go. This, for Cabrera, was a minimum condition for winding down the revolution, which he saw as urgently necessary if rebel leaders wanted to keep the revolution manageable. Two weeks later, Madero's restless military commander, Pascual Orozco, underscored Cabrera's anxiety when he disobeyed orders and seized Ciudad Juárez; ironically, this convinced the government that the departure of Díaz was a small price if it averted a radicalization of the revolution. Thus, the capture of Juárez handed Madero a victory that he parleyed into the resignation of Porfirio Díaz.

My very distinguished and esteemed friend: I cannot discuss whether you were right in taking up arms to assert the principles of no re-election and effective suffrage; that is the task of History. It is enough to say that the Revolution is a fact and the country finds itself enveloped in a conflagration more powerful and much vaster than you expected or desired.

Mr. Madero, you have an immense responsibility. Having unleashed social forces, you also implicitly assumed the obligation to restore peace and to satisfy the grievances that led to the war, so that the sacrifice of the homeland will not be sterile.

Revolutions are always painful operations for the social body; but before closing the wound the surgeon must clean the gangrene. Do not be intimidated by the sight of blood or distracted by the moans of our homeland, otherwise you will close the wound precipitously, without disinfectant and without curing the illness you set out to extirpate.

The sacrifice will have been in vain and History will curse your name. Not because you opened the wound, but because the homeland will continue to suffer the same evils as before—and it will be exposed to increasingly dangerous relapses, threatened with new operations, each time more exhausting, each time more painful. To speak without metaphors: you have caused the revolution, and you must extinguish it.

However, the desire for peace can be frustrated by a lack of accord or ineffective remedies. The rupture of the armistice will be a bad outcome; but perhaps it is worse to obtain peace too quickly or by half measures. A definitive peace must satisfy the grievances that constitute the discord between General Díaz and the people, and not just those expressed by the Revolution.

The Revolution must look beyond its own goals and satisfy national interests. Peace will be more lasting to the extent that the representatives of the Revolution are firm in their demands—and to the extent that General Díaz is liberal. Conversely, if the revolutionary negotiators are too lenient, or if General Díaz insists on narrowly-defined freedoms and reforms, peace will be incomplete or temporary.

The demands of the Revolution, namely amnesties, indemnities, conditions of submission, disarmament, and so on, must take into account the conditions of each region in rebellion. Only then can you end the revolution promptly. The demands in Chihuahua and Coahuila are different from those of Guerrero and Yucatán. Hence, southern rebels will not accept a deal that only satisfies Chihuahua or Coahuila. This will leave you exposed to repression, and a bloody and painful extermination.

After this, you must address the country's economic and political needs and suppress the causes of social unrest. This is tantamount to a vast program of government.

Your responsibilities are serious. If you fail to grasp the political and economic reforms required, you risk future disruptions. You can consult writers like Molina Enriquez who have catalogued the country's needs, and have discerned that political and democratic interests are basically manifestations of economic necessity.

From an economic standpoint the urgent need is restoring a balance between the many small interests (agricultural, industrial and commercial) who are oppressed by disadvantage, and the few big interests (agricultural, industrial and commercial), which are uniquely privileged.

In politics, the main requirement is guarantees to protect people's lives and their civil and political liberties. For this, we need political change, a point which is the most difficult to solve. The first and easiest way is to dictate legislation that reduces executive abuses, ensures meaningful electoral reform, and establishes the principle of no re-election. The second way—and this seems more practical—is to introduce men of the Revolution into federal and local governments, and even the cabinet, to monitor the government. But we are convinced that neither one is a strong guarantee, if Díaz remains.

Congress could reform the Constitution and tie the hands of the Executive, as it is now doing in a puerile way; it could proclaim new systems and fill state governments—and even the Cabinet—with anti-reelectionists. But this would not prevent General Díaz from restoring the old system. He is already seeking ways to circumvent the new laws, to nullify them, or to convince new men to do so. And within six months, when your revolution is perfectly suffocated, its leaders will be dismissed or discredited, or corrupt or tired, and the laws will be repealed or relegated to oblivion.

No. There is only one way to ensure the regeneration of government, and that is the resignation of General Díaz and the appointment of a Vice-president committed to the concessions won by the Revolution. Over the last two months, the idea of General Díaz's resignation has gained ground to the degree that few doubt that this radical remedy will relieve our political situation.

After proposing this to General Díaz, and by renouncing your own claim to the Presidency, the Government will have no reason to oppose the resignation, other than official scruples that this will reflect poorly on the dignity of the government.

Peace and the future of the country are above self-esteem and the propriety of governments. A country which does not hesitate to sacrifice the lives of its children when necessary, should not hesitate to sacrifice decorum if this guarantees its tranquillity, sovereignty and existence.

The resignation of General Díaz constitutes a personal act that does not reflect on the decorum of Government. Not everyone sees it this way. But if it was decent for General Díaz to remove state governors through local coups, why is a resignation unseemly when done constitutionally? If it was decent to dismiss six secretaries of state without due cause, why is it unseemly for the head of state to reign, when this can restore peace?

Some see changing banners as unworthy. However, the entire Government—the executive and the legislative houses—did not believe it undignified to declare against re-election even after supporting re-election in order to keep power. Why so many scruples for a resignation that is justified by the incompatibility between the republican system of the Revolution and the system of dictatorship practised by General Díaz?

There is no reason to stop insisting on the resignation of General Díaz. This is not only necessary and patriotic, but the most decent act that the Revolution can impose.

Government compliance will be ensured by completely transforming the dictatorial government into a democratic one composed of new people. To allow some revolutionaries to enter the Cabinet is a sort of vigilance that does not imply control over the government, and would lead to constant struggle. Real control will mean anti-reelectionists in the federal and local chambers and the renewal of legislatures throughout the country with truly independent representatives of popular origin.

Given the origins of every member of congress, and the loyalty they still show to General Díaz, perhaps we can dissolve the current Congress without causing a big scandal. However, this seems utopian, and less dignified for the Government than the resignation of General Díaz, for it would mean the sacrifice of power en masse. But separating them from Díaz will only affect the Chief Executive.

Another means is to keep the rebel forces under arms, but this would be the most dangerous mistake you and General Díaz can make. Political parties must control the government, always by orderly and peaceful means. Weapons in the hands of a political party are tantamount to establishing a system of force and endemic revolution rather than a constitutional regime.

The only sensible way to ensure a change is through one or more officially recognized and independent political parties whose relations with power are defined in law.

Your victory, or that of General Díaz, is only weeks away. One of you will triumph, depending on how long the truce lasts. If the truce breaks within a week, the fall of General Díaz is inevitable. But if the truce continues more than fifteen days without spreading to the rest of the Republic, this will strengthen the ability of General Díaz to fight the Revolution, which will have relaxed and divided its energies. Upon the renewed outbreak of hostilities, the government will easily win.

Weighing upon you are the greatest political responsibilities any man has had for thirty years in Mexico—not because you launched the revolution, but because a failure to satisfy the legitimate interests of the nation will plant the seeds of future revolutions.

To Maderista Soldiers: Repudiate Your Leaders! [8]

Ricardo Flores Magón, May 27, 1911

The Treaty of Ciudad Juárez changed the personnel leading the government but, as Limantour later recalled, it said "nothing, absolutely nothing" about "liberal principles, or political, social, or administrative reforms." [9] The entire Porfirian edifice remained. Maderistas like Cabrera believed that this would enable new leaders to run the system and introduce reforms without sacrificing modernization or altering social and economic structures. Some radicals rejected that as myopic optimism or outright betrayal. In the selection below, published on May 27, one day after Díaz left Mexico, Ricardo Flores Magón condemned the Treaty of Juárez and argued for pushing the revolution in a more radical direction; he ended his manifesto with an explicit appeal for a revolutionary mutiny in the Maderista army.

The Revolution has reached its climax and must follow one of two paths: either it will degenerate into a political movement that only benefits its leaders and the wealthy, leaving the poor in the same conditions as before; or it will end in a genuine economic revolution. The latter is what the Mexican Liberal Party fights for, and its triumph will mean taking control of land and production for the common benefit of all inhabitants of Mexico, men and women.

If the Revolution degenerates into a political movement that puts Madero or any other man in the presidential chair, the poor class will have once more generously given its blood to remain in political and economic slavery. The history of our revolutions is replete with examples of this. The working class has given its blood in all of them, only to be subjected to the misery, hunger and ignorance they suffered before taking up arms. That has been the result when rebel soldiers do not wage an unyielding struggle for the interests of its own class. The interest of the working class is to abolish bosses. To do this, it is necessary to renounce the rich and the right of property, and to seize with virile hands the land and the machinery of production.

The War of Independence and all other revolutions that have shaken Mexico—including the one that brought Porfirio Díaz to power—have not benefited the class that spilled its blood in these struggles. These struggles were a triumph only for those who want to be presidents, governors, political leaders, mayors, judges, parliamentarians, ministers, or simple hangers-on. But the working class wins nothing.

We must open our eyes, Mexicans. We must not be satisfied with putting Madero in the presidential chair. Our happiness can only be achieved through economic freedom, by taking possession of land and machinery of production and to use them in common.

Francisco I. Madero and Porfirio Díaz have signed a peace treaty.

They are asking all insurgent leaders to suspend hostilities in order to hold new elections, but that does not solve the problem of hunger. Perhaps a good man will be elected. But even a good man cannot end the misery of the vast majority of the Mexican people. Any ruler will have to protect the interests of the capitalist class. Governments have no other purpose.

Federal troops and Maderista forces are already pursuing all revolutionaries who reject the treaty or oppose the farce of a new election. Maderistas and federals troops have united to crush comrades in Coahuila. In the mountains of northern Chihuahua, the Maderista Gabriel Marquez disarmed comrade Miguel González along with twenty other comrades. The disarming of Silva and Alanis by Madero personally is still fresh in our memory.

What is going on? They are trying to suppress the emancipating movement of the Mexican Liberal Party.

Madero has paid its many lackeys to betray the libertarians. They mix with the Liberal forces, trying to gain the confidence of our comrades to then disarm and execute them. Madero has declared a war of extermination against the Liberal forces throughout the country.

Madero and Díaz have made a deal that unites Maderista forces with the federal army. Together they are crushing heroic Liberals who refuse to surrender their weapons.

Already there is talk of sending Orozco or Villa to suppress the Liberals in Sonora. Already Maderista leaders, combined with the federals, are crushing Liberals in central Mexico. Already Maderista leaders, combined with the federals, are crushing revolutionaries in Veracruz and Tabasco, Campeche and Yucatan, Chiapas and Oaxaca, Jalisco, Guanajuato and elsewhere.

Is not this a terrible betrayal of the revolutionary movement? Have proletarians spilled their blood so that a few bandits can benefit? Will this great movement end with the farce of elections? Have they no shame? Are we going to seize the land and the machines with ballots in our hands?

Maderista soldiers, turn your rifles against your leaders, as you did against the federals. Or else you will be changed overnight from soldiers of freedom to henchmen of despots. No. Maderista soldiers, you belong to the working class and you must refuse to shoot your disinherited brothers of the Mexican Liberal Party. Do not commit the infamy of murdering those who struggle for redemption, the Liberals who want to make all Mexicans equal.

Do not conspire against yourselves. Repudiate your leaders and fly the Red Flag of your class, inscribed with the Liberal motto: Land and Freedom.

Did you rebel for the pleasure of putting a new executioner in the presidency or did you rebel to win the material well-being of all Mexicans without exception? If you rose in arms to improve living conditions for the Mexican people, then you must unite resolutely with the phalanxes of the Red Flag, with the Liberal phalanxes.

Repudiate your leaders, who are already dreaming of a sweet and idle life, of parading with their swords in banquet halls with crosses and decorations on their chests, or occupying the seats of congress or the chairs of state governors, or becoming ministers and lords—while you return to the countryside, the workshop, the mine, or the factory to sustain your new masters.

Disinherited brothers who fought in Madero's ranks, we Liberals will not ask you to vote for parasites. When the land is finally in the hands of the dispossessed, we simply want to work at your side with the plough, the hammer, the pick and the shovel. We do not want to be better than you, but your peers, your brethren.

We have struggled for a long time against tyranny and exploitation. The best years of our lives have been spent in the prisons of Mexico and the

United States, and we have remained loyal to the cause of the people. If we only struggled for personal gain, we would have accepted long ago the tempting propositions to become executioners of the people.

Brothers in misfortune, brothers in chains: do not surrender your weapons. Repudiate the Maderista chiefs and officials. The Mexican Liberal Party is the only movement fighting for the well-being of all Mexicans, flying the Red Flag and shouting with enthusiasm: Long Live Land and Liberty!

Madero and the Counterfeit Revolution[10]

Francisco Bulnes, 1916

The Magonistas were not alone in condemning the Madero revolution. So too did the old guard, among them Francisco Bulnes, an intellectual and politician who had long been associated with the científicos and had served in the Porfirian government. Bulnes was an exponent of Comtean positivism and social Darwinism, and unapologetically advocated authoritarian rule in Mexico. To Bulnes, the success of Madero's revolution proved that Porfirio Díaz had lost his capacity to provide the strong hand that Mexico needed; Bulnes did not mourn its passing. However, Bulnes also argued that Madero's reliance on the lower classes—what Bulnes called the "popular or sub-popular classes"—revealed the degeneration of the middle classes and proved their incapacity to govern. For Bulnes, the revolution represented the triumph of "ignorant and primitive hordes" who threatened to undo the progress won by 36 years of Porfirian rule.

In 1911 the material victory was won by the leaders of the popular or sub-popular class, some of them reputable, others bandits. Among these were Pascual Orozco, Francisco Villa, Tomás Urbina, Emiliano and Eufemio Zapata, and others. A Venezuelan President, speaking of our burlesque democracies, said that in dictatorial Latin America their only serious feature is that by right of might they belong to the strong.

In Mexico, this bitter truth has been realized. The winner is the master of the situation, and Mexico had fallen from the feeble, tremulous grasp of General Díaz under the hoofs of the horses of ranchmen, cowboys and bandits in the north, and in the south into the clutches of a barbarous or semi-savage horde. Fortunately for the Mexican public the revolutionary press, with its illimitable power of suggestion over a credulous people, aiming to obliterate General Díaz's formidable personality, managed to pass Madero off as the saving hero, transforming him into a veritable idol in the eyes of the people.

This crusade of fanaticism was carried to such a point that it was impossible to create among the masses, rural or urban, an enthusiasm for any deserving revolutionary leader equal to the deified figure of Madero. The work of the press was bound to be ephemeral. Every revolutionary press that has forged an idol is fated to demolish it, and the counterfeited portrait of Madero as a Herculean reformer was destined to be shortly annihilated by the same press that had made him superior to all other public men.

The triumph of Madero revealed the nation's misleading position. The federal army, although it fought with bravery and discipline was routed and humiliated. Notwithstanding its reduced numbers, it might have conquered Madero and put an end to the revolution. Its failure proves its inefficiency, and in this light its failure must be attributed to its advanced state of degeneration.

The second is more significant and more deplorable. In our famous War of Reform [1858–1861], bloody and destructive in the extreme, liberal leaders were all professional men of the middle class. They suffered terrible defeats with fortitude, and carried on heroically until they were able to organize armies and to dominate the reactionaries. Their names deserve to be remembered.

In the Madero revolution we do not find a single lawyer converted into a hero by military feats, or as the leader of any important detachment. One or two young attorneys were attached to Madero, carefully hugging the rear, and the only professionals engaged in the struggle, Eduardo Hay, Roque González Garza, and Alberto Fuentes, never held important commands. The lawyer, José Maytorena, and the engineer, Manuel Bonilla, watched the bull-fight from behind the fence as civilians. From the sociological point of view this proves that the middle class, with few exceptions, was lost to shame or bravery and, consequently was no longer entitled to the right to govern.

The governing class should possess enough strength to be the fighting class, or to transform itself into it should occasion demand. A people is truly sovereign only when it knows how to discharge military duties, taking up arms for the defence of its legitimate rights according to ethical principles, which are nothing more than the principles of true militarism. The Madero revolution revealed the deplorable fact that the middle class had lost control of the country, and that it must henceforth belong to those who possessed the greatest military strength.

If Mexico fell into the hands of two hundred thousand bandits, it was because of the natural law which, all theories of jurists to the contrary, gives dominion to the strong over the weak. Since the triumph of the Madero revolution, the educated middle-class man, honest or dishonest, is destined to live as a courtier, a bawd, a lackey, or as a private secretary of the leading bandit chief of the popular or sub-popular class, who cannot feel anything but well-merited contempt for them.

No one noticed the change. The real revolutionists who had spent eight years in working out their plans and preparing their campaign, and those who had recently joined the ranks, expected that Madero would endorse their great principles, "vengeance and pillage"—vengeance against the Científicos, even to picking their bones with the greedy rapacity of vultures.

Falstaff's Revolution[11]

Henry Lane Wilson

Henry Lane Wilson was the U.S. ambassador to Mexico from 1909 to 1913. As a social Darwinist, Wilson admired the authoritarian politics of Porfirio Díaz and was an ardent advocate for U.S. imperialism in Latin America. Wilson believed that Mexicans, except for the upper classes, were unprepared for democracy and might not ever be. He expressed his contempt for Madero's revolution by comparing its political and military leaders to Shakespeare's Falstaff, a vainglorious and incompetent buffoon. During the Madero revolution, Wilson urged President Taft to follow a pro-Díaz policy.

The revolution of Madero sprang unarmed and motley from national discontent with the Díaz regime. This discontent was neither represented nor organized. Madero was a comparatively unknown person who appeared at a psychological moment and reaped a harvest which might have gone to stronger and abler men had any been prominent in the public eye. His previous history had been that of a dreamer of dreams, but he was more a mountebank [quack] than a messiah; an honest enthusiast with a disorganized brain. Madero managed, by disseminating literature of extremely ordinary but inflammable character, to increase discontent with the aid of American and European capital—enlisted by promises of concessions or preferential favours—and the Madero fortune, equipped a force on the border which, though inconsiderable in numbers, constituted a rallying point for unsatisfied spirits and a nucleus for action against the government. Nevertheless, the character of the revolution was formidable neither in numbers or organization. It gained strength from the weakness of the government; from the well-meaning but damaging overtures of Limantour who, having relations with the Madero family, was supposed to be a proper intermediary through which to influence their actions.

The revolutionary forces under Madero, Orozco, and other border chieftains were conglomerate border bandits, roving cattlemen, and American adventurers, falstaffian in numbers and equipment. In the earlier stages it was regarded by Mexicans and foreigners as a fanatical and impotent affair destined soon to failure because of lack of support among the really solid elements of the population and of the improbability of financial assistance. But as time went on the government remained inert and repressive measures were delayed or lacking in energy. At this juncture Gustavo Madero, and other members of the family joined the movement, and the considerable family fortunes of the Maderos were enlisted in the cause. Financial assistance was obtained from sources in the United States and Europe, notably from Paris and Frankfurt. The records of the Department of Justice of the United States carry revelations connecting Gustavo Madero with an oil company in Mexico and with an arms company in Washington. With this aid efforts at organization and discipline were made and victories of an unimportant character, largely exaggerated by the press, were gained.

As the army of Madero remained in the field gaining recruits and support, intrigue and discontent spread and the poorly organized machinery of government fell rapidly into the chaos.

I kept the government at Washington informed. As the situation became complex I went north for a consultation with President Taft. The President manifested the deepest interest. Taft was a firm believer in Díaz, and the action he took was inspired by a desire to afford protection to Americans living along the border and to sustain, as far as our obsolete neutrality laws would permit, the government of Díaz. Action came sooner than I anticipated, for as I was on my way to the railway station, I read in the *Evening Star* the story about the mobilization of 20,000 troops for concentration at San Antonio, Texas.

Triumphant Entry of the Caudillo of the Revolution Sr. Don Francisco I. Madero into the Capital of the Republic[12]

Anonymous, June 1911

Francisco Madero made his way from Ciudad Juárez to enter Mexico City on June 7, 1911, where he received a tumultuous hero's welcome. The enthusiasm was unquestionably genuine, but it had been well-prepared by his supporters. The following corrido bears all the hallmarks of a commissioned ballad, written by one of the writers retained by the publisher Antonio Vanegas Arroyo who printed it at the end of May in anticipation of Madero's arrival in Mexico City. Traditional corridos that emanated from popular culture were often composed extemporaneously, using memory aids like short stanzas, simple words, vernacular phrases, and repetition; these made corridos easier for illiterate and semiliterate Mexicans to remember and perform. None of these elements are present in this ballad, which strongly suggests the hand of an educated middle-class writer. This was not an innovation of the Maderistas, for the practice of commissioning corridos began with

Porfirio Díaz who understood that popular ballads were a form of ideological struggle. This ballad bears a stronger resemblance in tone, language, and structure to the "official" corridos that celebrated Díaz before the revolution than it does to more traditional ballads.

Homeland, oh homeland! How grand that your children protect you.
You are the goddess of the people, who love you with devotion.

Victorious, Madero advances from the hard-fought campaign that he won.
In his laws we can see his sincerity, upheld by his noble banner.

A banquet will be offered in your honour with myrtle and white orange blossoms,
and with stars of living radiance, as thousands bid you affection.

The sky will strum its blue curve with asteroids streaking across.
Your soul is an inspiration and you upheld your conviction with faith.

You are welcome at every estate by your friends, your noble brothers
because you won a hard struggle—the sanctified god of Mexicans.

Each station your train passes by will be adorned with a lovely mirage—
nymphs will be clad in white garments and they will give you a warm embrace.

And Madero, oh, how his grand profile expresses his deeds and nobility!
He's a citizen of such high culture, and a stoic of firmness and life.

Redeemer of my beloved homeland! You will be sublime in our history,
for your passionate gaze is an exemplar of living memory.

The streets will be adorned with flowers, and consulates with noble shields;
hard-working peasants in their fields will salute you with a brilliant dawn.

You will have a triumphal march, with the noble emotions of the people.
And on pages of gold will be written "Oh, Madero, your conviction is grand."

Receptions will welcome you warmly when you arrive at Buenavista.
Your bust has been venerated, Coahuilense, grandiose, altruistic.

Teberento, hydrangea, amaranth, bougainvillea, white lily and violet—
these are the flowers that will serve as a cloak for the lyre of every poet.

The neosotis and lovely agapando—these beautiful and fragrant flowers,
will fall to the street as you pass, with affection and love and in peace.

CHAPTER THREE

THE APOSTLE OF DEMOCRACY

Francisco Madero's victory did not bring an end to the revolution. It simmered for 19 months and reached the boiling point again when Madero succumbed to a military coup in February 1913. Madero was committed to electoral reforms and greater democracy, but his social and economic policies differed from Díaz's only in degree. In his own way, Madero was as dedicated to the positivist motto of order and progress. The main point of contention had been Madero's belief that Díaz's dictatorship had created a bottleneck that obstructed progress; Madero expected that political reform would allow Mexico to resume its economic and cultural modernization. This was similar to the view of científicos like Justo Sierra who had worried that the continuous reelection of Díaz would sooner or later act as a brake on progress. But most científicos, along with the rest of the Porfirian old guard, were convinced that Madero's democratic aspirations were reckless and dangerous, as was his reliance on the lower classes to win his revolution. Sharing this attitude were foreign investors and U.S. Ambassador Henry Lane Wilson. These critics insisted that Mexican peasants and workers were unfit for democracy and might always be. Clinging to scientific racism, the bourgeoisie and their foreign allies saw insurgents like Emiliano Zapata and Francisco Villa as atavists, primitive throwbacks with dangerous prehistoric instincts; they wasted no time in labelling Zapata as a modern-day Attila who threatened to destroy civilization in Mexico. They privileged order above democracy and spent the next 19 months seeking a formula that would restore authoritarian rule.

Madero himself contributed to instability when he signed the Treaty of Ciudad Juárez and allied with the científicos in order to govern Mexico. For the first four months, state power was in the hands of an interim government led by Díaz's ex-foreign minister Francisco León de la Barra. His cabinet of Porfirian and Maderista ministers was charged with pacifying the country and organizing the presidential election on October 1, 1911. This guaranteed a conservative approach to policies like land reform, and led to the early marginalization of ambitious middle-class Maderistas like Emilio and Francisco Vázquez Gómez, and lower-class leaders like Zapata, Villa, and Pascual Orozco who had won the military struggle. The first harbingers of turmoil appeared during this interregnum, when Madero approved De la Barra's use of Maderista and federal troops to suppress Mexican Liberal Party (PLM) insurgents in Baja California, while U.S. officials arrested Ricardo Flores Magón in Los Angeles and returned him to prison in the United States. Trouble also flared in Morelos when Zapata resisted disarming without guarantees of land reform. In the meantime political factions maneuvered for position, some hoping to undermine Madero or prevent his election, others hoping to influence his policies if elected. Some científicos saw Madero as an alternative to the presidential aspirations of General Bernardo Reyes, the ex-governor of Nuevo León, who saw himself as the heir apparent to Díaz. However, most científicos bolted to the conservative opposition, including the National Catholic Party (PCN). The election was the cleanest one in Mexico hitherto and it delivered 53 percent of the votes to Madero and vice-presidential candidate José María Pino Suárez. Their main opponents were Francisco Vázquez Gómez—Madero's running mate in the 1910 elections—and Reyes, who refused to accept defeat at the polls and launched an unpopular rebellion in December that collapsed on Christmas Day.

Despite victory at the polls, Madero's popularity was in decline when he took office on November 6. Encouraged by greater political tolerance, workers on railways, mines, factories, and plantations joined unions and organized strikes for higher wages and better working conditions. The upsurge in worker militancy created fertile soil for PLM activists who resurfaced to organize the Casa del Obrero Mundial. Although repression under Madero was much reduced, the government still relied on the army and police to suppress strikes. This weakened working class support for Madero, but it also stiffened the hostility of employers who criticized Madero for failing to crush unions. Meanwhile, the disintegration of the original Maderista coalition ignited new rebellions. At the end of November, the Zapatistas issued a manifesto called the Plan of Ayala that renounced Madero and launched an agrarian insurgency. The Vázquez Gómez brothers saw their ambitions for high political office evaporate in Madero's alliance with the científicos; they rebelled in December but surrendered in February to Chihuahua militia commanded by Pascual Orozco. One month later, Orozco himself rose against Madero with a plan that incorporated the PLM program. Orozco's revolt likewise failed, but it required five months of campaigning by General Victoriano Huerta and Francisco Villa, as well as an arms embargo imposed by U.S. President William Taft.

By autumn of 1912, Madero's government had put down the Reyistas, Vazquistas, and Orozquistas, but it was unable to smother the Zapatistas in Morelos. More than any other rebellion, the persistence of the Zapatistas galvanized the conservative opposition into an alliance among científicos, the PCN, and Reyistas. Added to the mix were U.S. President Taft and Ambassador Wilson who encouraged the opposition's desire to replace Madero with an authoritarian hand. The first try at a *cuartelazo*, or military coup d'état, came when General Félix Díaz, nephew of Porfirio Díaz, seized Veracruz in October. He expected the rest of the federal army to rally to his cause, but the attempt was hasty and poorly planned, and it failed immediately. Díaz ended up in a Mexico City prison where he contacted Bernardo Reyes, held in a different prison; the two began plotting a second coup attempt, this time with different results.

★ ★ ★

Corrido of the Meeting between Zapata and Madero[1]

José Muñoz Cota

Corridos were an important part in the war of words that accompanied the armed struggle. This was especially true for the Zapatistas. While they issued manifestos and published newspapers, ballads were an effective way to record their history, argue their points, and reach the ears of peasants in Morelos and beyond. No movement produced more corridos, except perhaps the followers of Francisco Villa. The following corrido, composed by a Zapatista balladeer, narrates the first meeting between Zapata and Madero on June 8, 1911. Also at this meeting were Maderista officials Emilio Vázquez (interior minister), Venustiano Carranza (a hacendado and ex-Porfirian governor of Coahuila), and perhaps Gildardo Magaña, a middle-class aide to Zapata. To Zapata's insistence on land reform, Madero promised only to consider the problem and insisted that Zapata disarm and repair his split with Ambrosio Figueroa, the Maderista chief in neighboring Guerrero. Zapata declined. Even though his forces had won the war in Morelos and had started to recover their land, the planters still ran the state government and had the ear of De la Barra. Zapata also had reason to distrust Figueroa. In the final stage of the war against Díaz, the planters bribed Figueroa to lead Zapata into a federal army ambush during an attack on Jojutla, a town near the Morelos-Guerrero border. Zapata caught wind of the conspiracy and withdrew at the last minute. The corrido captures a moment when Zapata still had faith in Madero, but was beginning to express his unease at the direction Madero was taking. It contains at least one inaccuracy—the meeting was in Mexico City, rather than in Cuautla. It has one explicit purpose: to justify Zapata's refusal to disarm until Morelos's peasants recovered lands usurped by the big planters.

On June 8, 1911, Madero, the chief of the rebellion
against the dictatorship came to the town of Cuautla.[2]

On that morning Zapata had a meeting with Madero.
Madero was from the North; Zapata was from the South.

We know about their meeting, and we know what they said
for Gildardo Magaña is the witness who told us.

Madero was a good man who loved the Revolution.
He was a man of conviction, but he lost our trust.

They spoke of Figueroa and Zapata accused him of
trying to betray him during the attack on Jojutla.

But Madero patiently asked that Zapata submit;
Zapata replied: "Only time will tell who is right."

But Madero insisted: "The Revolution is over
for we have defeated Porfirio Díaz.

"So disband the people who fought at your side.
For peace is assured now; that's my point of view."

Zapata was disciplined when he answered Madero:
"I am sure in my heart that would be a mistake,

"until we get what we want"; the General insisted.
"the return of our lands, just as you promised.

"The Indian rebelled for nothing but the land . . .
to take back the lands the hacendados usurped."

Zapata was Chief of the South, the apostle of conviction.
He was the voice of the land, the voice of liberation.

The good apostle Madero, the man who dreamed, who
just counselled patience and faith in law and order.

But Zapata the *ranchero*[3] had learned to be wary.
He saw danger for Madero, and so he insisted:

"I don't think that the federals will support you Señor;
so take every precaution against their betrayal."

Madero replied: "You must disband your troops,
for I already agreed in the treaty I signed."

Magaña told us that Zapata stood up
with his carbine in hand—his constant companion.

He stood before Madero and demanded his watch,
and gave him a lesson that astonished us all:

"If I have my carbine, I can steal your watch,
but if you have a weapon the next time we meet,

"would you take it back, Señor Madero?" he asked.
"Not only that," said Madero, "but with indemnity too."

"Well, that's what we want," Zapata concluded.
"Morelos wants the land the hacendados have stolen.

"My armed *campesinos*,[4] with respect but with strength
have told me to ask you for fair restitution."

Madero agreed this was righteous and promised once more
to fulfill the promise that he made in his Plan.

But he still hoped Zapata would surrender to a bribe,
so he offered a *ranchito*[5] to Emiliano Zapata.

The Chief of the South could not hide his disgust,
so he slapped his carbine and indignantly replied:

"I beg your pardon, Señor Madero,
but I didn't rebel to be a landowner or a boss.

"I am fighting for justice for the miserable peón;[6]
I won't abandon the people without winning their demand.

"And if we do not fulfill what we already promised,
they will rise up again in a new armed rebellion."

So Gildardo Magaña, who fought with Zapata,
witnessed this meeting and told us the story.

The Clash between Madero and General Huerta[7]

In June, Zapata reluctantly agreed to disarm when Madero privately
promised to appoint Zapata commander of the state police and to enlist
400 of his men. However, the planters objected and the promise was
never kept. Then in July, a crisis in nearby Puebla heightened tensions
in Morelos and in the interim government. Interior Minister Emilio
Vázquez Gómez sent Zapatista General Abraham Martínez to Puebla
City to investigate a rumored plot to assassinate Madero. Martínez
arrested three politicians he suspected of collusion. Federal troops led
by Colonel Aureliano Blanquet responded by attacking the bullring
where the prisoners were held, killing 50 Maderistas, including women
and children. A group of Maderistas withdrew from the city and
approached the Covadonga textile factory to find food; they received
fire and in the battle killed seven Spanish and two German employees,
as well as a woman. Fearing the worst, Zapata rearmed his forces and
waited. Meanwhile, the Morelos planters pressed De la Barra for
decisive measures to suppress Zapata. The interim president was
amenable, for Maderista political leaders were starting to split. Two
cabinet ministers—the Vázquez Gómez brothers—continued to resist
the demobilization of the revolutionary army.[8] Madero squeezed them

out by founding the Progressive Constitutional Party, where the Vázquez Gómez brothers had little influence. In short order, both left the cabinet, and the balance of power shifted to the científicos. On August 8, De la Barra made his move, sending General Victoriano Huerta and his troops into Morelos, along with federal police led by Ambrosio Figueroa.

The conservative plan to crush Zapata stumbled over Madero, who intervened to avert an expanded crisis that would benefit Reyes in the presidential elections six weeks away. De la Barra reigned in Huerta while Madero negotiated with Zapata. They reached agreement on August 18: Zapata would disarm if the government appointed an acceptable governor and state police commander. The disarmament was under way when Huerta suddenly advanced on Yautepec and Cuautla, hoping to encircle Zapata. Zapata slipped through and escaped to the mountains to regroup, while Huerta attacked the villages and drove peasant recruits into Zapata's forces. The conservative provocation failed to crush Zapata or undermine Madero's electoral bid. It did inflame Morelos and bring renewed fighting to within 15 miles of downtown Mexico City. Furious, Madero forced De la Barra to relieve Huerta of his command.

The following selection is an exchange of letters that illustrates how this incident strained relations between Madero and Huerta. Their enmity opened a breach between Madero and the federal army, even as Madero came to rely on the professionalism and loyalty of federal military commanders to sustain his government.

October 28, 1911
To: Señor don Francisco I. Madero

I have seen a message with your signature on it, which reads: "If the federal forces have failed against Zapata, this is: first, because it is very difficult for troops of the line to pursue parties like those of Zapata's; second, because the commander was General Huerta, whose conduct was truly inexplicable. For this reason, I suggested that Huerta be replaced. My recommendation was ignored at first, but after convincing the President, General Huerta was relieved of his command."

So you have said. Now I say to you, refuting your accusations, that as General in Command I had the honour of leading the troops for eleven weeks in that State, with the *unconditional approval of the President of the Republic and without reprimand from the Secretary of War.* I did nothing more than victoriously defeat any rebels I encountered, open schools, re-establish police services, and establish security for railways and on the roads, to the point where the State was completely pacified. I had the honour of reporting this to the President in a letter I sent upon leaving Morelos at the express order of the Secretary of War.

I am surprised that a person as respectable as you would make such charges against me, and I reject them with all my energy. With all due respect, I urge you to explain how my conduct was inexplicable. I have nothing personal to gain in my request since, as you know, I am a son of the people, *a soldier and father to my family with no more capital to leave my children than my honour and my loyalty.*

Thus I reiterate my request that you shed light on the charges you made against me, understanding that I already wrote to the President declining an appointment to the Supreme War Council and to the Assistant Secretary of War asking for my absolute discharge from the Army. I wish to be free of suspicion and, as I have always been, to remain a loyal citizen serving the country unconditionally, and to defend my conduct as General in Command of the troops I led in Morelos.

Respectfully Yours,
Brigadier General Victoriana Huerta

October 31, 1911
To: Señor Brigadier General don Victoriano Huerta

Today I learned of the letter you wrote to me and had published in the press. I am pleased to oblige you and explain why your conduct in Morelos seemed inexplicable. At the moment you arrived in that State, I was trying to arrange a peaceful settlement of the issue. I carried a communication to you from the Assistant Secretary of War clearly explaining my mission, implying that you should work with me, so as not to hinder my efforts. I prefer to win over worthy persons, military or otherwise. Therefore, I gave you every possible consideration, dining with you in my lodging and inviting you on my visits to towns and villages, in the hope of forming a friendship between us. Everything led me to believe you shared the same attitude. Your reaction to me and my pledges of friendship left no doubt in my mind.

This is precisely why I was painfully surprised by the following: when I thought I understood the situation in Morelos, I wanted to confer with the President in the capital; just before taking an automobile to the capital I learned your columns were approaching Yautepec. I asked you to explain this, and you assured me that the troops were on a military exercise to the outskirts of this town and that they would soon return. When I arrived in the capital I discovered that you had deceived me. Your troops had indeed advanced on Yautepec. In itself, this would not have had much importance if you had not stated otherwise to me.

Then, as I was in Cuautla negotiating with Zapata, you continued to advance on Yautepec and Cuautla without orders from the President or the Assistant Secretary of War. This complicated my efforts to end hostilities and made them fruitless. It also put my life in danger, for Zapata understandably believed that I had deceived him; I had telegraphed him from Cuernavaca to repeat what you told me—that your troops were only training and not advancing on Yautepec, that they were not near Cuautla. But it was not true. It is even said that you captured the escort that Zapata had sent to welcome me near Cuernavaca, although I could not confirm that. But anyways, this might have aroused suspicion in Zapata and his soldiers.

I have my doubts about your claim that the State was completely pacified when you were relieved of command, for even now newspapers report depredations committed by Zapata's forces. Concerning the skill of your operations against Zapata, I do not wish to express my judgement at the moment. I only note that when Zapata's hordes sacked Jojutla, the inhabitants asked you for help. They suffered three days of arson and looting, and you did not aid them, even though you were only a day's march away. I do not know why. You had 3,000 men and could have despatched 300 or 400 to protect that village. To say you were under broad instructions, does not explain why you failed to protect Jojutla. Even if you were following instructions to the letter, this does not explain why you marched out of Cuernavaca. This only inflamed the people of Morelos and increased recruits to Zapata's forces who then rose up and looted Jojutla.

I would not have referred to your attitude in Morelos, except that I was unjustly attacked by General González Salas, then-Assistant Secretary of War. I thought it right to say the truth about who provoked that war and was then unable to end it. From the first moment I went on this mission, you knew my business even though it was extra-official. If you had been inspired by the same patriotic sentiment, you would have worked with me instead of hampering my plans. I hope you are satisfied with my response.

Francisco Madero

Plan of Ayala, November 28, 1911[9]

Insurgent Army of the South

The Zapatistas made one last effort to negotiate when Madero assumed office in November. Madero's emissary arrived in Morelos on November 8. Three days later they had a draft agreement. Zapata would disarm in exchange for: Figueroa's resignation as governor of Morelos, the withdrawal of federal troops, a state police force composed of revolutionaries, guarantees to solve the land problem, and amnesty for the rebels. Madero refused and demanded unconditional surrender. On November 28, the Zapatistas declared war and issued the Plan of Ayala, named for the village where the rebels were headquartered.

The Plan was drafted by a local schoolteacher influenced by the PLM, Otilio Montaña, and signed by Zapata and other rebel chieftains. They renounced Madero and conferred leadership of the Revolution on Pascual Orozco; they pledged to fight until death for the lands usurped by the Morelos planters.

Having formed a Revolutionary Junta to carry out the promises of the revolution of 1910, we solemnly declare before the civilized world and the nation the principles we have formulated to end the tyranny that oppresses us and to redeem our homeland from the dictatorships imposed on us. These principles are the following:

The Mexican people, led by Francisco Madero, shed their blood to recover their liberties and rights, not so that one man could appropriate power, violating the sacred principles he swore to defend under the slogan "Effective Suffrage—No Re-election," thus betraying the faith, the cause, the justice, and the liberties of the people.

Francisco Madero initiated the revolution and the people hailed him as a liberator, but he imposed his will through the Provisional Government of Francisco L. de la Barra. This caused the fatherland bloodshed and misery in a confused and ridiculous manner, and had no purpose but to satisfy his personal ambitions, his immoderate instincts as a tyrant, and his profound contempt for the Constitution of 1857, written with the blood of revolutionaries from Ayutla.

Francisco Madero did not successfully conclude the revolution that began with the support of God and the people. He preserved the powers and corrupt elements of oppression from the dictatorship of Porfirio Díaz. This is provoking unrest, opening new wounds in the bosom of the Motherland.

Francisco Madero has evaded the promises he made in the Plan of San Luis Potosí, restricting himself to the Treaty of Ciudad Juárez. Using false promises and intrigues, he is persecuting and killing revolutionaries who raised him to the high post of President.

Francisco Madero has repeatedly used the brute force of bayonets to silence and drown in blood people who demand that he fulfil the promises of the revolution—calling them bandits and rebels, condemning them to a war of extermination, refusing to concede any of the protections prescribed by reason, justice and law.

Francisco Madero has made "Effective Suffrage" a bloody mockery. He imposed Vice-President José María Pino Suárez on the people. He did likewise with the States, by naming Governors like General Ambrosio Figueroa who is a tyrant and the executioner of Morelos. He scandalously colludes with those he once proclaimed as enemies of the revolution—the científicos, feudal hacendados, and oppressive caciques[10]—in order to forge a shameful and terrible dictatorship. He has violated the sovereignty of the states, debasing laws without respect for people's lives and interests in Morelos and elsewhere. He is leading us into the most horrifying anarchy in recorded modern history.

We declare Francisco Madero unfit to fulfill the promises of the revolution, unfit for betraying his principles and deceiving the people. He is incapable of governing and has no respect for the law or justice for the people. He is a traitor to Mexicans who seek freedom, for placating científicos, hacendados, and caciques who enslave us. Thus, we continue the revolution until we overthrow the existing dictatorial powers.

We repudiate Francisco Madero as Chief of the Revolution and as President of the Republic for the reasons above. We seek his overthrow.

We recognize as Chief of the Liberating Revolution, the illustrious General Pascual Orozco. In the event that he declines this post, Citizen General Emiliano Zapata will be recognized as Chief of the Revolution.

The Revolutionary Junta of Morelos declares: to benefit the oppressed people, it endorses the Plan of San Luis Potosí with the additions below, and will defend these principles until victory or death.

We will not negotiate or compromise until we have defeated the dictatorial elements of Porfirio Díaz and Francisco I. Madero. The Nation is tired of false men and traitors who pose as liberators, only to become tyrants when they come to power.

As an addition, we state: that the lands, forests and waters that the hacendados, científicos, and caciques usurped, will return to the villages and citizens who have Titles to them, but were despoiled by our oppressors. These properties will be protected at all costs, with weapons in hand. When the Revolution wins, special tribunals will hear the claims of usurpers who believe they own these properties.

The majority of villages and citizens no longer own the land upon which they stand. They suffer the horrors of misery without the power to improve their condition, unable to dedicate themselves to industry or agriculture because a few have monopolized the lands, woods and waters. For this reason we will expropriate, with indemnification, a third of these monopolies to allow the villages and citizens to have ejidos, colonies, legal foundations for villages, fields for sowing and labouring, and to bring prosperity and well-being to all Mexicans.

The hacendados, científicos, or caciques who oppose this Plan will have their property nationalized. Two-thirds of their property will pay war indemnities or pensions for the widows and orphans of victims who succumb in the struggle for this Plan.

The insurgent Military Chiefs who oppose this Plan are traitors to the cause and the Fatherland. By indulging tyrants for a handful of coins, or through bribery and graft, they are spilling the blood of brothers who demand that Francisco Madero fulfill his promises.

Once we carry the Revolution into triumphant reality, a Junta of the main revolutionary Chiefs in the States will designate an interim-President, who will then convene elections for a new Congress, as well as elections for other federal powers.

The main revolutionary Chiefs will designate a provisional Governor for the States to which they belong. This official will convene elections, avoiding the imposition of officials who work against the people—like the appointment of Ambrosio Figueroa in Morelos who has driven us to the edge of bloody conflict, sustained by the caprice of the dictator Madero and the circle of científicos and hacendados who influence him.

If President Madero wishes to end the misfortune that afflicts the Fatherland, he should immediately resign his office. By so doing he can staunch the grave wounds he has opened. But if he does not, the blood of our brothers will be on his head.

Mexicans: the cunning and bad faith of a man unfit for governing is causing bloodshed. His government is choking the Fatherland and trampling our institutions with the brutal force of bayonets. Just as we raised our weapons to bring him to power, now we rise against him for failing to keep his promises and betraying the revolution. We are not *personalistas*.[11] We are partisans of principles and not of men!

The Planters' Complaint: Savages and Bandits in Morelos[12]

Lamberto Popoca y Palacios, 1912

The following excerpt is from a pamphlet in January 1912, commissioned by the planters of Morelos to demonize the Zapatistas and to press Madero for a campaign of extermination. They got their wish. In January, Madero suspended the constitution and imposed martial law in five of the states surrounding Mexico City: Guerrero, Mexico, Morelos, Puebla, and Tlaxcala. In February, Madero ordered General Juvencio Robles into Morelos to wage war against the civilian population—burning whole villages and conducting mass executions— and so deprive the Zapatistas of any moral and material support. Some aspects of the pamphlet merit attention. The first is that it seeks to deny the Zapatistas any legitimate political motive by comparing them to the bandits known as *Plateados*,[13] who preyed upon Morelos in the 1860s. The second is the unabashed use of the racist epithet "kaffir" to describe the Zapatistas; the term is borrowed from Afrikaans in South Africa and is analogous to the term "nigger." This was not unique to author Lamberto Popoca y Palacios; the Morelos planters used such terms freely in public and private discourse. For example, the Porfirian ex-Governor of Morelos, Pablo Escandón, wrote to Porfirio Díaz in March, to complain that "if things go on as they, surely we will retro- gress to our former position as ... a true niggerdom."[14] The third is the author's use of scientific racism to justify his call for extermination; the Zapatistas, in his view, were not only bandits but atavists who had recapitulated—or reverted—to a state of savagery.

In the unfortunate state of Morelos, fifty years after the extermination of the Plateados, the morbid germs and perverted idiosyncrasies of those old bandits have crawled out from the sludge of buried sewers. Rabid criminals have emerged once more with the decomposed features of Cain and the ferocity of wild jackals. Apparently, only the iron fist of Porfirio Díaz—a man of steel—had prevented until now the explosive ferment of crime from maturing in the black minds of these dark souls.

How did these so-called defenders of a political ideal become bandits? What cause do they serve, anyway? How can they call themselves "saviours of the oppressed" when [they] are really the destroyers of the oppressed? Perhaps they are merely bandits at war with the rich to satisfy their lust for money. Unfortunately, they are worse than bandits—they are savages!

Everybody knows about the terrible events committed in Cuautla by these hordes of kaffirs. They plundered, destroyed and burned fifty-two homes of businessmen and middle-class citizens. They murdered wounded soldiers convalescing in the hospital. Is this how they liberate oppressed people? Do mere bandits burn and destroy the homes of innocent families, helpless children, and feeble old people? No! The word "bandit" is a generous description for people who commit such deeds!

The example of Jojutla speaks eloquently to the instincts of these men. Dynamite thrown by hellish hands destroyed peaceful homes and completed the bloody picture. The tears of their innocent victims cried out for mercy, but in vain. And then, Covadonga in Puebla! Oh, Covadonga, where they violated the wife of a victim, then killed and robbed them. Why do these monstrous criminals treat their wretched victims as terrible enemies? They could fight in the fields, in the plazas and in the streets against armed men who want to destroy them. Why do they murder defenceless hard-working people? Why do they destroy the homes of people who toil for the wellbeing and progress of the country?

The bandits of old—the famous Plateados—never committed such savage acts, but they were still hounded tenaciously until they were destroyed.

But the current government doesn't want to suspend constitutional guarantees in order to suppress them. The law imposes the death penalty on those who kill with perfidy and premeditation, but the highwayman and the arsonist are already outside the law from the moment they commit an offence. These reprobates don't feel the slightest pity for their victims, and yet the government seems to think they deserve God's mercy. Decent society in Morelos needs to find someone to hunt bandits, someone like Rafael Ortega Arenas who finished off the bandits of Huamantla many years ago, whether or not they possessed safe-conduct passes.

Those ferocious murderers in Morelos are called Zapatistas, because they enter a village and commit their iniquities to the cry of "Viva Zapata," looting and burning estates, and killing defenceless people like cowards.

If Emiliano Zapata fought in the last revolution to win a democratic government, then why does he allow frenzied hordes of savages and kaffirs to use his name and soil it with vile outrages? If he needs people to join his rebellion, why does he not require them to respect the laws of humanity, if not those of war? Surely it is not the fault of their hard-working and innocent victims if President Madero has not kept his pledges, or that the Plan of San Luis Potosí was a deception. They are not responsible for the lies of the politician or the falsehoods of his men.

No! Don Emiliano Zapata must reverse his path and repair, if possible, all the injustice, all the evil, all the iniquities committed by his followers.

Don Emiliano Zapata must remember the brave men of Mapaxtlán who followed the worthy Don Rafael Sánchez in 1860. He should remember that his own uncle Don Cristino Zapata was never a coward who killed defenceless people. He must know that in those days, men fought "face to face" as revolutionaries; they only killed the enemy in combat. They never killed defenceless and peaceful citizens. Nor did they burn houses and properties as reprisals against villages or individuals.

In Guillermo Prieto's immortal words: "brave men are not murderers." The men of old were disgusted by cowardice and villainy. Back then, Mapaxtlán—today known as Ayala—was famous for its brave men. But nature has its vagaries, and so a wise man can be born to a fool and vice versa; so too can an honest man be born to a thief. It is likely, though, that after fifty years, the environment and the lack of worthy examples to emulate has allowed that race to degenerate.

In any event, Zapata cannot be defending a good cause if he has to win followers by offering impossible things, when their rewards and incentives are looting, arson and murder. A cause thus defended is only worthy of bandits. This is anarchy and socialism, with impractical principles and ideas that only the insane defend and promote. Remember that insane men have degenerate minds! Remember that degenerates are criminals! This is why their weapons are dynamite bombs that cause cowardly murders and despicable destruction.

Decent men of sound mind struggle heroically to defend justice, progress and wellbeing. But criminals with degenerate minds only struggle for personal ambition. Their ideal is to prey upon spoils in any form. To which of these two classes do the so-called Zapatistas belong? Without question: to the second class. Their deeds are eloquent proof. Who knows what will happen to Emiliano Zapata and the lavish promises he has made to his hordes of felons? It cost Ché Gómez of Juchitán his life when he could not fulfil the promises he made to his men.[15] Who knows if poor Emiliano Zapata will suffer the same fate, for in Morelos it will be impossible to divide up other people's properties.

Meanwhile, there will be an avalanche of outlaws who want to destroy the world and to entertain themselves with looting, murder and arson, while waiting for Zapata to fulfill his promises to them.

What can we say about the burning of public records offices and the destruction of files, committed first by illiterate Maderistas—or rather, by Maderista convicts—and then, by Zapatista criminals? In the ashes of the public records offices are files that attest to the unblemished efforts of law and order. How many proofs of assets were destroyed by these perverts? How many records of large and small fortunes were lost to the looting? How many children lost the evidence of their legal inheritance? And how many black stories about those vampires will haunt decent society? To destroy those records, to burn files that legally secured the social wellbeing and the rights of individuals and villages—are these not the acts of the wildest savages?

Wherever these punishable acts have occurred, everyone has suffered immense and irreparable injury, creating great difficulties in administering justice and governing. The honour of Mr. Madero's government demands an investigation to uncover the arsonists, and to apply the severe punishment they deserve.

What has the government done to exterminate the Zapatistas and remedy the afflicted situation of people who demand justice and protection? It has sent thousands of men with all kinds of weapons to Morelos, but without any practical result. This desolate region cannot yet see the desired moment of safety from predation. The liberating army that followed Mr. Madero in his struggle for democracy freed the country in four months from a dictatorship of thirty years. But in six months, it has failed to liberate the tiny state of Morelos from a handful of rebels, outlaws, murderers and arsonists that have caused immense harm to so many peaceful citizens.

This situation—so disastrous for industry, trade and general tranquillity—must end soon. If the government is powerless to remedy these ills and protect Morelos, then the citizens of that state must arm themselves with the support of the government. The hacendados must help with everything at their disposal and find leaders, like the bandit hunters of old, to wage a tenacious campaign to exterminate the bandits, imitating the people of Mapaxtlán in 1860 who defended their lives and interests from the terrible but courageous *Plateados* led by the noble bandit Salome Placencia.

The Zapatistas: A People in Arms[16]

Rosa King

The English hotelier, Rosa King, who adopted Morelos as her home, offers a sharp contrast to the Morelos planters. General Robles wreaked death and destruction in Morelos from February to July 1912. Despite a scorched-earth campaign, Robles failed to suppress the Zapatistas.

Witnesses like King, who were horrified by the brutality of Robles, credit his failure to the inability of federal forces to adapt to the guerrilla tactics used by the Zapatistas, to the dogged determination of Morelos peasants to sustain the quest to recover their lands, and to the popular character of the insurgent army, which was, in her words, "a people in arms." Robles might have succeeded but only at the cost of a veritable holocaust. This he was prepared to do, but Madero recalled Robles and replaced him with General Felipe Angeles, a soldier of humane instincts and socialist leanings who nearly pacified Morelos by ending the assault on the civilian population. In this Angeles was aided by the midsummer elections in Morelos when Maderistas sympathetic to agrarian griev-ances defeated the planter candidates, and by a shift in Mexico City where Madero was preparing for a decisive break with the científicos. In this passage, King describes her revulsion for the atrocities commit-ted by Robles and the reaction by the Morelos peasants.

I was vexed by the turn affairs had taken. We were safe in Cuernavaca, as Zapata had moved out of town before his break with Madero, and the new governor, Ambrosio Figueroa, and his troops were well established. Yet we were inconvenienced by raids in the outlying country. Traveling became unsafe and few people ventured from home. My hotel business suffered. At the same time, I simply did not believe what the newspaper said, that the Zapatistas, who had lived among us peaceably for weeks, had turned overnight into villainous desperadoes. Victim of the hacendados, Emiliano Zapata had been exasperated by landowners, who reigned with the despotism of feudal lords over the peons and working classes of the rural population. His personal experiences had inspired an ideal—"Land and Liberty" for the downtrodden Indian—which was perfectly clear to him, and which his followers comprehended to an extent that preserved their faith in their leader through all the strife that followed.

The townspeople sympathized with the Zapatistas, but were too sensible to say so openly. The newspaper talked constantly about the bravery of the Federal troops and how the ragged rebels fled when they met them. The trouble was that the ragged rebels ran as far as the nearest shelter, from behind which they sniped at the Federals; the professional soldiers could never quite stamp out this guerrilla warfare. Madero's weak and vacillating will did not help our situation. The morale of the soldiers was impaired by the suspicion that the government was not squarely behind them. Some deserted and went over to the Zapatistas. The Zapatistas raided with new boldness and confidence, closer to the town.

None of the generals who followed Huerta were able to cope with the wily Zapata and his constantly growing bands of untrained Indians. The rebels knew the mountains and *barrancas* [ravines] and shot from ambush. The tactics of the Federals were useless and the ease with which the rebels picked off their comrades maddened the federal soldiers. They burned the crops that sustained the rebels and the houses or huts that sheltered them, and shot anyone wearing the white *calzones* [white cotton trousers] of the peon. Zapata's men not only fought; they had to work to provide for their families, cultivating patches of corn and beans. Many of these men were surrounded by Federals while working unprotected in the fields. They were made prisoners and forced to dig their own graves before they were shot.

One day I had occasion to go to Mexico City with my daughter. We were going on the military train, since regular trains were often attacked in the mountains. As I stood looking at the soldiers who filled the first car, a young colonel I knew proudly invited me to see some prisoners he had captured. Never shall I forget those poor wretches tied together, not one uttering a word; looking like the farmers they were, caught unprotected in their milpas.

"The only way we can quiet down Morelos," the Colonel explained, "is to ship out these Zapatistas." The soldiers were hustling the poor wretches into a cattle car, till there was not even standing room. They boarded up the doors and nailed them shut. I saw Pepe, an Indian who had worked for me faithfully, and I began to protest very bitterly.

I saw the commander, General Robles, inspecting the guard on the train. I rushed up to him, "Oh, General Robles," I said, tears streaming down my face, "you don't know what they're doing. Make them let those poor people go."

To my horror he smiled. "Now, now, Señora," he chided, "you must not take it so hard. You are only a woman and you do not understand these things. Why, I am trying to clean up your beautiful Morelos for you. What a nice place it will be once we get rid of the *Morelenses* [citizen of Morelos]! If they resist me, I shall hang them like earrings to the trees."

And being what they are, the people of Morelos did resist his will to wrench them from their beloved soil. The women cooled and reloaded guns and scoured the country to feed the fighting men, and old people and young children endured the hardships of their lots without complaint. The Zapatistas were not an army; they were a people in arms.

Those of the rebels he caught, General Robles strung up on trees, where their companions could see them. I often saw the sickening sight of bodies swinging in the air. At that high altitude they did not decompose, but dried up into mummies, grotesque *things* with the toes hanging straight down in death and hair and beard still growing.

The savage persecution by the Federals, who seemed to have lost sight of the fact that they were supposed to be Revolutionaries, champions of freedom and justice, turned the Zapatistas into fighting demons. Our newspapers lashed on the Federals with tales of atrocities by the rebels. I think this was largely propaganda, but if there was truth in the tales, the acts were retaliation for the cruelty of the Federals, and if I had been one of those ignorant hounded people, I would have acted as they did.

Mexicans Must Rally to the Government[17]

Francisco Madero, March 3, 1912

Francisco Madero issued the following manifesto on March 3, 1912, the day that Pascual Orozco rebelled against his government. It does not mention Orozco by name, but it was intended to rally Mexicans to support the government against the uprising in Chihuahua. Like the Zapatistas, Orozco posed a serious threat for he enjoyed genuine popular support in a state that had been, until then, a bastion of pro-Madero sentiment. Also like the Zapatistas, the principal issue driving the insurgency was access to land. Unlike Zapata, Orozco also received financial aid from the state's landed oligarchs, the Terrazas family who played a dangerous game by manipulating the rebels in order to weaken Madero's hold over Chihuahua. At the end of March, quick action at the city of Parral by Francisco Villa, who remained loyal to Madero, blunted Orozco's drive to the south and bought the government time to mount a counteroffensive. Madero sent federal troops north, under the command of General Huerta. Together, Villa and Huerta turned the tide and reduced the rebellion to scattered pockets of resistance by early summer. But the campaigning also generated friction between Villa and Huerta, and heightened Huerta's enmity towards Madero.

In this manifesto, Madero accused all rebels of being demagogues who lacked real political principles and who deceived the people with false promises. He urged patience with his government, insisting that only time would deliver economic and social improvement. Although Madero protested that he had kept the promises made in the Plan of San Luis Potosí, he made no mention of restoring stolen lands; instead he proposed a limited and vague policy—still under study—to finance the purchase of public lands at reasonable rates.

Mexicans: The moment has arrived when all good Mexicans must rally to the Government they freely elected. It will not be easy, but it is [the] only way to restore peace, which the nation needs to follow the path of progress and democracy. The situation is not as grave as it seems despite false reports that spread to all corners with such speed. Nevertheless, there are alarming symptoms which reveal that some Mexicans will not hesitate to send the Republic back to the tragic era of intestine rebellion.

The States of Morelos, Chihuahua, and Durango, as well as adjacent districts in Zacatecas and Coahuila, are currently the scenes of lamentable vandalism. Those who have rebelled are not guided by any definite political or military plan. They proclaim the Plan of San Luis Potosí and assert that I have not complied with it. They hope to seduce the ignorant classes, deceiving them with the promise of creating small rural properties. It is simply foolish to expect that the Government can solve the agrarian problem under the pressure of anarchic movements. The Zapatistas were in arms before I was elected and they still refuse to submit. The Vazquista movement began the very day that I took office, while the defeated Reyista revolution began shortly after.

These movements are unlike the revolution of 1910, which was a reaction against a Government rejected by the majority of citizens. The authors of these movements have not even waited to see if the Government will faithfully develop my political program or not. The great majority, which freely elected me, will not condemn me before seeing how I carry out its mandate. Those who have rebelled are a handful of ambitious and spiteful men.

The presiding Government is not the product of armed imposition. I did not call the people to revolution in order to satisfy my own personal ambition but to win political freedom. For that I was rewarded with election. My opponents were General Bernardo Reyes and Francisco Vázquez Gómez, who obtained a small number of votes. If we allow candidates who were defeated in a fair election to dispute the results by force of arms, then we abjure our political constitution and invest power in the mob and the coup.

The consolidation of my Government will firmly root our political rights and freedoms, because my Government is based on democracy. The immense majority understands this. Therefore my appeal intends to make it clear that ambitious minorities disrupt order when they disregard the law and take up weapons.

I have received countless offers from patriots who wish to defend order. Their offers will be more efficacious if they submit to military discipline and join the ranks of the Federal Army. The army has covered itself in glory on the field of battle, defending republican institutions with courage and admirable constancy. It has demonstrated such loyalty to the Government that it has evoked admiration at home and abroad. When the time comes, the Government will reward the chiefs, officers, and soldiers who have so honoured themselves. I invite all Mexicans to enlist in the ranks of this glorious Army, to fight the enemies of order and peace, to raise the sword of the law and let its weight fall on those ill-intentioned sons of the Father-land. This will guarantee order and tranquility. It will ensure that Mexico, free from the yoke of tyranny, does not become a prisoner of anarchy or ban-ditry, and that it will develop serenely along the path of liberty, within the law—the unshakeable base of democracy.

I appeal to Mexicans of all social spheres: to civil and military authorities, to individuals, to attorneys, to workers and humble peons. Everyone should help to raise a powerful army. The humble must not be deceived by agitators and ambitious men. Conditions cannot be improved as quickly as they promise. Remember what we said when the revolution triumphed: "If your political situation has undergone a radical change in a few months, it is because the plight of the pariah has won the august rights of the citizen. However, your social and economic situation cannot be changed so quickly, for this requires constant and prolonged effort. No one can learn or enrich themselves except through work and thrift. Liberty is the foundation since the people no longer face obstacles that keep them from their own prosperity. Rather than oppressing the people, as dictatorships did in the past, this Government will dedicate its effort to teach them, help rid them of their vices, and offer them a means to achieve economic wellbeing." Since then, I issued a decree to make national lands available to small landowners, at moderate prices with easy terms of payment. The Government of General Díaz alienated nearly all the national lands, but some escaped the clutches of monopolies, while others have been recovered during my administration when concessionaires failed to meet the obligations they contracted in return for these extensive tracts.

For this reason, the Government has considered establishing a Credit Bank, an institution that acquires large properties to re-divide among small-holders, and provides them with the ability to pay. Only by these combined means can we constitutionally solve the agrarian problem. But even so we cannot carry out this plan without studying it, unless we wish to precipitate a financial crisis.

Remember that I have always been faithful to my promises, the most important of which is to obey the Constitution. For this reason, I will do everything constitutionally for the prosperity and wellbeing of the Republic. But outside the Constitution, I will do nothing. The demand to despoil landowners of their legitimate property is absurd and unconstitutional

Ultimately, it must not be forgotten that I am President because you elected me. In fulfilling the sacred duties of citizenship you must sustain and respect a government that represents the triumph of liberty over dictatorship, of law over force. I pledge to fulfill all my duties and promises. Since the principle of Effective Voting has been established, I will ensure that the principle of No Re-election is also definitive. I consider it cowardice and treason to abandon my office to those who demand it without any justification other than personal ambition, or under pressure from an anarchic movement. I will firmly defend the banner of legality entrusted to me by the people. I will know how to die at my post, fulfilling my duty.

Will the Army Remain Loyal to Madero?[18]

Marion Letcher, October 16, 1912

Doubts about the loyalty of the federal army circulated openly by autumn 1912, as attested in a report on October 16 by Marion Letcher, U.S. Consul in Chihuahua. At that time, Zapata was campaigning in Morelos, but federal General Angeles had significantly reduced the level of violence. Meanwhile federal forces had broken Orozco's rebellion and were bringing the coup by Félix Díaz in Veracruz to its denouement. But if the tide was turning toward pacification, Madero's dependence on the federal army made him more vulnerable to mutinous attitudes among his commanders. One such threat was emerging from General Huerta's hatred of Madero. Huerta's enmity deepened during the Orozco campaign when Madero kept him from executing Francisco Villa on spurious charges of theft and rebellion. The execution of Villa would have eliminated one of the last remaining revolutionary military veterans willing and able to defend Madero. Villa ended up in a Mexico City prison, from which he escaped and fled to Texas.

I have had the opportunity to gain an insight into the animus which moves the Mexican army and which explains the peculiar indifference and lack of spirit in the campaign against the rebels in the north.

In the first place, frankly and without concealment, the army has no love for, nor patience with, the new régime. General Huerta shared this attitude completely and was in full accord with the army's feelings until the northern campaign was begun. This officer was in command of field operations against the Zapatistas in Morelos and, loyal to the constituted Government and an enemy of rebellion, while still by no means a partisan of the new régime, planned a campaign against the rebels which would have been effective had not Mr. Madero interfered when victory was within reach and ordered a change in plans which resulted in the escape of the rebels. This interference occurred during the operations in the neighbourhood of Cuautla. As a consequence General Huerta asked to be relieved from command and retired to Mexico City, where he remained, sulking and disgruntled, until placated by Mr. Madero and sent to put down the Orozco rebellion with the promise of promotion, free rein in conducting the campaign, and a lump payment for successfully concluding the campaign. The second of these considerations was broken when Francisco Villa, the Maderista partisan and ex-bandit, was ordered shot by General Huerta for serious crimes and insubordination. Mr. Madero ordered a stay in the summary execution of the ex-bandit until the matter could be submitted to the President. Villa was ordered to Mexico City, where he remains in prison. This episode came near to causing a breach between General Huerta and the President. Granting even General Huerta's full adherence to the Government it is probably true that he was quite unable to drive his troops more than he did, and we thus find the perplexing and disappointing inactivity of the Federal army after entering Chihuahua in July. Up to the present time the entire campaign has been left to irregular Government partisans and the regular forces have rested completely idle. Another cause of disgust in the army is that General Huerta and the civil authorities have joined in a policy of pacification which the officers of the army know to be impracticable and visionary. This lack of firmness is disappointing to loyalists and earns the contempt of the erstwhile rebels. General Huerta himself no longer has the entire confidence and cordial respect of his officers. The official personnel of the army, without exception, believe that he degraded himself in submitting to the slights and affronts to his dignity by Mr. Madero.

Madero Might Have Pacified Mexico[19]

Francisco Bulnes, 1916

The científico politician and intellectual Francisco Bulnes, ever conservative and pragmatic, offers a frank assessment of Madero's regime, written after it fell in February 1913 to a second cuartelazo by Generals Félix Díaz and Bernardo Reyes. For Bulnes, the central problem with Madero was the political incompetence and inflexibility of the President and his government, including his failure to compromise, bribe, or suppress his opponents at the appropriate moments. Underlying his assessment, however, is his persistent belief that Mexico still required an authoritarian government to maintain order.

The Government of Madero was far from a democracy; but it was also far from representing the dictatorship of General Díaz. The Madero Government gave something better than what it overthrew. Yet the dreadful failure of this regime was the lack of peace, which is essential as the fundamental basis of government and society. Without peace the brink of the abyss is soon reached, and the mere fact that a Government is impotent to restore peace is enough to justify a revolution.

Why was Madero unable to pacify the country and prevent the revolutionary movements of Zapata, Orozco, Vázquez Gómez, Félix Díaz and Reyes? All these could have been avoided if Madero had been able to count on politicians of high calibre. When Zapata issued his Plan of Ayala, I wrote in *El País* that this plan is worthy of study and approbation, with the exception of one absurd clause: "The claimant is to be put in possession of the disputed property, rural or urban, from the moment he makes his claim, unless the dispossessed has proved his claim to it before a revolutionary tribunal."

The Plan of Ayala required the planters to hand over one-third of their arable land to the villages or to the poor. The planters of Morelos developed only one-fifth of the arable land in cultivating sugar cane and rice, and could, without hurting their own interest in the slightest, meet the requirements of the Plan of Ayala, always provided, of course, that the absurd clause referring to disputed titles was omitted. I have stated that the distribution of land in general is not feasible, because the greatest portion of it is in the temperate and cold zones, and cannot be advantageously cultivated without irrigation. It is precisely in Morelos that the land might be distributed because the climate is semi-tropical, and the land not completely exhausted. It is not exposed to frosts, and the rainfall is less irregular and more abundant than elsewhere. Morelos is one of the few states where the distribution of land might be undertaken at once with great possibilities of success.

Zapata demanded that the Federal army not set foot in Morelos, and that elections be entirely free. It is evident that the acceptance of the first condition was humiliating for the Government, but political situations sometimes present humiliating circumstances that must be met with courage and patriotism. As editor of *La Prensa*, I upheld Zapata's demands and insisted upon the necessity of sometimes bowing to the inevitable.

I may be quite mistaken, but it is my conviction that if Zapata's demands, with the exception of the one absurd clause, had been granted, Zapata would have submitted. But it would have been an honourable submission, because a deed of justice or of intelligent patriotic policy cannot be anything but an honour to the one who executes it.

The first revolt of Reyes could have been prevented by not permitting him to return in 1911. This, however, was not a serious mistake, because when General Reyes raised the standard of revolt in December, 1911, he found that he stood alone, or, more properly speaking, disillusioned for he saw the country no longer wanted him and that he was unpopular, if not more so, than the Científicos.

As Orozco was the "military genius" of the Madero revolution, following historic precedents he had to rebel against Madero and demand the presidency. Madero, in the days of his popularity was irresistible and could have annihilated any rival, and should have settled the Orozco problem definitely. Instead of giving him only 50,000 pesos when he asked for 100,000, "the Apostle" should have given the "military genius" 500,000 pesos, on condition that he go to Europe for two years and educate himself in order to receive the post of Division General or Grand Marshall of the army. This might not have pleased the army chiefs, but this would not have occasioned any serious trouble.

With regard to Generals Bernardo Reyes and Félix Díaz, their inordinate ambition, their indomitable spirit of intrigue, their endless conspiracies, and their decision to take the presidency by storm was well known. Reyes and Díaz never would have overthrown Benito Juárez or Porfirio Díaz, because they would have found it difficult to carry out a first revolt; and a second revolt would have been impossible, because dead men cannot revolt. Madero captured Reyes and Díaz knowing that they were conspiring against him. Nevertheless he scorned them. The ruler who scorns the greatest danger in countries where the government is constantly endangered by military power, is not fit to rule.

CHAPTER FOUR

THE TEN TRAGIC DAYS AND THE MURDER
OF MADERO

The military coup that deposed Madero and led to the murder of the president and vice president took place in Mexico City, February 9–18, 1913. However, the stage was set the preceding summer when state and national elections hastened the split between Madero and the científicos. In Morelos, the balance of power shifted from the planters toward the Maderistas; the willingness of Maderista legislators to consider "the agrarian problem" buoyed the efforts of General Felipe Angeles to reduce violence. The Zapatista insurgency was waning, making pacification a real possibility when the national congress convened in September. Maderista deputies hoped to further this by mooting plans for agrarian reform. But the balance in congress was less decisive. Madero's Progressive Constitutional Party enjoyed a majority in the Chamber of Deputies, but the senate went to a conservative "triple alliance" of científicos, Reyistas, and *católicos* of the National Catholic Party. By then, Madero's conservative opposition had decided he must go, by fair means or foul. Many therefore welcomed the coup attempt by General Félix Díaz when he seized Veracruz on October 16. However, the cuartelazo failed and Díaz ended up in a penitentiary in Mexico City. Some historians perceive U.S. involvement in the Felicista attempt, but the evidence is circumstantial. It is clear that Ambassador Henry Lane Wilson tried to open a breach between Washington and Madero by sending alarmist and exaggerated reports about worsening violence and banditry, attacks on U.S. property, and an anti-U.S. turn in Madero's foreign and economic policy. However, it is less clear that the U.S. State Department supported the coup; it ordered warships to stand off the coast ostensibly to evacuate U.S. residents—but it also refused to recognize the right of Mexico to close the port to commercial vessels, including those bearing munitions.

The second attempt almost failed too, but was saved by General Huerta and Henry Lane Wilson, with timely support from De la Barra and conservatives in the senate. The new coup was hatched by Díaz and General Reyes, still in the Tlatelolco military prison after his rising in December 1911. Plotting from their prisons, Díaz and Reyes developed a plan that would see Reyes become provisional president, with Díaz elected to the post afterwards. Early on, they tried to suborn Huerta who, for his own reasons, declined—but neither did he inform Madero. The coup unfolded on February 9 when General Manuel Mondragón freed Reyes and Díaz, but in the assault on the National Palace failed when troops loyal to Madero killed Reyes. The mutineers retreated to an armory known as the Ciudadela (Citadel). Madero named Huerta to crush the mutiny. What followed became known as the *Decena Trágica*—the Ten Tragic Days. The Ciudadela was indefensible, but Huerta opted for an artillery duel that did nothing but cause enormous damage to property and kill thousands of civilians. His tactics strengthened his negotiating position with Díaz rather than suppress the revolt; they also weakened Madero politically and decimated loyal troops with suicidal attacks on Felicista machine-gun nests. Meanwhile De la Barra and Wilson strove to salvage the coup. De la Barra established contact with Díaz by offering his services to Madero as a mediator; he then organized the senate to demand Madero's resignation and suborned Huerta. Meanwhile, the U.S. Ambassador suborned Madero's foreign minister, Pedro Lascurain, and lobbied other diplomats to insist that Madero step down—and threatened Madero with U.S. military intervention. The turning point materialized on February 18, when Huerta and Díaz met in the U.S. embassy to sign the Pact of the Embassy. But Wilson went further, advising Huerta how to manipulate the constitution to lend a veneer of legality to his accession to the presidency. After the arrest and forced resignation of Madero and Pino Suárez, Wilson then instructed U.S. consuls in Mexico to encourage state governors and rebels alike to recognize Huerta, and turned his attention to winning recognition from Washington.

However, Huerta and Díaz committed a grievous blunder by carrying out a spate of assassinations. Madero and Pino Suárez were murdered on February 22 as they were being transferred to Lecumberri Penitentiary. Their executioner was Captain Francisco Cárdenas of the Rurales; the official story was that they were killed by Maderistas who botched an attempt to free them. This was followed by the assassination of Chihuahua Governor Abraham González on March 7. The killings created a martyr out of Madero, cast a shadow over Huerta's government that ultimately prevented recognition by Washington, and undermined the effort to win submission from the governors of Sonora and Coahuila who feared they would meet the same end as Madero.

★ ★ ★

Remove Power from Madero's Bloody and Inept Hands[1]

General Félix Díaz, October 1912

General Félix Díaz was the nephew of Porfirio Díaz and an admirer of General Reyes. His followers were known as Felicistas, but his social base was very thin, limited to supporters in the military and the conservative elites. His coup attempt on October 12 was revanchist; that is to say, he hoped for a return to the political system established by his uncle. It was hasty and ill-prepared; its timing driven less by favorable conditions and more so, perhaps, by the approach of the U.S. presidential elections on November 1, which pitted Republican William Taft against Democrat Woodrow Wilson. In his manifesto, below, Díaz appealed to the deep disappointment of former Maderistas with the lack of reforms emanating from the Madero government, but he had no intention of summoning popular armed support; he therefore offered no economic or social program. His revolt was a classic pronunciamiento, aimed at mobilizing a military mutiny. But the army was not yet ready to move against the government. A week later, Díaz surrendered to General Joaquín Beltrán. A court-martial sentenced Díaz to death, but Madero commuted the penalty and had Díaz transferred to Lecumberri prison in Mexico City.

Mexicans: In this moment of supreme anguish for the homeland, I have come to raise my voice and call for the aid of all men of goodwill who wish to contribute to the rebirth of an era of peace and harmony. It is no longer possible to endure in silence the many ills inflicted on the Republic by the disastrous administration that emerged from the revolutionary movement of 1910.

Madero has now removed the mask of democracy and altruism that he cynically used to deceive the people in a moment of national madness and drag them into an armed movement, thus exposing the true face of the man who illegitimately proclaimed himself the leader and true soul of the revolution. It is the face of a greedy man enriching himself and his many family members, a man who lacks the ability to govern, a man whose weakness and indecision make him cruel and bloodthirsty, a man whose dubious state of mind makes him unfit for the responsibilities of the office he holds.

Arson, looting and killing are the weapons used by the current government, not to defend itself against aggression, but to silence the voices of former supporters who demand: Meet your promises! And those who were deceived by Madero retaliate with killing, looting and arson, driven to rabid heights by the impotence of their complaints. They are left with no road to follow other than to die fighting unless they wish to perish like wild savages, hunted in the ashes of razed villages that have been littered with the bodies of sisters, daughters, wives and mothers uselessly and ignominiously sacrificed.

Let there be no doubt: the current revolution is a provoked insubordination which is absolved even by harsh military laws, for it has been forced by the cruellest abuses of authority that threaten prosperity, honour and life. It is therefore necessary, for the prosperity and happiness of the Republic, to make a supreme effort and destroy the evil at its source, removing power from bloody and inept hands.

It is for this noble purpose that I am risking my life and that of the brave men who have rallied around me. If we die, it will be with the satisfaction of having done so for the good of the fatherland. But if we are favoured with victory, we will install an interim government whose members are persons of recognized probity, intelligence and prestige, regardless of political affiliation or belief. That government will work tirelessly for the ideal inscribed on the flag of our rebellion, "Impose Peace Through Justice." Upon the return of order, the interim government will convene elections, respecting and upholding the popular mandate on the basis of free suffrage and no re-election—which has been so vilely flouted by Madero's ambition—solemnly promising never to repeat the cruel mockery of a fake election which, being fraudulent and without legal value, makes the current presidency vacant.

To the Noble Army, which I have had the honour of belonging to since my youth; I now suffer the pain of separation from you as a vigorous protest against those who claim to be our equals or superiors—criminals rescued from the gallows, foreign adventurers and the relatives of Madero. To my comrades, and especially my brothers, sons of the glorious Military College: our discipline has a limit, which is the supreme good of the fatherland, but now, weapons for defending the nation have become an executioner's axe used by the current government to impose its tyranny. We call on you to join with us in our work of justice. Good sons of the current revolution, rally to me so that our action will be more effective. We pledge that, along with my life, my name will always follow the path of patriotism and honour.

To all Mexicans, lend me your material and moral support for the task of securing peace out of this war. I do not stand before you with impossible promises or deceptive appeals to your good faith, as did the infamous men of the previous revolution. I only promise peace and, when this is achieved, the elimination of those who started this war and spilt rivers of their compatriots' blood in order to loot the coffers of the Treasury. Your interests lie in the rule of law, serene and impartial, for only peace and order can produce material goods and the exercise of freedoms. Let our slogan be that which is stamped over my signature: Peace and Justice.

Twenty Months of Anarchy: Madero and His Enemies[2]

J. Figueroa Domenech, 1913

Politically, J. Figueroa Domenech was cut from similar cloth as Madero. He was a scholar in the late Porfiriato who published on Mexican geography. Figueroa Domenech supported the Anti-Reelectionists and became a chronicler of Madero's revolution. The next excerpt is from *Twenty Months of Anarchy*, a history of Madero's downfall written in 1913. Figueroa Domenech criticized the Felicista coup as a reaction against Madero by the wealthy classes—specifically the conservative senate, the press, and the military—but also argues that Madero was more fatally wounded by the popular revolts and unrest that dogged the regime from 1911 on, particularly the Zapatistas.

"Words, words, words" said the people, in a parody of Hamlet, when they read Díaz's manifesto. That much, at least, is clear from the profound indifference that greeted the adventure of the former brigadier. A manifesto without a programme or any new idea could not hope to relieve the afflicted homeland. To the contrary, it threatened to infect the army—the robust pillar of the State—with the terrible plague of insubordination and disorder, a contagion from which it had been hitherto free. But the Government did not look at the Veracruz movement with the same indifference as the people. From the outset, it perceived two terrible aspects. The first was that the Porfiristas had thrown down the gauntlet before the government. The second is that when it came time to suppress the movement, it would also have to proceed against the powerful and wealthy class whose conservative members had selfishly supported Félix Díaz. But fortunately, the subversive movement quickly collapsed without spreading. This averted a disastrous struggle between democracy and the wealthy classes, and also smothered the spark of indiscipline which hoped to link the army with the Porfirians.

Before discussing Madero's errors, we must gloss Díaz's manifesto to highlight its injustices and contradictions to support our thesis that, despite the many shortcomings of the Madero regime, any attempt at revolution was unjustified since Mexico's political and material conditions were improving.

The preamble of the document invites all men of good faith to help in regaining peace and harmony through armed struggle and by sowing discord in the army. This is a contradiction for one cannot impose peace by force unless one has a force greater than the disorder. And what power did Díaz have to counter the numerous groups of armed rebels? None. It goes on to say that Madero removed his mask of democracy and altruism to reveal his true face as the illegitimate leader of the revolution. This phraseology is taken from a libellous pamphlet called "Madero Unmasked," which appeared after the triumph of the revolution in 1911, which Madero allowed to circulate without harassing its author [Rafael Aguilar Olmos]. But it does not even attempt to explain why or how Madero ceased to be democratic and altruistic.

Díaz's first coup failed and, even though the next one succeeded, there were ultimately three powerful forces that defeated Madero: the Senate, the Army and the newspapers. The government was unable to resist them as Madero had lost his prestige, partly due to his own mistakes, partly the result of a campaign of defamation and slander undertaken by his enemies. The illegal and violent way in which these forces overthrew Madero's regime brought the fatherland to the brink of an awful abyss.

But how did Madero lose his prestige? Zapatismo was the most important factor for it served as a weapon of formidable opposition against Madero.

Everywhere the spirit of rebellion spread among the Maderistas and anarchy settled like an oil slick across the Republic.

Another mortal factor derived from the Maderista rebel leaders who had sustained their men's enthusiasm by promising benefits when the revolution triumphed in 1911. These were impossible to fulfill, but they were made in the name of the Revolution. For example, the Zapatista leaders promised to divide the land among proletarians. Those uneducated people believed that re-dividing the land was a legitimate form of restitution, without any regard for the sacred right of ownership. But the opposition press, and the political figures behind it, were careful not to point out this error. In fact, they welcomed the capricious promises as if they actually came from the Plan of San Luis, confident that by fostering and discussing these absurd promises, they would thereby create a dangerous obstacle for the government of Madero.

The Zapatistas' socialist preaching even impacted the Yaqui Indians who rebelled with the demand: "we want our land!" Some even implemented the infamous re-division of lands, while others went further, sharing crops as well as land, and formulating a new definition of their creed that stated: "socialism consists in sharing the products of each others' work." How was it possible to sustain Madero's popularity with such anarchy, such despotism, such turmoil, and such a relaxation of social discipline?

The Zapatistas, then, were the darkest nightmare of Mr. Madero. His major error is that he did not have the Zapatistas destroyed during the interim-Presidency of De la Barra! Outside the Zapatistas, nothing was important: not the war in Chihuahua against Pascual Orozco; not the other revolutionary hotbeds that died away with Orozco's defeat; not the Vazquista conspiracy that fell into disrepute; not even the rabid and dark plots against Madero. The Zapatistas! Zapatismo was the most fearsome threat.

In Mexico, we still don't know what impression the events of February, the Ten Tragic Days, have had in the interior, but a terrible doubt has assailed us all. Will the political change unite the nation and restore order, or will new revolutionaries appear in the battlefield still soaked with Mexican blood, some clamouring for revenge, others in pursuit of ambition? We believe that there can only be one answer. The Government of Francisco Madero was defective. But bad or not, it embodied a national aspiration. With the end of the democratic regime we will see a return of the old dictatorial regime of Porfiristas and oligarchs. The people will see the edifice of political liberty pulled to the ground, whose cornerstone was placed in Puebla by Aquiles Serdán. We received what could be expected from a dreamer and visionary. But war, lawlessness, and anarchy continued, creating a false impression that the nation was fed up with Madero as well as the democratic institutions that he brought to government. So now anarchy, chaos and war will continue!

The Charges Against Madero[3]

Rafael de Zayas Enríquez, 1914

Rafael de Zayas Enríquez was a Porfirian politician, jurist, and writer, a longtime friend and supporter of Porfirio Díaz until 1906 when, in his own words, "I separated myself from him" and went into exile in the United States, having concluded that his methods were "leading the country unavoidably towards revolution." Zayas Enríquez opposed Madero's revolution, but like many científicos he offered critical support when offered a post in the government, late in 1911. Ultimately, he condemned Madero's government as a disaster for Mexico and supported the Felicista revolt in October 1912, as well as the Huerta-Díaz coup in February 1913. In the following excerpt, he argues that the "counter-revolution was a necessity created by the government itself."

No man with a spark of common sense ever expected Madero to fulfill even one half of the promises he made as revolutionary leader or as presidential candidate; it would have been beyond the limits of the possible. But he was expected to inaugurate a regime of order and justice. Madero unfortunately was himself caught in the snares he had set. It is now recognized that his administration meant disaster for Mexico from every point of view, political, administrative, and international.

The whole country began to manifest its unrest. Revolutionary groups sprang up in the Northern, the Southern, and the Central States. They lacked coherence and leaders of prestige; however the same desire animated them all. They were bent on overthrowing Madero. The truth is that the nation gave no support to its government because it had no confidence in that government and resented its shocking machinations. Neither did the nation support the revolutionists because it failed to find among them one striking personality offering positive guarantees for the future.

There is not the slightest doubt that President Madero protected the Zapatistas. At first he did it to hold in check the provisional government of De la Barra, and later for purely sordid reasons. The existence of Zapatismo in Morelos had only one meaning for the Madero family; by keeping that region in a constant state of hostility it was possible to lower the value of real estate, and since the landowners were unable to protect their interests, the Madero family was in a position to acquire valuable sugar plantations at a ridiculously low price.

For these reasons, General Félix Díaz rebelled in the city of Vera Cruz, October 16, 1912. He intended to pacify the country. The revolt awoke sympathies among the Mexican population and in foreign countries. Pleasant hopes were built upon its possible success. Unfortunately its young leader, rich in valor and self-confidence, lacked experience and organizing ability.

He was betrayed and captured by Maderista troops which had promised him their assistance.

Félix Díaz was sent to the Lecumberri penitentiary in Mexico City. General Bernardo Reyes was in the military prison. They contacted each other and began secret preparations for another rebellion. It was necessary to select a chief to conduct military operations, and the unanimous choice was General Huerta. Joaquin Claussell, a young lawyer, and Fernando Gil, a partisan of Reyes and related to Huerta assumed the task of convincing Huerta to accept the leadership; but they could not break his allegiance to the government. General Manuel Mondragon also organized a group of officers and citizens. The alliance was concluded on the understanding that Reyes and Díaz would be the leaders, that the former would be commander-in-chief, assume the provisional presidency as a military dictator, and call for presidential elections, after which all would do their best to assure the election of Félix Díaz.

On February 8, everything was ready and General Mondragón decided to strike on Sunday. The officers fighting under General Huerta were hostile to the government. So were the soldiers, who felt a deep hatred for this ruler whom the press represented as a ridiculous person. General Huerta felt the terrible hostility of his subordinates towards the government, and he remembered the calumnies slung at him by Madero. He was unable, however, to take any radical decision, for the government distrusted him openly.

As the fighting continued, a group of senators met with Madero on February 18, seeking his resignation. He answered he would never resign. The senators decided upon a final step. They called on General Huerta to overcome his scruples. The senators told him that history would judge whether the army had done right or wrong in supporting a man who cost his country so many lives. The only alternative for the army, they said, was loyalty to Madero or the country. This impressed the old soldier so deeply that he said: "I have already told you that I cannot strike such a blow, but I could refuse to recognize President Madero if directed by the legislative and judicial powers. If these two bodies agree I will tell President Madero to resign at once." The senators returned soon with a majority of the justices of the Supreme Court who assured Huerta that they were agreeable to the proposition.

Later that day, General Huerta had Madero arrested and issued the following:

"In Mexico City, Generals Félix Díaz and Victoriano Huerta met together, the former assisted by Attorneys Fidencio Hernández and Rodolfo Reyes and the latter by Lieutenant Colonel Joaquin Maas and Engineer Enrique Zepeda.

"General Huerta stated that, as Mr. Madero's Government was unsustainable, in order to prevent further bloodshed and out of feelings of national fraternity, he had made prisoners of Mr. Madero, his Cabinet, and other persons. General Huerta expressed his good wishes to General Díaz to the effect that they might fraternize and unite to save the present distressful situation. General Díaz stated that his movement had no other object than to serve the national welfare, and that he is ready to make any sacrifice which might redound to the benefit of the country. After discussions had taken place, the following was agreed on:

"First: From this time on, the Executive Power which held sway does not exist and is not recognized. Generals Díaz and Huerta pledge themselves to prevent by all means any attempt to restore said Power.

"Second: As soon as possible, efforts will be made to adjust the situation under legal conditions. Generals Díaz and Huerta will make every effort within seventy-two hours to assume the Provisional Presidency of the Republic with a Cabinet.

"Third: While the legal situation is being determined and settled, Generals Huerta and Díaz are placed in charge of all authority in order to afford guarantees.

"Fourth: General Félix Díaz declines to be part of the Provisional Cabinet in case General Huerta becomes Provisional President, in order to remain at liberty to campaign for the Presidency at the next elections.

"Fifth: Official notice is immediately given to foreign diplomats that the former Executive Power has ceased; that provision is being made for a legal substitute; that full authority is vested in Generals Díaz and Huerta; and that all proper guarantees will be afforded to their respective countrymen.

"Sixth: All revolutionists are at once invited to cease hostile movements and to reach the necessary settlements."

I will now review my charges against Francisco Madero: he disturbed the peace and started a revolution in which the ills the Mexican Republic is suffering had their inception; he took control of the presidency merely on the strength of that revolution; he was too lenient with Zapata and other rebel chieftains whose troops are mere bandits; he repeatedly violated the constitution and the election laws, imposing unpopular officials; and his government was disastrous for the country. Therefore the counter-revolution was a necessity created by the government itself.

The Heart of the Conspiracy[4]

Márquez Sterling, 1917

Márquez Sterling was Cuba's ambassador to Mexico. Sterling entertained high regard for Madero and a correspondingly low opinion of U.S. Ambassador Henry Lane Wilson. Indeed, Sterling's was one of the few voices in the diplomatic corps to oppose Wilson's policy of undermining Madero. In the following selection, Sterling asserts that the U.S. Embassy was the heart of the conspiracy to overthrow Madero during the Decena Trágica.

Ambassador Wilson, as dean, met with the Diplomatic Corps and the meeting took place, as was natural, at the embassy. The ministers were punctual, arriving at the hour set by Mr. Wilson. The extraordinary severity of the circumstances was reflected in the faces of the diplomats.

I remember that, upon leaving the legation to take my automobile to the meeting, a sympathizer of Félix Díaz's, gave me some news which later proved accurate: "In the last exchange of gunfire at the gates of the Palace, the rebels injured Villar and the Minister of War appointed Huerta as Commander of Plaza."

The appointment of the hero of Bachimba was contrary to the wishes of Madero's family and friends, and was done without consulting the President. "I do not understand," continued this supporter of the Prince, "why the government put its trusts in Huerta or why Huerta decided to support the government . . ."

"Huerta," I asked, "is not loyal to Madero?"

"The situation, Minister, prevents loyalties that lead to disaster," replied the government's adversary, "and I know that Huerta has had dealings with the leaders of the coup . . ."

"Are you certain that this is true?"

"I am myself involved in the affair, and I know that Huerta has not yet reached an agreement with the rebels because he hopes for the Presidency if they succeed—but according to the pact of rebellion, the Presidency is supposed to go to General Bernardo Reyes. Oh, if Huerta guesses the details of the pact he will join Félix Díaz in organizing the final attack on the President!"

When I arrived at the meeting of diplomats, nobody questioned the loyalty of the new Commander of the Plaza and I withheld what I had learned. I was not certain that it was completely accurate, and the spreading of false information is repugnant to me.

Mr. Wilson appeared to be highly alarmed, and suggested we ask the government to undertake two measures: first, a ban on the sale of pulque; and second, to have regular soldiers provide police services. Everyone agreed. Pulque is the favourite drink of the Mexican people. Mr. Wilson feared that drunkenness would incite the rabble to commit the barbaric horrors of looting. The Apostle Madero had also preached about the harm of pulque in the period of his dominance. At a street demonstration, two men displayed bottles of pulque as if they were national symbols. Madero addressed them saying: "My friends, pulque is the best supporter of dictatorship, because it degrades and stupefies the people and delivers them, bound hand and foot, to their executioners." Such was the magnetic appeal of the Apostle that the electrified crowd shouted: "Down with pulque!"

The other measure proposed by the ambassador corresponded to the importance of the crisis. The rebels had quickly disarmed the police, many of whom were supporters of Félix Díaz anyways, and they joined his ranks. Madero's government had kept the police force of Don Porfirio Díaz; not surprisingly, the law enforcement officers of the old Dictator now abandoned Madero.

The diplomatic conference turned to discussing the government's position in the conflict with the rebels. "The government?" asked one minister ironically. "I do not know where it is or who forms the Mexican government!" Another one immediately replied: "Madero claims to be the President of the Republic. I do not know. I'm not satisfied with him either. I don't think anyone is." But no one paid any attention because the ministers were all talking at the same time. Then the U.S. ambassador reminded us to consider the urgent political problem: "We should address ourselves to the government . . ." But, his discourse was lost in the wind, for the ironic Minister interrupted again: "We cannot address ourselves to the government; there is no government . . ."

"To the Foreign Minister," said Mr. Wilson calmly.

"You can not go to the Foreign Minister, and he cannot leave the Palace; he cannot receive us, nor can he come to us. There is no Foreign Minister."

"The government is Madero," exclaimed a Latin American diplomat, "and the Diplomatic Corps cannot repudiate him. This is an uprising, nothing more. The Ciudadela does not appoint or depose constitutional governments in Mexico. It is our responsibility to respect the sovereignty of this nation; this means that our actions should not undermine the indisputable legitimacy of Madero's government."

Their Excellencies refused to listen to this diplomat's eloquent words in defence of Mexican sovereignty. Moreover, the ministers rose from their seats to confer around a certain foreigner who had arrived and wanted to talk to the U.S. Ambassador. He was a tall man, thick, blond, and German. His name? I've forgotten. His profession? Perhaps a consul, perhaps a trader, perhaps an industrialist, perhaps anything except his role as a supporter of Félix Díaz. "I come from the Ciudadela and the Presidency," he exclaimed, drowning out the others. "Madero's position is now untenable and desperate. There are no police to protect the city, which is now at the mercy of enraged troops and the rabble."

Mr. Wilson has said that "the U.S. embassy became the focal point of all activities on behalf of humanity." But honestly, my view then—and later with the testimony of the Spanish Ambassador Cologán—is that there is ample evidence that the U.S. embassy was nothing other than the heart of a real conspiracy against Madero's government. Its policy, even before the rebellion, and especially during it, was to spread false information and to raise false alarms. One of Mr. Wilson's obsessions, and one that most impressed his colleagues, was the imminence of looting by mobs. Even though no one saw any signs to support that fear, some ministers surrendered, pathologically, to panic.

Another obsession of Mr. Wilson was that the hordes of Morelos might invade the troubled capital. Female voices called the embassies by telephone to ask if it was true that Genevevo de la O had taken nearby Tacubaya. The consternation was so great that the most extraordinary phenomena appeared in the imaginations of some people who claimed to have seen the "bandit" leader with several bloody heads tied to the saddle of his horse, advancing on the city by way of San Angel—and not only Genevevo de la O but Zapata himself, unbroken by the forces of Federal General Felipe Angeles who had no desire to collaborate with Félix Díaz in the ruin of Madero.

I remember that Mr. Wilson showed me his list of the factions—including the Zapatistas—who were supporting the nephew of Porfirio Díaz. For Mr. Wilson, there was hardly a peaceful citizen anywhere in the Republic. "Madero," he exclaimed, "is insane, a hopeless dreamer, and his resistance to Félix is completely useless." Was Mr. Wilson merely deceived by the rebels? In Oaxaca, a battalion revolted and then returned to its barracks. In Puebla, things were quiet. A small group of rebels commanded by Benjamin Argumedo wandered around the outskirts of San Luis Potosí. Everywhere else the country was calm, except the capital. Thus, Madero had real hope of strengthening his government if Huerta would sink his claws into Félix Díaz. But Mr. Wilson transmitted his shocking reports to the State Department in Washington, just like the sensational reports of the foreign correspondents.

A Diplomatic Diary[5]

Henry Lane Wilson, 1913

The following selection is compiled and abridged from diplomatic reports filed by the U.S. Ambassador to Philander Knox, U.S. Secretary of State, during the coup. They illustrate the active role that Henry Lane Wilson played in the coup. At the same time, it is unclear to what extent Wilson acted on his own initiative or followed instructions from his superiors. On one hand, little suggests that Washington tried to reign in Wilson; on the other hand, Wilson acknowledged that he "assumed considerable responsibilities without instructions, but no harm has been done." Two points are worth noting. The first is that Wilson had prior knowledge that Huerta had been suborned but failed to warn the president of the country to which he was accredited as ambassador; the second is the discrepancy between Zayas Enríquez's account, which claims that Huerta was loyal up to February 18, and Wilson's account, which makes it clear that Huerta had decided to act against Madero at least by February 17.

February 12, 1913

I went with the Austrian and Spanish Ministers, and with the written authority of the British Minister, to the National Palace and saw the President. I stated that we had come to protest the hostilities. I informed him of the loss of American life and property, the destruction of the Consulate General, and that the President of the United States was concerned about the situation. President Madero was visibly embarrassed and tried to fix responsibility on Díaz. He added that measures were being taken to end the rebellion by tomorrow. These statements made no impression on us and we insisted on a cessation of hostilities until we could make representations to Díaz.

Joined by the British Minister, we then conferred with Díaz who received us with the honors of war. I made the same representations to him as to the President; urged that firing be confined to a particular zone, owing to the danger to non-combatants; stated that much damage had been done in the residential district by indiscriminate firing; that the President of the United States was concerned over the situation; that vessels had been ordered to the seaports, as well as marines which would be landed if necessary and brought to this city to keep order and protect the lives and property of foreigners.

Díaz replied that he regretted what was happening, but that his attitude had been one of defence, even though he could have taken the National Palace at any time. He considered the placement of Federal cannon in their present position as an utter disregard of all rules of civilized warfare. The morale of his troops was excellent, and he would be joined by about 2,000 soldiers now at San Lázaro station.

February 14, 1913

Pedro Lascurain, Foreign Minister, this morning expressed unofficially his conviction that something must be done to terminate the present dreadful situation. He intimated in confidence that the President ought to resign. I told him that public opinion, Mexican and foreign, was holding the Government responsible and urged him to take immediate action leading to a discussion between the contending parties. I suggested calling together the Senate and arranging an armistice. He is profoundly impressed with what he believes to be the threatening attitude of our Government.

The fighting has been mild since this morning, indicating that my conversation with Lascurain had the desired effect or that Federal ammunition is being exhausted. Information comes that the Cabinet urged the resignation of Madero but that he refused. I have asked the British, German, and Spanish Ministers and the French Chargé d'Affaires to come to the Embassy tonight for consultation. They are in accord with the policy I am pursuing and I believe also the rest of my colleagues. The Embassy automobile en route to bring colleagues here was held up a few minutes ago by Federals and robbed. I have asked for a Federal escort.

Mexico, February 15, 1913

In order to supplement the work done with Lascurain, I requested the British, German, and Spanish Ministers to come to the Embassy to resolve upon some action. The opinion of the assembled colleagues was unanimous that we should at once, even without instructions, request President Madero to resign in order to save further bloodshed and international complications. The Spanish Ambassador Bernardo Cólogan y Cólogan was designated to bear to the President our views, it being understood that his representations were in the way of advice and supposedly unofficial. This morning he went to the palace and entered in advance of thirty Senators, who were on a similar mission. Cólogan went over the points, saying that it was our unanimous opinion that the President should resign. The President replied that he did not recognize the right of diplomats to interfere in a domestic question; that he was the Constitutional President and would never resign, but would die in defence of his rights. At this moment the Senators announced that they were coming to ask for his resignation. He replied: "Tontería!" [Foolishness], and vanished through the doors. The Senators were told that the President had gone with General Huerta to examine firing points. The Senate had voted to ask Madero to resign by a vote of 27 to 3, a majority but not a quorum. Lascurain had worked very hard to bring this movement about, and the attitude of the President moved him so profoundly that he broke down and wept.

This morning a battery was sent to the block where the Embassy is situated. The whole American colony became panic-stricken. I wrote a courteous note to Huerta asking him to remove the battery. He sent me a courteous reply, saying that orders in compliance with my request had been issued, and the battery was removed.

The German Minister told me the Federals are now being manoeuvred to fire over the foreign residential district against the Ciudadela; also that the French school which I filled with women and children had been filled with Federals, and a battery stationed there. He asked me to join him to visit Huerta and we have asked for a cessation of firing, we ask for a daily armistice and a definite limitation of the firing zone. There is no question of removing Americans to a safer place. There is no safe place. Our only point of weakness is defence, as I have not been able to secure entirely satisfactory results, on account of obstacles which the Department will recognize.

Mexico, February 17, 1913

Huerta notifies me to expect action to remove Madero at any moment; plans fully matured, the purpose of delay being to avoid violence or bloodshed. I asked no questions and made no suggestions beyond requesting that no lives be taken except by due process of law. I am unable to say whether or not these plans will materialize; I simply repeat the word sent to me.

February 19, 1913

It is evident that the public believes that the storm is over. The city has been quiet all day, though many looters were abroad last night. There are very few people about the Embassy. The storm may or may not be over, so long as Díaz and Huerta continue to work in accord. To that end I am now devoting myself.

The originals of the agreements between Huerta and Díaz last night are on record in this Embassy. These documents provide for convening Congress, naming the new Cabinet, stipulating the election by Congress of General Huerta as Provisional President, and other provisions to maintain order. There are three agreements which I stipulated but are not in writing: first, the release of the Madero Ministers; second, liberty of the press and an uncensored telegraph; third, joint action between the two generals for maintaining order. Congress is now in session; its ratification of the agreement in the Embassy last night will be a formality.

The President and Vice President are in the guardhouse of the palace, as are General Delgado, General Angeles, and the Minister of War. The report this morning was that Gustavo Madero [Francisco's older brother] was killed by the simple process of the *ley de fuga* [shot while trying to escape].[6]

I have assumed considerable responsibilities without instructions in many matters, but no harm has been done. I believe great benefits have been achieved for our country. Our position here is stronger than ever.

The President and the Vice President have resigned and their resignations are before Congress, which of course will accept them. By law the executive power will devolve upon Lascurain, who will hold office a few moments and then General Huerta will be proclaimed Provisional President and will immediately announce the Cabinet.

February 20, 1913

The installation of the Provisional Government took place amid great popular demonstrations of approval. A wicked despotism has fallen, but what the future contains cannot be safely predicted. The new Government will be inaugurated this afternoon. So far no other executions have come to the knowledge of the Embassy. At the request of the wife of Madero I visited General Huerta today, with the German Minister, to unofficially request that utmost precautions be taken to prevent taking the lives of the President and Vice President, except by due process of law. General Huerta replied that he would have sent them out of the country last night but feared the possibility of an attack on the train. He said that every precaution was being taken to guard the life of these two persons and that they would probably be tried, but on what charges he did not state. Madero, the Vice President and some generals are still confined in the National Palace and I understand Madero is being severely treated. This should be brought to the attention of the President; I suggest that instructions be sent for me to deal unofficially with Díaz in the matter of reprisals. I urgently recommend retention of all American warships in Mexican waters.

February 26, 1913

The Government of Madero was anti-American; neither appeals nor veiled threats affected its incomprehensible attitude. In the last months of its existence its despotism was infinitely worse than Porfirio Díaz. Though the new Government resulted from an armed revolution and, at certain critical stages events occurred which must be deplored by civilized opinion, it nevertheless assumed office according to constitutional precedents and therefore is a representative Government. The new administration is accepted by Mexican public opinion and especially the more respectable part; it is equally accepted by foreign elements in Mexico. The Cabinet is united, active, and moderate, acting in full concert with the President, with public opinion, and the army. Anti-American sentiment has almost disappeared and the new Government is pro-American. The prospects for settling our existing complaints against Mexico are excellent. If this Government cannot be maintained, chaos will result and the necessity for intervention can hardly be resisted.

I am endeavoring to aid this Government establish itself firmly and to procure the submission and adhesion of all parties in the Republic. I assume I have the approval of the State Department and the President, and an expression to that effect will enable me to proceed with great vigor and confidence in a delicate question, work which I believe is in the interest of our Government.

Madero's Death Was a National Necessity[7]

Rafael de Zayas Enríquez, 1914

The murders of Madero and Pino Suárez were a shock to many Mexicans, as well as citizens of the United States where the assassinations gave President-elect Woodrow Wilson a reason to deny recognition to the provisional government of General Huerta. Almost nobody believed the official version that Madero and Pino Suárez died from a botched rescue attempt. Nevertheless, Huerta's supporters promoted the official story. Writing for a U.S. audience, Rafael de Zayas Enríquez attempted to absolve Huerta and Díaz as part of a broader effort to change President Wilson's policy.

As soon as President Madero and Vice-President Pino Suárez were arrested there was speculation as to the fate that awaited them. Both were the object of deep hatred. Army officers and soldiers were in favour of their execution; the people were incensed over the slaughter of harmless folk and the many executions that had taken place without process of law. The lives of both men were in great danger, and therefore the government decided to transfer them from the Palace to the penitentiary, where they would be safe against any attempt on the part of the mob or the army. This decision was agreed upon by Generals Huerta, Díaz, Mondragón, and Blanquet, and Rodolfo Reyes. Then, on February 23, the Mexico City press published the following item:

"The President called a meeting of his cabinet to report that Francisco Madero and José Pino Suárez, who were held in the National Palace, were being moved to the penitentiary, which had been placed under the command of an army officer for more safety; the automobiles carrying them were only a short distance from the penitentiary when they were stopped by a group of armed men; the men of the escort stepped out to defend themselves; the number of the aggressors increased and the prisoners tried to run away; a shooting affray took place in which two of the aggressors were wounded and one killed and both prisoners lost their lives.

"The president and his cabinet ordered a judicial inquiry into this attempt against the life of military prisoners. A very thorough inquiry was conducted under the personal direction of the military attorney general. The minister of justice ruled that, considering the exceptional character of the case, the Attorney-General is to take up the case after the preliminary inquiry is terminated.

"The government deplores this incident and promises that justice shall take its course. The officers commanding the escort have been held and all evidence is being collected. The whole truth shall be known regarding this disgraceful incident, which, however, is not unexplainable under the present painful circumstances."

Major Francisco Cárdenas of the 7th Rurales, in charge of the prisoners, informed the press that a first attack had been at Lecumberri Street where a group of men opened fire upon the automobiles. Those men were in ambush only a few yards from the prison. The men who fired the first shots were lying flat in the gutter.

"The prisoners tried to take advantage of the confusion and to run away. That cost them their lives, for the men who had set out to free them fired shots rather carelessly. The Rurales of the escort discharged their guns in self-defence. Madero and Pino Suárez fell down, probably struck by bullets from both sides."

Such is the official version.

A different version was circulated, according to which the prisoners had been shot by their escort. The authors of the "Bloody Ten Days" give credence to this version and add: "The news of Madero's death did not create much of an impression, nor did it cause any disturbance. A few people from the lowest classes and a few workingmen were the only ones to cheer

Madero's body when it was removed from the penitentiary where the autopsy had been held."

Carlos Toro expressed himself as follows: "Let us say it quite frankly: nobody cared to preserve the lives of these dangerous apostles of violence and anarchy, and their death was considered by friends and enemies alike as a national necessity. The bitterness, the anger, the feuds kept up by those two men ended with them. Plain common sense demanded their extermination. There was plenty of deplorable evidence that those men, incapable of governing, were dangerous agitators. Whether this was a genuine assault or a premeditated execution, the nation's will was done. If a crime was committed it was a collective crime, for society was demanding the suppression of the two men responsible for the disorder affecting the Republic."

José Fernandez Rojas writes: "the official version has not found acceptance; there is nothing incredible about it, however, and it is perfectly possible. A group of Maderistas may have tried to free their chief with the result of satisfying the public's greatest need. Madero's and Pino Suárez's deaths were essential to the welfare of the country. It is a sorry thought that only their tragic fate insured permanent peace for our country."

Thus we find two contradictory reports. The first can be suspected on account of its official origin. The second is quite as suspicious, for it is little more than gossip. In favour of the official version, the government did not have to resort to such stratagems. It could have proceeded as it did with Gustavo Madero, or it could have sent Madero and Pino Suárez to a court-martial which would have tried them summarily and ordered their immediate execution. Moreover the case was referred to the court, which declared that no one could be held on account of the shooting. From the point of view of the court, the legal truth was that no crime had been committed and that the official version was the truthful one.

I Accuse Henry Lane Wilson[8]

Luis Manuel Rojas, 1914

Madero's supporters also engaged public opinion in Mexico and the United States. Luis Manuel Rojas, a Maderista deputy in congress, at no small risk to his own life, accused Ambassador Henry Lane Wilson of moral culpability for the murder of Madero and Pino Suárez, as well as having played a central role in facilitating the coup that led to the fall of Madero's government.

I accuse Mr. Henry Lane Wilson, Ambassador of the United States in Mexico, of being morally responsible for the death of Francisco Madero and José Pino Suárez, who were elected by the people in 1911, as President and Vice President of the Mexican Republic.

I accuse Ambassador Wilson of having thrown the weight of his influence as the ambassador of Washington into the balance, tilting Mexico's destiny towards a military government.

I accuse Ambassador Wilson of having argued against the legality of the Madero government, of threatening armed intervention by the U.S. Army during the combat in streets of the capital, and at a time when all liberal and democratic Mexicans hoped for sympathy and moral support from the one of the freest and most democratic nations on earth.

I accuse Ambassador Wilson of having had timely knowledge of the coup against constituted order, and of having received at the Embassy envoys from the leaders of the coup who counted on his support to attack a legally-constituted government.

I accuse Ambassador Wilson of having shown bias in favour of the reactionaries from the time that Félix Díaz rebelled in Veracruz. Mr. Wilson gave interviews to the American press frankly praising the rebel leader. This was outside the normal conduct of an ambassador and is evidence that he is not worthy of such a high mission.

I accuse Ambassador Wilson of a personal resentment toward President Madero; of not using his moral influence to aid the prisoners. Clearly, the men of the new order would not have refused a frank and genuine request by Ambassador Wilson, which was the only way to save the lives of Madero and Pino Suárez. He failed to do so despite instructions from Washington, despite the impassioned pleas of Mrs. Madero and Mrs. Pino Suárez, despite the desires of other diplomatic representatives, despite the formal request I made at the Embassy as Grand Master of the Lodge of the Valley of Mexico, and despite the people's clamour for clemency.

I accuse Ambassador Wilson of knowing that Madero and Pino Suarez would be sacrificed on the pretext of urgent political necessity, even though Huerta and Díaz promised to respect the lives of their prisoners and allow them to leave the country, provided they consented to resign.

I accuse Ambassador Wilson of having washed his hands like Pilate, when the authorities refused to let Madero and Pino Suárez leave immediately for Europe—keeping their wives and family waiting vainly at the Railway Station in Veracruz—even after the House of Deputies accepted their signed resignations.

I accuse Ambassador Wilson of lacking a natural sense of humanity for failing to protect the prisoners under the American flag on the pretext that he did not want to bear responsibility for what Madero and Pino Suárez might do afterwards.

I accuse Ambassador Wilson of having been two-faced in his behaviour. He showed one face to the new powers, and another one to Mrs. Madero and Mrs. Pino Suárez.

I accuse Ambassador Wilson of having misled his own government about the events in Mexico, and of having justified the need for a change of power.

I accuse Ambassador Wilson of having personally interfered in the politics of Mexico, of having contributed significantly to the fall of President Madero, and of having advised General Huerta that Congress should legalize the new government.

I accuse Ambassador Wilson of having used members of the American colony in Mexico City to convince Washington to keep him in his high post, contrary to the desires of Mexicans after the role Mr. Wilson played in our homeland's recent political tragedy.

I make these specific charges against Ambassador Wilson, under oath as an honest man and despite the danger to my life, placing my hopes for justice in the American people.

Everything Was Done to Save Madero[9]

Henry Lane Wilson, March 12, 1913

The day after the murder of Madero and Pino Suárez, Ambassador Wilson filed a peremptory report noting the atrocity and stated his conviction that the government version was truthful. However, the issue came back to haunt him. On March 4, President Woodrow Wilson and Secretary of State William Jennings Bryan assumed office, both adopting a different attitude towards Mexico than their predecessors. President Wilson and Bryan were unconvinced of the legality of Huerta's government and they rejected the official version of the assassination of Madero and Pino Suárez. They called on the U.S. Ambassador to account for his actions and, finding his explanations dubious they recalled him from Mexico. The following is Ambassador Wilson's response on March 12, 1913, to Secretary of State Bryan's queries about whether the ambassador bore any responsibility for the assassinations.

I never for a moment believed the lives of Madero and Pino Suárez to be in danger. Immediately after the arrest and imprisonment of Madero and his Ministers I asked General Huerta that no further violence be committed or blood shed, and that he release the Ministers. I received the assurances of General Huerta that no violence against the President and Vice President was contemplated and that he had immediately placed all of the Ministers of the Cabinet at liberty. Later on he asked my opinion as to what disposition should be made of the President; I did not think it expedient to assume the responsibility of advising him, but answered that he must do what was best for Mexico.

Later, I remonstrated with the President, and I think with De la Barra, against the unnecessary severity of the ex-President's confinement, and suggested that he and the other prisoners be transferred to more comfortable quarters. The Provisional President informed me that the ex-President and ex-Vice President would be put in a place of safety and later tried for unspecified crimes.

I also went to the President with the German Minister and had a very serious conversation, requesting assurances that the lives of the ex-President and the ex-Vice President would be saved. These were given, and I believed, and the German Minister believed, as did many of our colleagues, that there existed no reason for apprehension as to the attitude of the Government toward the deposed President and Vice President.

I also, at the request of Mrs. Madero, verbally asked the Provisional President to permit her to see the ex-President and that he should be furnished more palatable food. At the request of Mrs. Pino Suárez, I addressed a letter to General Blanquet, interceding for the life of the ex-Vice President, who I believed to be in danger from unofficial enemies.

Not content with these efforts, I personally visited members of the Cabinet to express deep concern for the ex-President's life and my desire that his treatment be more humane and considerate. If I had been apprehensive of any intention to deal foully with the ex-President I might have been more agitated and vehement, but not more active.

At the request of the family, I sent two messengers to General Mondragón to recover the body of the unfortunate Gustavo Madero, and obtained authority to search for the remains near the Ciudadela, which they did without success. Believing at one time that the life of Ernesto Madero [uncle to Francisco Madero] might be in danger, I sent him a letter inviting him to come, with his family, to the Embassy; and I afterwards caused the soldiers (who were ugly and threatening) to be removed from the house of his brother-in-law, where he was staying.

I am warranted in saying that everything was done to save the life of Francisco Madero that humanitarian considerations, public opinion in the United States, and the instructions of the Department could demand.

Concerning the deplorable death of the ex-President and ex-Vice President it is not possible to furnish the Department with a reliable account beyond the official version, which, in the absence of any other, I felt obliged to accept. A dozen different accounts by "eyewitness," all differing in details, have been offered, but are lacking in probability, and none convincing or positive. My own opinion is that the Government was not privy to killing these men, but that their deaths resulted as in the official version or from a subordinate military conspiracy, actuated by sentiments of revenge.

History will undoubtedly straighten out this tangle. While the crime was revolting it is not evident to me that the death of these two Mexicans should arouse greater disapproval in the United States than the murders of some 75 or 80 Americans in Mexico during the last two years.

Corrido of the Death of Madero[10]

Anonymous, 1914

In 1913, U.S. journalist John Reed crossed the border into Mexico to cover the campaign being fought by Francisco Villa against Victoriano Huerta. Reed discovered that Madero had already become an icon of martyrdom to the soldiers fighting alongside Villa. He recorded the lyrics of the following corrido sung by Villa's troops.

In Nineteen hundred and [thirteen] Madero was imprisoned
in the National Palace, on the eighteenth of February.

Four days he was imprisoned, in the Hall of the Intendancy
because he did not wish To renounce the Presidency.

Then Blanquet and Félix Díaz martyred him there.
They were the hangmen feeding on his hate.

They crushed . . . until he fainted
with play of cruelty to make him resign.

Then with hot irons they burned him without mercy
and only unconsciousness calmed the awful flames.

But it was all in vain because his mighty courage
preferred rather to die; his was a great heart!

This was the end of the life of him who was the redeemer
of the Indian Republic and all of the poor.

They took him out of the Palace and tell us he was killed in an assault.
What a cynicism! What a shameless lie!

O street of Lecumberri, your cheerfulness has ended forever,
for through you passed Madero to the Penitentiary.

That twenty-second of February will be remembered in the Indian Republic.
God has pardoned him, and the Virgin of Guadalupe.

Good-bye Beautiful Mexico, where our leader died.
Good-bye to the palace, when he issued a living corpse.

Señores, there is nothing eternal, nor anything sincere in life.
See what happened to Don Francisco I. Madero!

THIS IS A DICTATORSHIP
RAFAEL DE ZAYAS ENRÍQUEZ, 1914

For or against Huerta, to recognize his government or not; this was the question facing everyone—political parties, organized labor, state governors, rebel forces, and foreign governments—in the aftermath of the Decena Trágica. Huerta and Díaz seized power promising to restore the order and stability that had eluded Francisco Madero. It was not to be. The reaction against Huerta triggered a ferocious opposition within Mexico that surpassed the scale of the rising against Porfirio Díaz, and acquired characteristics of a social revolution that threatened to uproot the political and economic edifice. Moreover, Huerta's coup and the policies of his government offended the moralizing sensibilities—and the strategic interests—of U.S. President Woodrow Wilson who refused to recognize the new regime. As a result, Huerta's government survived for 20 months—slightly longer than the Madero government—and failed in even more spectacular fashion to subdue the country.

In the first year, Huerta had an upper hand. Most state governors capitulated and recognized his government, many intimidated by the example of Chihuahua Governor Abraham González who almost certainly would have resisted. Federal soldiers arrested González and put him on a train to Mexico City where he expected to be imprisoned; at Bachimba his escort stopped the train and applied the Ley de Fuga to Gonzalez, and for good measure hurled his body beneath the train as it departed. The only exceptions to the governors' capitulatory spirit were in the north. In Sonora, José María Maytorena hesitated and then fled for his life to Arizona. In Coahuila, Venustiano Carranza hesitated briefly, but chose to fight, repudiating Huerta and forming the Constitutionalist Army. In Mexico City, the Casa del Obrero resisted with work stoppages and civil disobedience, although Huertista repression compelled the flight of some of its leaders: Antonio Díaz Soto y Gama found refuge with the Zapatistas, while others joined the Constitutionalists in the north. Huerta also tried to induce the submission of anti-Madero rebels with bribes and offers of amnesty. The Zapatistas spurned the offer, but Pascual Orozco cashed in his fight for social reform to accept a large lump sum payment and a commission as one of Huerta's main military commanders. None of this was very surprising to Huerta, but the reaction of U.S. President Wilson was a rude shock for it inhibited recognition from those Latin American governments who followed Washington's lead and, while most European governments did extend recognition, the hostility of Washington weakened Huerta's credit abroad.

Meanwhile, Huerta moved quickly to consolidate power, excluding his erstwhile allies in the cuartelazo and imposing a military dictatorship. Like Porfirio Díaz, Huerta was imbued with the authoritarian culture of military command. Unlike Díaz, he lacked the ability or the desire to cultivate the political alliances that helped to sustain Díaz for 35 years. If the Porfirian dictatorship governed with a republican veneer, Huerta's was naked and unvarnished by any such pretensions. One by one former collaborators exited the inner circles. Huerta packed off Félix Díaz into exile with a diplomatic post in Japan, and then purged his cabinet of Felicistas like General Mondragón and científicos like Francisco De la Barra. In the autumn, Huerta dissolved congress—thereby dispersing opposition from científicos, Reyistas, and the Progressive Constitutionalists. A carefully managed election in October provided Huerta with a pliant congress dominated by the católicos who reaffirmed him as provisional president of Mexico. The dictatorship was in place.

★ ★ ★

The Choice Is Huerta or Anarchy[1]

Henry Lane Wilson, March 12, 1913

Diplomatic recognition might not have been an issue had outgoing President Taft and Secretary of State Knox acted before their terms expired. Their decision to delay had nothing to do with discomfort over Huerta's coup, nor even with the murders of Madero and Pino Suárez. To the contrary, they hoped to use recognition as a lever to extract a more compliant attitude from Huerta in anticipated negotiations over boundary disputes, claims for damages, and the like. They did not expect President-elect Wilson to use nonrecognition as an instrument to depose Huerta. A week after Woodrow Wilson assumed office, the Ambassador began to press his superiors for action. In the following report, on March 12, 1913, Henry Lane Wilson recited the arguments for recognition; he insisted on the legality of Huerta's succession, and emphasized his pro-U.S. attitude and capacity for pacifying Mexico. The argument did not persuade President Wilson. By the end of July, Washington permanently recalled its Ambassador.

There can be no doubt as to the legal constitution of the Provisional Government in conformity with precedents and the Mexican Constitution. The incumbency of Huerta is as legal as the incumbency of De la Barra after the resignation of Porfirio Díaz. If De la Barra was recognized by the United States as constitutionally inducted into office, the Provisional Government of Huerta is entitled to the same.

Without our recognition, upon which recognition by many other governments depends, it will be constantly exposed to attacks from enemies; and our attitude will take on a color of constructive sympathy with those conspiring against the reestablishment of order and peace in a neighboring and friendly Republic.

By hesitating too long, therefore, we might contribute to the weakening and possible demolition of the present Government and re-invoke the movements of disorder and anarchy which brought us to the verge of intervention in the affairs of this Republic.

The present Provisional Government has shown remarkable activity and energy in restoring order, in subduing rebellious elements and in consolidating different political factions and revolutionists in arms against the Government of Madero.

In two weeks the whole of the Republic to the south and west of the Federal District has been brought into a state of comparative peace. A small district in Guerrero is still in arms under Genevevo De la O, but a strong force of Federals has been sent against them and they will soon be defeated and brought to submission. Zapata remains inactive south of Cuernavaca, but negotiations with him indicate his early submission. In the north all of the leading rebel chieftains have submitted and most are now enrolled in its service.

The whole of the north is at peace with the exception of isolated brigandage, and in Sonora and Sinaloa where the governor is hostile to the present administration. The Sonora situation is not a Maderista movement, but the remains of the movement in which Carranza, then Governor of Coahuila and now a fugitive from justice, was the originator and prime mover.

General Huerta is pre-eminently a soldier who knows what he wants and how to get it, and is not overly particular as to methods. He is a firm believer in the policy of General Porfirio Díaz and believes in the closest and most friendly relations with the United States. I believe him to be a sincere patriot who will cheerfully relinquish the responsibilities of office as soon as peace is restored in the country.

The new administration is not popular, but it is respected. It has given birth to a new feeling of confidence which will permit the resumption of peaceful occupations in the cities and throughout the agricultural districts. Ultimately, unless the same type of government as that of Porfirio Díaz is again established, new revolutionary movements will break forth and general unrest will be renewed.

Now More Than Ever You Must Strike[2]

Emiliano Zapata, February 22–28, 1913

Contrary to the assertions of Ambassador Wilson, the Zapatistas had no intention of submitting to Huerta. Some minor Zapatista chieftains did accept amnesty, but the bulk of Zapata's forces remained in the field. The Zapatistas knew Huerta too well from his 1911 campaign in Morelos. The following two letters—respectively dated February 22 and February 28—that Zapata sent to one of his generals, Genevevo de la O, urged him to reject negotiations and to strike hard against Huerta. These are supplemented by an account written by an anonymous Maderista, and published in a compilation of anti-Huerta documents in 1914, that described Zapata's break with Orozco and the subsequent revision of the Plan of Ayala.

To Citizen General Genevevo de O:

This urgently informs you that the Government of Citizen Francisco Madero, has ended with his imprisonment as well as José María Pino Suárez, and other members of the government, leaving the Provisional Government in the hands of General Victoriano Huerta as Interim President and a Cabinet of members from past Governments, and which in no way satisfies the Revolution of the South, Centre and North of the Republic.

Consequently, I recommend that you refrain from entering into treaties with absolutely anyone outside of the Revolution who appears in your camp. In any case, you must adhere to the orders and instructions you receive from this headquarters. These recent events are no reason to stop your military activity. Now more than ever you should engage in hostilities with this evil government, not losing any opportunity to strike.

My esteemed General Genevevo de la O:

I recommend you carefully consider my argument; you will see that I am in the right. It is of the greatest importance that all insurgent leaders remain united and avoid any last minute difficulties. This is especially so with respect to political developments in the capital of the Republic, where a group of ambitious revolutionaries recently betrayed their patron Madero and seized government by illegal means. Otherwise the Government will outwit us.

This is it: continue fighting as you have until now for the ideals of the Plan of Ayala. We will soon succeed, for the current illegal government was established by treachery, has no elements of life, and lacks money to continue the war, as the country has lost its credit with foreign nations and cannot borrow even a single peso.

Above all: the Revolution of the South, Central and North is not in accordance with the traitors who seized the government. Revolutionaries should not believe anything they say nor have any confidence in them whatsoever. That would expose us to failure. What else can we expect from those who have notoriously betrayed and murdered their masters, to whom they owe all their wealth and the position they now have? No, in no way whatsoever can we believe these villains; you must strike them until you exterminate them.

I hope you will be fully satisfied with the foregoing and wish you every success in your military work, and that you always emerge victorious in combat. I take my leave and wish you happiness.

The Attitude of Zapata

Anonymous

[When first proclaimed in 1911], the Plan of Ayala recognized Pascual Orozco as Chief of the Revolution. When this frontier revolutionary submitted to Huerta and arrived in the capital city, he tried to establish contact with Zapata, and commissioned his father, Pascual Orozco Sr., to negotiate with the southern rebel. The military regime hoped that this would lead to the surrender of Zapata. Very soon, however, these hopes vanished. Zapata withdrew recognition of Orozco and arrested the peace commissioners. Some escaped, but the Zapatistas executed Pascual Orozco Sr. as a traitor. The regime then tried to use other southern revolutionaries [like Juan Andrew Almazán], who already submitted, to isolate Zapata. Huerta and Orozco urged Almazán to issue the following manifesto to the population of Guerrero [on March 31, 1913]:

In the tradition of the great independence heroes José María Morelos, Vicente Guerrero, Juan Alvarez, and Nicoás Bravo—we today uphold the prestige of our state's heroism, grasp the banner of patriotism and launch ourselves into the struggle against banditry.

The Zapatista nucleus rooted in Morelos believes that it is invincible. Our arms have emerged victorious on other more difficult occasions. We do not hesitate. Zapatismo is the flag of bandits, the flag of those who kill, of those who steal, of those who plunder. It is a black flag that must be totally exterminated and never again appear anywhere. Zapatismo is shameful and a threat to our country. The Zapatista rebellion has no ideals to follow. They have proved this with all of their repugnant deeds, with all their contemptible acts.

The submission of the rebel chiefs in Guerrero is palpable evidence that we are not connected to those bandits. Our only goal was to defeat Mr. Madero. Now we turn the weapons of Guerrero against the bandits. As they were in the old era of glory during the war of independence, our weapons are on the side of our country. We invite southerners to form a corps of volunteers to battle Zapatismo. Soon we will sign up recruits at the Hotel San Carlos. Citizens of Guerrero: will you measure up to the standard of courage?

Pascual Orozco Jr. also wrote to Juan Andrew Almazán on March 31, expressing his views on the current regime:

My dear friend and comrade:

In addition to the recommendations and orders sent to you by the President of the Republic, I am writing to ask that you inform your comrades in Guerrero, in my name, that they must have absolute faith in the current Government. It is inspired by a sincere desire for the welfare and prosperity of the country, and wishes to comply, before long and as much as possible, with the high ideals of the revolution of 1910, but which were betrayed by ex-President Francisco Madero.

The best way to bring our work of progress to a close is for all Mexicans, and especially revolutionaries, to act as one man to support the Government, to pacify the country, and to prepare for the coming elections. I wish you success in your patriotic mission and embrace you as a comrade and friend.

On May 30, 1913, Emiliano Zapata adopted an openly hostile attitude to General Huerta, and accordingly revised the Plan of Ayala. At the same time, he declared that Pascual Orozco was unfit to be Chief of the Revolution. Below are the relevant articles:

The first article of this Plan is amended thus:

Article 1: The ideas expressed in this article now apply to the usurper of public power, General Victoriano Huerta. With each passing day, his presence in the Presidency magnifies the contrast between his character and everything that stands for law, justice, rights, and morality. In this, he is much worse than Madero. As a result, the revolution will continue in complete accordance with the principles embodied in this Plan until it defeats the pseudo-President. Inspired as a trust of the supreme national will, the principles of the revolution will be sustained with the same fortitude and magnanimity that have been shown to this point.

The third article of this Plan is amended thus:

Article 3: Pascual Orozco is declared unworthy of the honour conferred on him by the revolution of the South and Centre. As for his compromise with the illicit and ill-fated government of Huerta, Orozco has lost the respect of his fellow citizens, to the point of becoming a social non-entity, without any meaningful significance. He is traitor to the principles he swore to uphold.

Consequently, the Chief of the Revolution, based on the principles in this Plan, is General Emiliano Zapata, leader of the Liberating Army of the Centre and South.

Carranza's Resistance and the Plan of Guadalupe[3]

Phillip Holland

On the same day—March 12, 1913—that Ambassador Wilson wrote to Bryan urging recognition of Huerta, the U.S. Consul in Coahuila,

Phillip Holland, forwarded the following compendium to Washington; it narrates the decision of Carranza to repudiate Huerta. What emerges is an indictment of Ambassador Wilson for misleading his consul on the imminence of U.S. recognition and for acting on behalf of Huerta by instructing U.S. consuls to win submission to Huerta. The portrait of Huerta is also unflattering; his actions come across as a deliberate attempt to provoke Carranza rather than to win his support. Following Holland's report is Carranza's Plan of Guadalupe—adopted on March 23, 1913—which formally repudiated Huerta and named Carranza as First Chief of the Constitutionalist Army. The Plan was narrowly political and contained no program for social or economic reforms; this reflected the politics and social status of Carranza who was a Porfirian-era liberal and a hacendado, who had been a reluctant and conservative supporter of Francisco Madero.

February 21: immediately after the announcement of General Huerta as the Provisional President, Governor Carranza of Coahuila denounced the new administration. He insisted that Huerta unconstitutionally assumed office, and that he would resist with armed forces. Then at noon the Governor decided to accept the Provisional President.

February 22: the Consul urged the Governor to announce his conformity with the new administration, but by the night the situation became tense as the Governor had not issued a bulletin of acceptance. That night this Consulate received the following telegram from the Embassy:

"A Provisional Government is installed with General Huerta as President. There is general public approval in the city. There are reassuring reports from other places. President Madero is a prisoner awaiting the decision of the Congress. The Senate and House of Representatives are in full accord with the new administration. You should urge general submission to the Government, which will be recognized by all foreign governments today."

The Consul called at the Palace to deliver the message. The Governor stated that he had been willing to accept the Provisional Government, but had been cut off from communication by the Provisional President. The Governor requested the Consul to urge Huerta to open communication. In pursuance of this the Consul sent the following to the Embassy:

"The Governor advises me that communication with Mexico has been cut by order of the President, and he believes federal troops are approaching to depose him. He reiterates his conformity. If the President deposes him he will lose the strongest man in Northern Mexico and a serious mistake will be made."

February 23: The Governor's overtures to the Government have been ignored; he does not propose to meet the fate of Madero; he will not resign but will go into the open and fight. It is reported he will attack the Federal troop train reported to be en route.

February 25: It would be advisable for the Embassy to counsel the President to communicate immediately with the Governor and to avoid a conflict with the combined northern States. It would be consummate folly to send Federal troops. Governor requests that the Embassy advise whether President Madero has been killed. Fighting reported to have begun. All hope of peaceful settlement abandoned.

March 1: The Governor is in open and armed opposition. Local conditions could hardly be worse. Governor has over 1,000 well-armed men. He has disarmed the city police and has liberated and armed prisoners.

March 3: The Governor has proposed: immediate resignation of Huerta; that the President and his chief of artillery leave the country; that Pedro Lascurain form a new government. The Governor says he has 11,000 men. Probably he has half the number. The Governor says that the miners of the north are joining his forces and begging for arms. There appears no longer any hope of the Governor submitting.

March 4: the following instruction was received from the Embassy:

"Assure the Governor he is rebelling against a legally constituted government which is strongly fortified; that his overthrow and defeat appear to the Embassy to be inevitable. Urge the necessity of making terms with the Provisional Government and avoiding further shedding of Mexican blood, destruction of property and the disturbance of the peace."

Immediately the Consul and Vice Consul met with the Governor. While the Governor received us with his usual gracious manner, it was evident that the Embassy's communication provoked resentment. He said: "The Consul can report that the Governor is in the fight to stay; that the Governor believes the Embassy to be at fault for the present state of affairs; that the Governor does not care to receive any further communication from the Embassy."

The Governor said that he knew that the Embassy's statement, that all countries will acknowledge Huerta, is incorrect. He said that the United States had not recognized the new administration. The Consul could only reassure the Governor that the United States had recognized Huerta as he had received no advice to the contrary. The Governor resents and declines the suggestions of the Embassy.

Plan of Guadalupe[4]

Hacienda de Guadalupe, Coahuila

General Huerta is repudiated as president of the Republic. The legislative and judicial powers of the federation are repudiated. State governments are repudiated if they continue to recognize the federal government 30 days after the publication of this plan.

In order to organize an army to carry out their goals, Citizen Venustiano Carranza, Governor of Coahuila, is appointed first chief of the Constitutionalist Army. Upon the occupation of Mexico City by the Constitutionalist Army, Citizen Venustiano Carranza, or his designate, will become provisional president. When peace has been established, the provisional president will convene general elections and hand power over to the civilian elected. When elected civilians have assumed office in the federal government, the citizen acting as first chief of the Constitutionalist Army in states that recognized Huerta, will assume the post of provisional governor and convene local elections.

Pancho Villa: The Rise of a Bandit and His Dream[5]

John Reed

John Reed was a U.S. journalist who crossed into Mexico to travel with Francisco Villa's army as it campaigned against Huerta. As the following illustrates, Reed admired Villa and saw him as the embodiment of the revolution, in contrast to Carranza who Reed saw as aristocratic and conservative. Reed brings out a key aspect to Villa's motives in fighting Huerta. Villa was steeped in the culture and ethics of northern Mexico—this explains his dream of establishing "military colonies." Villa had in mind the tradition of the military colonies like Tomóchic, whose traditions and ethics were valued among the *fronterizos* (frontier inhabitants) lower classes. This included "a frontier code of loyalty and reciprocity," which meant that if Villa "felt that his attitude was reciprocated, Villa would remain loyal to both his superiors and his subordinates." [6] The inverse meant that betrayal and treachery would transform Villa into an implacable enemy. These factors—his loyalty to Madero and his enmity toward Huerta—guaranteed that Villa would return from exile in 1913. He had a personal score to settle with Huerta.

When Madero took the field in 1910, Villa was still an outlaw. Perhaps, as his enemies say, he saw a chance to whitewash himself; perhaps, as seems probable, he was inspired by the Revolution of the peons. Anyway, about three months after they rose in arms, Villa suddenly appeared in El Paso and put himself, his band, his knowledge of the country and all his fortune at the command of Madero. The vast wealth that people said he accumulated during his twenty years of robbery turned out to be 363 silver *pesos*, badly worn. Villa became a Captain in the Maderista army, and as such went to Mexico City with Madero and was made honorary general of the new Rurales. He was attached to Huerta's army when it was sent north to put down the Orozco Revolution. Villa defeated Orozco with an inferior force in the only decisive battle of the war.

Huerta put Villa in command of the advance, and let him do the dangerous and dirty work while the old line Federal regiments lay back under the protection of their artillery. In Jiménez Huerta suddenly summoned Villa before a court-martial and charged him with insubordination—claiming to have wired an order to Villa, which Villa said he never received. The court-martial lasted fifteen minutes, and Huerta's most powerful future antagonist was sentenced to be shot.

Alfonso Madero, who was on Huerta's staff, stayed the execution, but President Madero, forced to back up the orders of his commander in the field, imprisoned Villa in the penitentiary of the capital. During all this time Villa never wavered in his loyalty to Madero—an unheard-of thing in Mexican history. Now he wasted no time in regrets or political intrigue. He set himself with all his force to learn to read and write. Villa hadn't the slightest foundation to work upon. He spoke the crude Spanish of the very poor—what is called *pelado*.[7] In nine months he could write a very fair hand and read the newspapers. Finally, the Madero government connived at his escape from prison.

From then to the outbreak of the last revolution, Villa lived in El Paso, Texas, and it was from there that he set out in April 1913, to conquer Mexico with four companions, seven horses, two pounds of sugar and coffee, and a pound of salt. He recruited in the mountains near San Andrés and so great was his popularity that within one month he had raised an army of three thousand men; in two months he had driven the Federal garrison all over the State of Chihuahua back into Chihuahua City; in six months he had taken Torreón; and in seven and a half Juárez had fallen to him; Mercado's Federal army had evacuated Chihuahua, and Northern Mexico was almost free.

It seems incredible to those who don't know him, that this remarkable figure, who has risen from obscurity to the most prominent position in Mexico in three years, should not covet the Presidency of the Republic. But that is in entire accord with the simplicity of his character. When asked about it he answered as always with perfect directness, just in the way that you put it to him. He didn't quibble over whether he could or could not be President of Mexico. He said: "I am a fighter, not a statesman. I am not educated enough to be President."

He never referred to Carranza except as "my Jefe," and he obeyed implicitly the slightest order from "the First Chief of the Revolution." His loyalty to Carranza was perfectly obstinate. He seemed to think that in Carranza were embodied the ideals of the Revolution. This, in spite of the fact that many of his advisors tried to make him see that Carranza was essentially an aristocrat and a reformer, and that the people were fighting for more than reform.

Carranza's political program, as set forth in the plan of Guadalupe, carefully avoids any promise of settlement of the land question, except a vague endorsement of Madero's Plan of San Luis Potosí, and it is evident that he does not intend to advocate any radical restoration of the land to the people until he becomes provisional president—and then to proceed very cautiously. In the meantime he seems to have left it to Villa's judgement, as well as all other details of the conduct of the Revolution in the north. But Villa, being a peon, and feeling with them, rather than consciously reasoning it out, that the land question is the real cause of the Revolution, acted with characteristic promptness and directness. No sooner had he settled the details of government of Chihuahua State, and appointed Chao his provisional governor, than he issued a proclamation giving sixty-two and one-half acres out of the confiscated lands to every male citizen of the State, and declaring these lands inalienable for any cause for a period of ten years.

It might not be uninteresting to know the passionate dream—the vision which animates this ignorant fighter, "not educated enough to be President of Mexico." He told it to me once in these words: "When the new Republic is established there will never be any more army in Mexico. Armies are the greatest support of tyranny. There can be no dictator without an army.

"We will put the army to work. In all parts of the Republic we will establish military colonies composed of the veterans of the Revolution. The State will give them grants of agricultural lands and establish big enterprises to give them work. Three days a week they work and work hard, because honest work is more important than fighting, and only honest work makes good citizens. And the other three days they will receive military instruction and go out and teach the people how to fight. Then, if the country is invaded, we will just have to telephone from the palace at Mexico City, and in a day and a half all the Mexican people will rise from their fields and factories, fully armed, equipped and organized to defend their children and their homes.

"My ambition is to live my life in one of those military colonies among my compañeros[8] whom I love, who have suffered so long and so deeply with me. I think I would like the government to establish a leather factory there where we could make good saddles and bridles, because I know how to do that; and the rest of the time I would like to work on my little farm, raising cattle and corn. It would be fine, I think, to help make Mexico a happy place."

The United States Will Not Recognize Huerta[9]

Woodrow Wilson, August 27, 1913

President Wilson is remembered as a moralizing politician who felt revulsion at the brutality of Huerta's coup and its violation of legality.

This attitude was evident in his statement on U.S. policy in Latin America when he declared, "We have no sympathy with those who seize the power of government to advance their own personal interests or ambitions." [10] Yet Wilson's protest that political principle outweighed U.S. commercial interests in Mexico was a misstatement; Wilson believed that the interests and profits of U.S. businesses operating in Mexico—or anywhere in Latin America—were best served by governments solidly established on liberal democratic foundations. From this vantage point Wilson found Huerta both morally reprehensible and incapable of satisfying U.S. commercial interests. This and a third consideration—the willingness of Britain and British capital to fill the U.S. void—stiffened Wilson's resolve to isolate Huerta. After recalling Ambassador Wilson, the President sent envoy John Lind to Mexico to propose U.S. recognition contingent on an armistice with the rebels, to be followed by national elections in which Huerta would not be a candidate. Huerta refused, so on August 27, 1913, Wilson announced his policy of watchful waiting: a continuation of nonrecognition and an arms embargo against both Huerta and the revolutionaries.

The deplorable posture of affairs in Mexico I need not describe, but I deem it my duty to speak very frankly of what this Government should seek to do in fulfillment of its obligation to Mexico as a friend and neighbour. We are glad to call ourselves the friends of Mexico, and to show that our friendship is genuine. The peace, prosperity and contentment of Mexico mean more to us than an enlarged field for our commerce and enterprise. They mean an enlargement of the field of self-government and the realization of the hopes and rights of a nation with whose best aspirations, so long suppressed and disappointed, we deeply sympathize.

The future has much in store for Mexico but the best gifts can come to her only if she be ready and free to receive them and to enjoy them honourably. The development of Mexico can be sound and lasting only if it be the product of a genuine freedom, a just and ordered government founded upon law. Mexico has a great future, if only she attains the path of honest constitutional government.

The present circumstances do not promise the foundations of such a peace. We have waited for the conditions to improve, and they have not. They have grown worse. The territory controlled by the provisional authorities has grown smaller. The prospect of pacifying the country grows remote and is impossible by any other means than force. War and disorder, devastation and confusion threaten. It was our duty to volunteer our good offices to assist in effecting an arrangement which would bring peace and a universally acknowledged political authority.

I took the liberty of sending John Lind as my personal representative to Mexico City with the following instructions:

"Press very earnestly upon the attention of those who are now exercising authority in Mexico the following:

"The Government of the United States does not feel at liberty any longer to stand inactively by while it becomes evident that no progress is being made towards establishing a government in Mexico City which the country will obey and respect. The present situation in Mexico is incompatible with international obligations on the part of Mexico, with the civilized development of Mexico, and with tolerable political and economic conditions. All America cries out for a settlement.

"A satisfactory settlement seems to us to be conditioned on: a) an immediate cessation of fighting throughout Mexico; b) an early and free election in which all will agree to take part; c) the consent of General Huerta to not be a candidate for election as President of the Republic at this election; and d) the agreement of all parties to abide by the results of the election and cooperate in supporting the new administration.

"The Government of the United States will be glad to play any part in a settlement honorably and consistently with international right. It pledges itself to recognize and assist the administration chosen in Mexico. The Government of the United States can conceive of no reasons to decline the friendship offered. Can Mexico give the civilized world a satisfactory reason for rejecting our good offices? If Mexico can suggest a better way to serve the people of Mexico, and meet our international obligations, we are more than willing to consider the suggestion."

But the proposals were rejected, partly because the authorities in Mexico City were grossly misled upon two points. They did not realize the desire of the American people that some just solution be found for the Mexican difficulties; and they did not believe that the present administration spoke for the people of the United States. This leaves them singularly isolated and without friends who can effectually aid them.

Meanwhile, what is it our duty? Clearly, everything must be rooted in patience and done with calm and disinterested deliberation. We can afford the self-restraint of a great nation which realizes its own strength and scorns to misuse it. It is now our duty to show how neutrality will enable the people of Mexico to set their affairs in order again. The door is closed against the resumption of the effort to bring order out of the confusion by friendly co-operative action.

For the rest, I deem it my duty to see to it that neither side in the struggle in Mexico receive any assistance from this side of the border. I shall follow the best practice of nations in the matter of neutrality by forbidding the exportation of arms or munitions from the United States to any part of Mexico. We cannot be the partisans of either party, or constitute ourselves the virtual umpire between them.

President Woodrow Wilson Is Deluded[11]

Federico Gamboa, August 16, 1913

Huerta declined to meet with John Lind, but did consent to an interview between Lind and Foreign Minister Federico Gamboa, a católico in Huerta's cabinet. Gamboa's reply on August 16 rejected Wilson's proposals. At this juncture, U.S. nonrecognition was an irritant —serious to be sure—but not fatal or decisive. Huerta enjoyed recognition from the major European powers and Japan, and would find it useful to play the anti-American card to drum up moral support and recruits for the campaign against the rebels. The imposition of an arms embargo on Mexico would injure the Constitutionalists far more than it would Huerta; indeed Huerta simply placed orders for more weapons from other countries.

The imputation that no progress has been made toward establishing a government enjoying the respect and obedience of the Mexican people is unfounded. The Mexican Republic is formed of twenty-seven States, three Territories, and one Federal District. Of these, eighteen States, the three Territories and the Federal District are under the absolute control of the present Government. Its southern frontier is open and at peace.
My Government has an army of 80,000 men to insure complete peace in time Republic.

The conditions of Mexico are neither doubtful nor secret; it is afflicted with an internal strife which has been raging almost three years. With reference to what might happen in Mexico no one can prognosticate. My Government appreciates the good offices tendered by the Government of the USA; it recognizes that they are inspired by the noble desire to act as a friend. But we have to decline them in the most categorical and definite manner.

Inasmuch as the U.S. Government is willing to act in the most disinterested friendship, it will be difficult to find a more propitious opportunity than the following: If it would watch that no material and monetary assistance is given to rebels who find refuge, conspire, and provide themselves with arms and food on the other side of the border; if it would demand from its local authorities the strictest observance of neutrality, I assure you that complete pacification would be accomplished within a short time.

However, Mr. Wilson is under a serious delusion when he declares that the present situation of Mexico is incompatible with her international obligations, with the development of her civilization, and the maintenance of tolerable political and economic conditions. To date no charge has been made by any foreign government accusing us of lack of compliance; we are punctually meeting all of our credits; we are maintaining diplomatic missions in almost all countries and we continue to be invited to international congresses and conferences. With regard to our interior development, a contract has just been signed with Belgian capitalists, which means the construction of 5,000 kilometres of railway. In one thing I do agree, and it is that the whole of America is clamoring for a prompt solution of our disturbances.

Consequently, Mexico cannot for one moment take into consideration the four conditions which Mr. Wilson has proposed. An immediate suspension of the struggle in Mexico is not possible due to the many bandits who are marauding toward the south and committing the most outrageous depredations; and I know of no country which has ever dared to propose an armistice to individuals who are beyond the pale of divine and human laws. Bandits are not admitted to armistice; the first action against them is one of correction, and when this fails, their lives must be severed, then the useful sprouts should grow and fructify.

With reference to the rebels who style themselves "Constitutionalists," what could be more gratifying than if they put aside their rancor to add their strength to ours, so that we would undertake national reconstruction? Unfortunately they do not avail themselves of the amnesty law enacted by the Provisional Government. Were we to agree to the armistice this would recognize their belligerency, something which cannot be done for reasons which cannot escape the Government of the USA, which has also classed them as rebels. It is an accepted doctrine that no armistice can be concerted with rebels.

The assurance asked of my Government that it will promptly call free elections is the most evident proof and unequivocal concession that the Government of the United States considers it legally constituted and that it is exercising the perfect civil operation of a sovereign nation. Inasmuch as our laws provide such assurance, there is no fear that the latter will not be observed during the coming elections. The present Government will cede its place to the Government which may be elected by the people.

The request that General Victoriano Huerta not appear as a candidate for the Presidency cannot be taken into consideration, because, aside from its strange and unwarranted character, there is a risk that this might be interpreted as a personal dislike. This point can be decided only by Mexican public opinion at the polls.

The pledge that all parties agree beforehand to support the new administration is something to be tacitly desired; the experience of this internal strife in loss of life and the destruction of property will cause all political factions to abide by the results; but no one can forecast the errors men are likely to commit under the influence of political passion.

We hasten to signify to the USA our appreciation of its aid but we deplore the present tension with your country. The legality of the Government of General Huerta can not be disputed. As will be seen, the point of issue is exclusively one of constitutional law in which no foreign nation, no matter how powerful and respectable it may be, should mediate in the least.

My Government considers a suspension of relations abnormal and without reason; abnormal, because the Ambassador of the USA congratulated General Huerta upon his elevation to the Presidency, and on his departure left the First Secretary of the Embassy of the United States of America as Chargé d'Affaires ad-interim, and the latter continues here in the free exercise of his functions.

Because of our sincere esteem for the people and the Government of the USA my Government consented to answer President Wilson's proposals. Otherwise, it would have rejected them immediately because of their humiliating character, hardly admissible even in a treaty of peace after a victory. My Government has confidence that when the justice of its cause is reconsidered by the President of the USA, whose sense of morality and uprightness are beyond question, he will withdraw from his attitude and will contribute to firmer bases for sincere friendship and good understanding.

With reference to the final part of the instructions of President Wilson, which say, "If Mexico can suggest any better way in which to show our friendship, serve the people of Mexico, and meet our international obligations, we are more than willing to consider the suggestion," we propose the following equally decorous arrangement. One, that our Ambassador be received in Washington; two, that the USA send us a new ambassador without previous conditions.

The Zapatistas Welcome Nonrecognition[12]

Emiliano Zapata, August 1913

Anti-Huerta rebels welcomed nonrecognition by the United States for it added weight to their claim that Huerta had illegally usurped the presidency. However, the embargo complicated access to arms for the rebels who relied far more heavily on suppliers in the United States. But this was not insurmountable, for smuggling was a long-established tradition along the frontier. Moreover, this consideration caused little concern for the Zapatistas, for they were landlocked and had to obtain weapons and ammunition from defeated federal troops. For them, Wilson's policy was a boon, plain and simple.

The Revolutionary Junta of the South and Center of the Republic of Mexico invites briefly the attention of the Embassy to its sentiments of gratitude and marked admiration, on account of the following:

The Revolution in the South and Center of the Republic is pursuing, with tenacity and constancy, the realization of the principles contained in the Plan of Ayala.

Therefore it is natural that we should be watchful of everything which in any way might affect the maintenance of our Creed, whether for our welfare or ruin.

We refer to events emanating from the White House in Washington, of great significance in favor of our country and therefore all we could desire in behalf of our revolutionary cause.

The national press has published news that the Government of the White House will not recognize the Pseudo-Government of General Victoriano Huerta, because he has been unable to restore peace in Mexico.

Reason, judgment, political expediency and everything pertinent are on the side of the Government of the United States when proceeding as it has in the matter, because General Victoriano Huerta never will carry into realization the cherished ideal of peace on our soil.

The Revolutionary Junta, cognizant of what it means, economically as well as politically, that the Government of the United States should not have recognized the false Government of Huerta, we pray the Embassy under your Excellency's worthy charge to convey to the Government and people of the United States our sincere gratitude, assuring the United States that our statements bear the approval of the whole nation.

The Working Class Resists Huerta[13]

Rosendo Salazar and Jose G. Escobedo, 1923

The labor movement in 1913 had two principle tendencies. One was associated with "economism," the view that unions should concentrate exclusively on economic demands; the other was anarcho-syndicalism, expressed in the Casa del Obrero, which rejected political action in favor of militant direct action against employers to achieve workers' demands, leavened by a commitment to an egalitarian future minus the state and capitalists. The Huerta regime tolerated both, so long as they avoided giving support to Zapatistas or Constitutionalists. Thus, organized labor was able to mount the first-ever May Day demonstration in 1913 and present demands for an eight-hour day to congress. It was a different story when workers adopted radical or revolutionary postures, as the Casa del Obrero discovered when it mounted an anti-Huerta rally on May 25; this started a year-long duel between Huerta's regime and Casa members who felt increasingly drawn toward the armed struggle. On May 27, 1914, the government suppressed the Casa when it resisted conscription. The following excerpt chronicles the beginning of this struggle between radical labor and Huerta.

The rise of Victoriano Huerta made many politicians afraid for their lives since the new leader had come to power through treachery. Maderismo found itself in the claws of militarism. The Casa del Obrero Mundial had many justified grievances against the Maderistas—for closing its school, for the suppression of its newspaper *Luz*, and for the expulsion of Moncaleano— but it was horrified by the crimes perpetrated by the Huertista administration and it had no objection to accepting into its ranks parliamentarians like Serapio Rendón, Hilario Carillo, and Jesús Urueta.

The Casa del Obrero Mundial was an antithesis, then, to the suffocating state of affairs created in Mexico by military vandals. It erected Red barriers from which sprouted the optimism of distinguished guests. And so it happened that some Maderistas, including the editors of *Nueva Era*, joined the Casa del Obrero Mundial, which they had previously hated.

After a successful public demonstration of 15,000 workers on May 1, the Casa del Obrero summoned the unions to a mass meeting at the Juárez hemicycle on May 25. The Maderista deputies and labor leaders were invited to address the crowd. All the unions attended as well as a multitude of individuals who had strong sympathy for the work of the Casa del Obrero and its campaign to support popular rebellions. So the working class, humbled but not degraded, awoke from the lethargy of servitude.

The orators spoke harshly but reasonably, lashing the despots and exciting the crowd to once and for all rebel against their tormentors. Antonio Díaz Soto y Gama opened the meeting with a discourse that was like a tempest of strident curses against Tyranny. He said:

"The workers have already formed powerful bonds that no human or divine force can break, despite all the traitors and all the cuartelazos; the Mexican people are revolutionary by nature and for this reason are seizing the land; they are coming from the North and South to destroy the spurious and vile Government of Victoriano Huerta."

Pioquinto V. Roldán spoke about the vile and criminal treatment of workers in the workshops and fields, of the horrendous conditions facing serfs in every nation—especially in Mexico—and whose destiny is not to remain on the margins of life, but to enjoy a maximum of happiness and minimum of suffering; of their precarious existence in a world turned dark and painful by usurpation and privilege; and finally of the urgent need for the international proletariat to win a system of distributive justice, where human wisdom provides for the common good of all, for social progress and the perfection of the species.

José Colado, member of the commercial workers union, attacked hard-hearted bosses who exploited plebeians to their last drop of energy only to discard them to hunger and neglect. Colado's speech also drew the attention to the significance of the situation created by the fall of the Maderista Government and the rise of militarism.

Serapio Rendón courageously spoke of the contemptible acts committed by Huerta and Blanquet, the acts of ruffians and assassins. He roused the workers with a detailed account of the conditions prevailing in the country, arising from the cuartelazo and which culminated with Huerta's coup d'état and the killing of Madero and Pino Suárez.

Other speakers took the floor, urging union organization of workers around the categorical imperative of radical socialism: the social revolution. Afterwards, the crowd marched to the centre of the city, shouting out "Death to Huerta, Death to Blanquet . . ." Hours later, the authorities arrested leaders of the Casa del Obrero and others who had addressed the meeting, a total of 28 persons. Six were expelled from the country.

The insinuations of the prostituted press were not needed by Huerta who very clearly heard the speakers, particularly deputy Rendón. But, would he order the closure of the Casa del Obrero Mundial for having planted the roots of rebellion?

On July 2, *El Independiente* published an entirely calumnious version of the meeting, intended to discredit the Casa del Obrero Mundial and to portray it as a hotbed of conspiracy which the authorities must destroy. The next day the administrative council of the Casa del Obrero responded with a statement:

"The person who gave the newspaper that false report or makes such a perfidious complaint to the Government, invents a fantastic story: it speaks of Maderista deputies who, after visiting Madero's tomb, went to the La Piedad barracks where they spoke with several officers, before concluding their tour at the Casa del Obrero where they held a mysterious conference with the directors of that institution.

"This portrays us as conspirators in order to provide our enemies with a pretext to impede the efforts of workers and to brutally stifle our work to organize unions.

"We have a treasure to protect, the ideals of the proletariat which today we are beginning to develop in our midst. Therefore we must defend the work we have started, to strongly protest against such slanderous insinuations, against this reprehensible and cunning accusation.

"The Casa del Obrero not does conspire. Moreover, it does not and cannot engage in politics, because its statutes prohibit trade unionists from so doing. This Casa has always professed the theory of the current intellectual leaders of the international workers' movement who preach "direct action" of the worker against the capitalist. That is to say, the struggle supported by unions who lead strikes, express the demands of the proletariat, and who sustain them in practice, brandishing like a weapon the unwavering solidarity of the majority of workers against the greed and privileges of the capitalist minority."

Huerta Is Stained by the Stigma of Treason[14]

Belisario Domínguez, September 23, 1913

The Maderista legislators who joined with the Casa were not the only politicians to publicly resist Huerta. On September 23, Senator Belisario Domínguez from Chiapas, attempted to deliver the following speech in which he condemned Huerta and called on congress to depose him. Not surprisingly, the senate chair refused to give Domínguez permission to read the speech. Knowing that he courted death by doing so, Domínguez had the speech printed and circulated to members of congress and the press. Two weeks later, the government arrested Domínguez and applied the Ley de Fuga.

Dear Senators:

All you have read the report submitted by Victoriano Huerta before Congress on September 16. Undoubtedly you are filled with indignation at the falsehoods contained therein. Who is he trying to deceive, gentlemen? The Congress of the Union?

No, gentlemen. All its members are enlightened people involved in politics. They are abreast of events in the country, and cannot be deceived on the matter.

Perhaps he intended to deceive the Mexican nation, this noble homeland which is confident enough in our honesty that it placed its cherished interests in our hands? What does it mean to represent the nation in this case? We must fulfill the trust that the country has honoured us with, to tell the truth and not allow it to fall into the abyss that opens at its feet.

The truth is this: the government of don Victoriano Huerta has not only failed to pacify the country, but the current situation of the Republic is infinitely worse than before.

The Revolution has extended to nearly all the States, and many nations, formerly friends of Mexico, regard his government as illegal and refuse to recognize it. Our currency has depreciated in foreign countries and our credit is agonizingly poor. The entire press in our country has been muzzled or has sold out like cowards to the government and systematically hides the truth. Our farmlands are abandoned; many have been razed. And finally, every form of hunger and misery threatens to spread across our unfortunate country.

Why do we face such a tragic situation? First and foremost, because the Mexican people cannot resign themselves to Victoriano Huerta, the soldier who seized power through treason and whose first act in the presidency was to cowardly murder the President and Vice-President. Both had been legally elected by popular vote. They showered Victoriano Huerta with promotions, honours and distinctions; he publicly vowed loyalty and unswerving fidelity.

Secondly, this tragic situation results from the methods that have been used to achieve peace. These methods you already know: death and extermination for all men, families and villages who do not sympathize with his government.

Peace at any cost, said Victoriano Huerta. Have you seriously considered what these words mean in the selfish and ferocious criterion of Victoriano Huerta? These words mean that Victoriano Huerta is ready to shed Mexico's blood, to cover the country with corpses, to convert our entire country into an immense ruin, so long as he does not lose the presidency or spill a single drop of his own blood.

In his mad zeal to retain the presidency, Victoriano is committing another infamy: he is causing an international conflict with the United States which, if resolved by force, will bring death to Mexicans, if not to Victoriano Huerta and Aureliano Blanquet. These two wretches are stained by the stigma of treason; the people and the army will eventually repudiate them.

That is the reality. To weak-spirited people it seems that our ruin is inevitable, for Victoriano Huerta has expanded his hold over power to ensure his victory as a candidate in the farcical presidential elections announced for October 26. Nor has he hesitated to violate the sovereignty of the States, removing constitutional governors and imposing military governors to circumvent the people through the criminal use of force.

However, gentlemen, a supreme effort can save it all. If the country's elected representatives fulfill their duty, the country will be saved and blossom bigger and more beautiful than before. The national representatives must depose Victoriano Huerta, for our brothers have risen against him with their weapons; this is why he cannot establish peace, the supreme goal of all Mexicans.

Some will say that the attempt is dangerous, because Victoriano Huerta is a fierce and bloody soldier who murders, without hesitation or compunction, anyone who gets in his way. It does not matter! Gentlemen, the Homeland demands that you fulfill your duty despite the danger and even in the certainty of losing your life.

This Is a Dictatorship[15]

Rafael de Zayas Enríquez, 1914

Huerta's dictatorship reflected his own understanding of leadership, inculcated in a lifetime of service in the most authoritarian of all state institutions, the military. But the shift was not merely a matter of preference; it also satisfied the bourgeoisie, which calculated that its interests—the suppression of an emerging social revolution—were best served by an "iron hand." For all the individual ambitions that were

smothered—Félix Díaz, Manuel Mondragón, or Francisco De la
Barra—the elites, as a class, supported Huerta's subordination of
civilian politics to military rule. As historian Alan Knight has pointed
out, "on the coat-tails on the military came many old Porfiristas, eager
both to resume their interrupted careers and to serve the new, congenial
administration." [16] This included Rafael de Zayas Enríquez who, in the
following selection, clearly expressed his preference for a dictatorship.

After the fall of Madero, Mexico was no man's land; it was at the mercy of
the first who would dare to take it. No civilian, however, was able to
accomplish that feat. That was a soldier's job. Then appeared General
Huerta, who saw his opportunity when so many were hesitating, so many
afraid, and so many indifferent. He felt it was his patriotic duty to take the
situation in hand.

The rebels of the Ciudadela thought that Huerta was the last card they
should play in order to win the game, and they played it; they thought that
the victorious general would be a tool in their hands; he became, instead, the
supreme arbiter with well-defined plans in his head. He had not longed for
the supreme authority, but when it became his, he had the will-power to
exert it.

Once established in the presidency, he set out to remove, without haste
but quickly and cleverly, whatever constituted an obstacle to the realization
of his political and patriotic projects. The pact of the Embassy, owing to
which he had become leader of the revolution and arrived at the presidency
through the regular constitutional procedure, was a binding agreement.
He did not break it, but he saw to it that both parties agreed to let it remain
a dead letter.

After cancelling the pact he eliminated one minister after another,
retaining only one he could work harmoniously with him. Even this one,
however, was eliminated as soon as Huerta came to consider him as useless
and dangerous. He prevailed upon Félix Díaz to join again the army, thus
retaining him as a subaltern. He entrusted him later with a most flattering
mission abroad, which made it difficult to return in time for the general
elections.

The houses of Parliament proved to be an obstacle to the pacification of
the country. When he saw that nothing could be accomplished through
suasion and that the Chamber of Deputies was becoming a nest of
conspirators, when he was convinced that the only alternative was to
eliminate Parliament or be eliminated by it, he resolved upon another coup
d'état.

Viewed from the proper angle, the actions of the rebels did not trouble
him; on the contrary, they rather served his purpose; the rebels were such a
burden to the country that the population would finally rise in anger against
them and become a powerful weapon in their destruction. General Huerta

considered that the rebellion, with its orgy of brutality, carried its own death sentence.

Francisco Bulnes published, a few days after the dissolution of the Chambers, an article in which we find, if not approval of that exceptional act, at least an explanation and a general justification. "A coup d'état," Bulnes wrote, "is a hygienic measure against the demagogic rabble when it seizes the powers of government and keeps the population terrified by its excesses. A coup d'état is also a weapon against dreamers and deluded reformists."

The reader may remark: "This is a dictatorship!" Well, it is.

In an article I published on May 13, five months before the coup d'état, I made the following statement:

"I shall be absolutely frank. I am opposed to dictatorship, but I am more strongly opposed to anarchy; if it is anarchy we are facing, I prefer a Mexican dictator to a foreign invader and conqueror; for it is a foreign invasion which is being precipitated by the machinations of the revolutionists, bandits, conspirators, and the miserable intrigues of many men whose sacred duty it would be to save their own country."

CHAPTER SIX

THE VICTORY OVER HUERTA AND THE SOCIAL REVOLUTION

Victoriano Huerta reached his apogee of strength in January 1914, controlling two-thirds of Mexico with nearly 200,000 troops. He also counted the support of the Catholic Church and the bourgeois classes. Internationally, Huerta enjoyed recognition from Britain and other European powers. However, Huerta's position deteriorated in the face of an opposition that acquired domestic and international dimensions and on July 20 the ex-dictator embarked for exile in Europe. On August 20, Venustiano Carranza entered Mexico City, inaugurating a new struggle to create a new social and political order in Mexico.

The insurgency involved two distinct movements: the Zapatistas based in Morelos and, in the north, Venustiano Carranza's Constitutionalist Army. The two movements cooperated loosely. The Zapatistas were committed to the Plan of Ayala and remained independent of Carranza whom they saw as a conservative hacendado. By the spring, the Zapatistas controlled all of Guerrero and Morelos, except Cuernavaca, and extended their influence into the other states around Mexico City. In the north Carranza organized his army into three wings. The Division of the North in Chihuahua, led by Francisco Villa, was the most powerful. In Sonora, Alvaro Obregón led the Army of the Northwest, while Pablo González commanded the Army of the Northeast. The Constitutionalists, however, were more heterogeneous than Zapata's peasant revolutionaries, giving rise to tensions rooted in conflicting visions for the future of Mexico. The principle point of friction lay between Villa's ardent but elementary desire for a more egalitarian society, and Carranza who maneuvered between his need for Villa's military skills and his desire to smother any radicalism. To hold the loyalty of his commanders, Carranza had been compelled in the autumn of 1913 to promise a vague program of social reform. Nevertheless, the first fissure between Villa and Carranza opened when Villa confiscated the large haciendas in Chihuahua to finance his army and reward his soldiers with land after the final victory. Tensions mounted as the Constitutionalists pushed south in 1914, and by the spring two more developments widened the split. The first was the return of Sonora governor José María Maytorena to restore his control over the state, backed by the Madero clan. This threatened the ambitions of Constitutionalist General Obregón; he aligned with Carranza who saw the Maderos as a danger to his political eminence. For their part, Maytorena and the Maderos cultivated their own alliance with Villa. The second development concerned U.S. intervention at Veracruz in April: Carranza opposed it, while Villa supported it.

Meanwhile, U.S. policy shifted away from "watchful waiting"— neutrality and nonrecognition—to active opposition to Huerta.

In February, President Wilson revised his arms embargo, allowing the sale of weapons and munitions to the Constitutionalists. As the Constitutionalists gained momentum and pressed south, the Zapatistas encircled Mexico City. Wilson decided the time was ripe to force mediated negotiations to replace Huerta with a president acceptable to Washington. Wilson ordered the occupation of the port of Veracruz at the end of April. This led to the ABC conference in Niagara Falls, Canada, involving Argentina, Brazil, and Chile as mediators among the United States, Huerta, and Carranza. Meanwhile, the race was on for Mexico City. Carranza and Obregón conspired to slow Villa's advance by diverting his forces and cutting off coal for his military trains. Obregón arrived in Mexico City first and negotiated the surrender and withdrawal of federal troops.

★ ★ ★

We Shall Not Alter Our Policy of Watchful Waiting[1]

Woodrow Wilson, December 2, 1913

On December 2, 1913, President Woodrow Wilson addressed the U.S. Congress and reiterated the policy of neutrality and nonrecognition of Huerta, including an arms embargo against the contending parties. But the efficacy of this required a weaker Huerta and a stronger opposition. Thus, in February, Wilson allowed the sale of war material to Carranza and expanded Huerta's isolation by misleading the British government into scaling back diplomatic ties with him; Wilson allowed the British to believe he was abandoning the goal of mediation in favor of an escalated conflict that might harm British interests in Mexico. Britain maintained official relations with Huerta but withdrew its ambassador. The option of intervention was now on the table; Wilson simply needed a pretext, however flimsy.

There is but one cloud upon our horizon. That has shown itself to the south of us, and hangs over Mexico. There can be no certain prospect of peace until General Huerta has surrendered his usurped authority in Mexico; until it is understood on all hands, that such pretended governments will not be countenanced or dealt with by the Government of the United States. We are the friends of constitutional government in America; we are more than its friends, we are its champions; because in no other way can our neighbors, to whom we would wish in every way to make proof of our friendship, work out their own development in peace and liberty. Mexico has no such Government. The attempt to maintain one in Mexico City has broken down, and a mere military despotism has been set up which has hardly more than the semblance of national authority. It originated in the usurpation of Victoriano Huerta, who, after a brief attempt to play the part of constitutional President, has at last cast aside even the pretence of legal right and declared himself dictator. As a consequence, a condition of affairs now exists in Mexico which has made it doubtful whether even the most elementary and fundamental rights either of her own people or of the citizens of other countries resident within her territory can long be successfully safeguarded, and which threatens, if long continued, to imperil the interests of peace, order, and tolerable life in the lands immediately to the south of us. Even if the usurper had succeeded in his purposes, in despite of the constitution of the Republic and the rights of its people, he would have set up nothing but a precarious and hateful power, which could have lasted but a little while, and whose eventual downfall would have left the country in a more deplorable condition than ever. But he has not succeeded. He has forfeited the respect and the moral support even of those who were at one time willing to see him succeed. Little by little he has been completely isolated. By a little every day his power and prestige are crumbling and the collapse is not far away. We shall not be obliged to alter our policy of watchful waiting. And then, when the end comes, we shall hope to see constitutional order restored in distressed Mexico by the concert and energy of such of her leaders as prefer the liberty of their people to their own ambitions.

The Tampico Affair and Huerta's Protocol[2]

José López Portillo y Rojas, April 19, 1914

Wilson's opportunity arrived on April 9, and the pretext was flimsy indeed. As the Constitutionalists lay siege to Tampico, a group of ten sailors from the USS *Dolphin* put ashore in a whaleboat to purchase gasoline amidst the shelling and burning oil tanks. The port was under martial law, but U.S. Rear Admiral Henry Mayo did not ask permission to land; Mexican troops therefore arrested the sailors. General Ignacio Zaragoza ordered the sailors released and verbally apologized to Mayo. But Mayo insisted that Zaragoza salute the American flag with 21 guns within 24 hours. Huerta was willing to apologize, but not to salute the U.S. flag given Washington's policy of nonrecognition. On April 14, Wilson ordered the Atlantic Fleet to Tampico, including seven battleships, two cruisers, and one transport bearing marines; Wilson then gave Huerta until April 19 to comply. On the deadline, Huerta offered a protocol whereby Mexico would salute the U.S. flag if the United States would salute the Mexican flag.

The next two documents are the proposed protocol and the response by U.S. Secretary of State William Jennings Bryan rejecting the protocol.

José López Portillo y Rojas, Foreign Minister of Mexico, presents compliments to Mr. Nelson O'Shaughnessy, Chargé d'Affaires of the United States of America, and, after talking with General Victoriano Huerta, interim President of Mexico, begs to inform him that the Government of Mexico is not disposed to accede to the unconditional demands of the American Government, but is disposed to act on the terms of the draft protocol which was left in his hands last night by López Portillo:

Nelson O'Shaughnessy, Chargé d'Affaires of the United States of America, and José López Portillo y Rojas, Minister for Foreign Affairs of the United Mexican States, for the purpose of putting an end to the lamentable incident which occurred on the 9th of April at the port of Tampico arising from the detention of nine marines and one officer of the United States from the crew of the Dolphin, considering:

That said marines were immediately released by General Ignacio Zaragoza, Military Commander of the Port; that the same officer sent his apology to Rear Admiral Mayo, Commander of the American Fleet anchored in the harbor; that later on, when the incident became known to the Provisional President of the Republic of Mexico, General Victoriano Huerta, he expressed his regrets through the Department of Foreign Affairs and directed that a full investigation should be made in order to punish the person guilty of the offence, should there be one; and in conclusion, that the detention in question was inspired by the zeal of the inferior officer, who carried the same into effect, a thing which can be easily understood if it is borne in mind that when the above-mentioned marines were detained they had landed without having permission from the military authorities, and at a time when the port was not only in a state of war but was being attacked by revolutionary forces.

The above-mentioned Chargé d'Affaires of the United States of America and the Minister for Foreign Affairs of Mexico, acting in their respective characters, hereby agree to the following: First, the Mexican Government, moved by a desire to show friendliness towards the people of the United States of America and acting in a manner similar to that in which the United States has acted in like cases, hereby agrees to salute the American flag at the port of Tampico with twenty-one guns from the coast battery or from that of a Mexican man of war anchored in the harbor. Second, the salute shall be made at the moment at which the American flag shall be hoisted to the top of a staff on the Mexican coast. Third, the Government of the United States of America hereby agrees to salute the Mexican flag immediately afterwards with twenty-one guns from the battery of the Dolphin or of any American battleship anchored in the harbor. Fourth, the salute shall be made at the moment when the Mexican flag shall be hoisted to the top of the mainmast of the above-mentioned vessel or of any battleship anchored in the harbor.

To the U.S. Chargé D'Affaires in Mexico:

On receipt of your telegram, saying that Huerta had acceded to the demand but only on condition that you sign a protocol, I talked with the President. He repeats most emphatically his objection to any protocol or agreement. He is not willing that the salute shall be fired as a matter of contract, or upon condition that we return it. It must be fired in accordance with international custom as an apology for the insult offered. When it has been fired it will then be the duty of this Government, according to invariable custom, to return the salute; but General Huerta must trust this Government to live up to the requirements of international courtesy.

The proposed protocol of which you sent a copy is especially objectionable because it is so worded that General Huerta might construe it as recognition of his Government, whereas the President has notified General Huerta and the foreign nations that he does not expect to recognize General Huerta's Government. General Huerta's acceptance of Admiral Mayo's demand should be unconditional. As soon as he announces his intention to comply with this demand he can arrange the details directly with Admiral Mayo. Please make plain to him that further negotiations are unnecessary and that the President expects him to accept at once in order that the incident may be closed.

The Situation in our Dealings with General Huerta[3]

Woodrow Wilson, April 20, 1914

On April 20, President Wilson asked the U.S. Congress to support his decision to intervene in Mexico. He received it but the original plan failed. It called for simultaneous landings at Tampico and Veracruz. From Veracruz, the marines were to take Mexico City and depose Huerta. However, the resistance at Veracruz forced the diversion of marines from Tampico and prevented any breakout toward Mexico City. Diplomatically, the plan was slightly more successful; it led to the Argentina, Brazil, and Chile (ABC) Conference, but this failed to resolve the issue of presidential succession, let alone an armistice. Huerta participated only at the urging of Britain, while Carranza insisted that the agenda exclude discussion of Mexico's internal affairs, including the naming of a new president, leaving the U.S. occupation of Veracruz as the sole topic for discussion.

Gentlemen of the Congress:

It is my duty to call your attention to a situation which has arisen in our dealings with General Victoriano Huerta in Mexico City which calls for action, and to ask your advice and cooperation in acting upon it. On the 9th of April a paymaster of the USS *Dolphin* landed at the Iturbide Bridge landing at Tampico with a whaleboat and boat's crew to take off certain supplies needed by his ship, and while engaged in loading the boat was arrested by an officer and squad of men of the army of General Huerta. Neither the paymaster nor anyone of the boat's crew was armed. Two of the men were in the boat when the arrest took place and were obliged to leave it and submit to be taken into custody, notwithstanding the fact that the boat carried, both at her bow and at her stern, the flag of the United States. The officer who made the arrest was proceeding up one of the streets of the town with his prisoners when met by an officer of higher authority, who ordered him to return to the landing and await orders; and within an hour and a half from the time of the arrest, orders were received from the commander of the Huertista forces at Tampico for the release of the paymaster and his men. The release was followed by apologies from the commander and later by an expression of regret by General Huerta himself. General Huerta urged that martial law obtained at the time at Tampico; that orders had been issued that no one should be allowed to land at the Iturbide Bridge; and that our sailors had no right to land there. Our naval commanders at the port had not been notified of any such prohibition; and, even if they had been, the only justifiable course open to the local authorities would have been to request the paymaster and his crew to withdraw and to lodge a protest with the commanding officer of the fleet. Admiral Mayo regarded the arrest as so serious an affront that he was not satisfied with the apologies offered, but demanded that the flag of the United States be saluted with special ceremony by the military commander of the port.

The incident can not be regarded as a trivial one, especially as two of the men arrested were taken from the boat itself—that is to say, from the territory of the United States—but had it stood by itself it might have been attributed to the ignorance or arrogance of a single officer. Unfortunately, it was not an isolated case. A series of incidents have recently occurred which cannot but create the impression that the representatives of General Huerta were willing to go out of their way to show disregard for the dignity and rights of this Government and felt perfectly safe in doing what they pleased, making free to show in many ways their irritation and contempt. I have heard of no complaints from other Governments of similar treatment. Subsequent explanations and formal apologies did not and could not alter the popular impression, which possibly had been the object of the Huertista authorities to create, that the Government of the United States was being singled out with impunity for slights and affronts in retaliation for its refusal to recognize the pretensions of General Huerta to be regarded as the constitutional provisional President of Mexico.

The manifest danger was that such offences might grow from bad to worse until something happened of so intolerable a sort as to lead directly and inevitably to armed conflict. It was necessary that the apologies of General Huerta should go much further, that they should attract the attention of the whole population, and impress upon General Huerta himself that no further occasion for explanations and professed regrets should arise. I, therefore, felt it my duty to sustain Admiral Mayo in the whole of his demand and to insist that the flag of the United States should be saluted in such a way as to indicate a new spirit and attitude on the part of the Huertistas.

Such a salute General Huerta has refused, and I have come to ask your approval in the course I now purpose to pursue. This Government can in no circumstances be forced into war with the people of Mexico. Mexico is torn by civil strife. If we are to accept the tests of its own constitution, it has no government. General Huerta has set his power up in Mexico City without right and by methods for which there can be no justification. Only part of the country is under his control. If armed conflict should unhappily come as a result of his attitude toward this Government, we should be fighting only General Huerta and those who give him their support, and our object would be only to restore to the people of the distracted Republic the opportunity to set up again their own laws and their own government.

But I earnestly hope that war is not now in question. I believe that I speak for the American people when I say that we do not desire to control in any degree the affairs of our sister Republic. Our feeling for the people of Mexico is one of deep and genuine friendship, and everything that we have so far done has proceeded from our desire to help them, not to hinder or embarrass them. The people of Mexico are entitled to settle their own domestic affairs in their own way, and we sincerely desire to respect their right. The present situation need have none of the grave implications of interference if we deal with it promptly, firmly, and wisely.

There can be no thought of aggression or of selfish aggrandizement. We seek to maintain the dignity and authority of the United States only because we wish always to keep our great influence unimpaired for the uses of liberty, both in the United States and wherever else it may be employed for the benefit of mankind.

The Intervention Violates Mexican Sovereignty[4]

Venustiano Carranza, April 22, 1914

The presence of U.S. troops on Mexican soil agitated Mexican nationalists on all sides, particularly so since Veracruz was where marines had landed during the U.S.-Mexico war of 1846–1848, leading to the annexation of one-half of Mexico's national territory. The landing was a short-term boon to Huerta, who rode a crest of patriotic fervor. From Morelos, Zapata announced he would resist any U.S. troops that entered territory under his control. Meanwhile, on April 22 Carranza denounced the intervention as a violation of Mexican sovereignty, and likewise pledged to resist any movement of U.S. troops into areas under control of Constitutionalist forces.

To President Woodrow Wilson:

Pending the action of the American Senate on Your Excellency's message directed to that body, caused by the lamentable incident which occurred between the crew of a whaleboat of the cruiser *Dolphin* and the soldiers of the usurper Huerta, certain acts of hostility have been executed by the naval forces under the command of Admiral Fletcher at the port of Vera Cruz. In view of this violation of national sovereignty, which the Constitutionalist Government did not expect from a Government which had reiterated its desire to maintain peace with the Mexican people, I comply with a duty of high patriotism in directing this note to you with a view of exhausting all honorable means before two friendly powers sever the pacific relations that still unite them.

The Mexican nation—the real people of Mexico—have not recognized as their executive a man who has sought to blemish national integrity, drowning in blood its free institutions. Consequently the acts of the usurper Huerta and his accomplices do not signify legitimate acts of sovereignty, they do not constitute real public functions of domestic and foreign relations, and much less do they represent the sentiments of the Mexican nation, which are of confraternity towards the American people. The lack of representative character in General Victoriano Huerta as concerns the relations of Mexico with the United States as well as Argentina, Brazil, Chile and Cuba has been clearly established by the justifiable attitude of these nations, who have refused to recognize the usurper, thus lending a valuable moral support to the noble cause that I represent.

The usurped title of "President of the Republic" cannot invest General Huerta with the right to receive a demand for reparation from the Government of the United States, nor the right to grant a satisfaction if this is due.

Victoriano Huerta is a culprit within the jurisdiction of the Constitutionalist Government, today the only one which represents national sovereignty in accord with the Constitution of Mexico. The illegal acts committed by the usurper and his partisans, be they of an international character such as those at Tampico, or of a domestic character, will be tried and punished with inflexibility and promptness by the tribunals of the Constitutionalist Government.

The individual acts of Victoriano Huerta will never be sufficient to involve the Mexican nation in a disastrous war with the United States for the fundamental reason that he is not the legitimate organ of our national sovereignty.

But the invasion of our territory and the landing of your forces in Vera Cruz, violating our existence as a free and independent sovereign entity, may indeed drag us into an unequal war, with dignity but which until today we have desired to avoid.

In the face of the real situation of Mexico—weak in comparison with the formidable power of the American nation and even weaker after three years of bloody strife—and considering the acts committed at Vera Cruz to be highly offensive to the dignity and independence of Mexico; considering also that the hostile acts already committed exceed those required by equity to the end desired; considering, furthermore, that it is not the usurper who should have the right to make reparation—I interpret the sentiment of the Mexican people, so jealous of its rights and so respectful of the rights of foreigners, and invite you to suspend the hostile acts already begun, to order your forces to evacuate Vera Cruz, and to present to the Constitutionalist Government, which I represent as Constitutional Governor of the State of Coahuila and First Chief of the Constitutionalist Army, the demand on the part of the United States in regard to acts recently committed at the port of Tampico, in the security that the demand will be considered in a spirit of elevated justice and conciliation.

Keep Veracruz and Hold It Tight[5]

George Carothers and William Jennings Bryan

Francisco Villa was the only important revolutionary leader to welcome the U.S. occupation of Veracruz. Whatever he felt as a patriot, it made military sense to him. Villa also had pragmatic reasons. The Division of the North depended on access to the United States for revenue from the sale of beef and cotton, and for weapons and munitions. His attitude had two important consequences. It widened the breach with Carranza, and put Villa in good standing with Washington at the moment it was beginning to search for a "suitable" leader to replace Huerta. On April 23, George Carothers, a U.S. representative assigned to Villa's camp, apprised Secretary of State Bryan of Villa's positive attitude. Bryan welcomed Villa's posture as one that would preserve U.S. policy in Mexico and move Carranza to a friendlier attitude.

To Secretary of State:

I have just dined with Villa. He said there would be no war between the United States and the Constitutionalists; that he is too good a friend of ours, and considered us too good friends of theirs, to engage in a war which neither side desired; that other nations would laugh and say, "The little drunkard has succeeded in drawing them in"; that as far as he was concerned we could keep Vera Cruz and hold it so tight that not even water could get in to Huerta and that he could not feel any resentment. He said that no drunkard, meaning Huerta, was going to draw him into a war with his friend; that he had come to Juárez to restore confidence between us.

My impression is that he is sincere and will force Carranza to accept his own friendly attitude. He was much pleased that the embargo had not been restored, saying that he must secure his ammunition for the Monterrey campaign through El Paso and that the report that the embargo had been restored had worried him. His residence is within two hundred yards of the international bridge guarded by ten men. He told me that he realized that if we were to go to war, the United States would crush them, but that they would do much damage and fight as long as they could continue to exist on herbs and live in the hills; but that even though we were to cross into Mexico he would still ask us to withdraw and talk it over. He asked me what the extensive military activity in El Paso meant, to which I replied that the American forces had much to contend with on this side, with five thousand prisoners at Fort Bliss and ten thousand refugees in the city, and that the activity meant prevention of rioting in El Paso. He expressed satisfaction at this and said he would do the same thing under similar conditions.

In comparing his conversation with me to a published interview with newspaper reporters please bear in mind that those interviews have been edited by the Carrancista junta here which is striving to show that Villa upholds Carranza's note to you. Villa's attitude is that Carranza may write pretty notes from Chihuahua but that he is here to do the work. If we can hold Villa in Juárez a few days, and provided the proposed embargo does not change his attitude, I hope to establish the neutrality of the Constitutionalists through Villa. As indicative of his frame of mind he handed me a beautiful blanket with the request that I forward it to General Scott with his compliments. Carothers.

To Carothers:

Your dispatch was received with gratification. You are at liberty to tell General Villa that the action of the United States on that part of the border controlled by the Constitutionalists will be governed entirely by the attitude of General Carranza, General Villa and their associates. We earnestly desire friendly relationships and are reassured by what General Villa said. It shows a largeness of view and a comprehension of the whole situation which is greatly to his credit. We sincerely hope that he represents the views of the Constitutionalists. Public opinion in the United States has been disturbed by General Carranza's attitude and has felt a very considerable degree of resentment about it. I have so far taken leave to believe that General Carranza did not mean real hostility. I hope that we may be assured of that in a very short time. Bryan.

Statement of Francisco Villa to President Woodrow Wilson

Villa issued his own statement on April 25, reiterating support for the occupation of Veracruz. At the same time, Villa paid careful attention to the volatile politics underlying the issue. Villa distanced himself from Carranza's opposition, but avoided a break by acknowledging Carranza's patriotic motives. At the same time, the statement warns Wilson against being drawn into a futile conflict by Huerta's "machinations" or by Carranza's "haughtiness." Villa needed an open border, but not to become an instrument for U.S. policy.

The great majority of the Mexican people, comprising all of the liberal party of warm democratic aspirations, recognize the greatness and power of the American people and are thankful for the sympathy they have shown for Mexico and their desire for its progress, manifested by their moral support of democratic Mexicans in the Revolution of 1910 and this one of 1913–14. They believe in the sincerity of the declarations of President Wilson that no war with Mexico is desired, and on their part aspire to live in good friendship with the United States.

They are sure that the difficulties between the United States and the United Mexican States have originated in the deliberate attempt of the usurper Huerta to force a war, and it would be very lamentable if the satanic abilities of this perfidious man should launch into war two brotherly countries which have so long desired to live in the most harmonious fraternal relations.

It is true that the situation has been aggravated by the note of the First Chief of the Constitutionalist Army; but this note was the attitude of one person, and whatever his momentary authority, cannot carry such weight as to bring war between two countries desiring to continue at peace, disdaining the machinations of Huerta, whom both countries consider a common enemy.

The worthy pride of the Mexican chief of a great party is quite excusable even if it should expose the country to a lamentable war. The President of the North American nation should measure up to his noble antecedents and the greatness of the country he represents, because our sister countries of Latin America hang on his words. He has before him the judgment of history, which shall decide whether he has been truly great, and moved only by his high ideals of justice and democracy, or was in the end influenced by the satanic machinations of one man and the haughtiness of another.

I can assure you that our Chief, Mr. Carranza, is animated by the keenest desire to avoid difficulties between our respective countries; and we, following his patriotic impulses and as faithful servants of our country, are of the same inclination. Mr. Carranza in his note has only endeavored to defend the dignity of the Republic, without the least intending his attitude to be considered as a hostile act against the United States, from which country we have received great demonstrations of consideration and sympathy.

Francisco Villa or Venustiano Carranza?[6]

Martín Luis Guzmán

In between the unpolished frontier politics of Villa and the aristocratic elitism of Carranza, there lay a small but significant stratum of urban intellectuals—some more radical, some less so—who gravitated to one camp or the other depending on preference or circumstance. A small handful served in a military capacity, but most were advisors, administrators, politicians, or journalists in Constitutionalist rear areas. One such was Martín Luis Guzmán, a supporter of Francisco Madero. Like many Maderista civilians, Guzmán gravitated to Villa, not from deep enthusiasm for Villa, but because he felt Villa would be more pliable than Carranza. Guzmán underestimated Villa and broke with him in late 1914. The following excerpt speaks to the dilemma that Guzmán and others like him felt as the split between Villa and Carranza became imminent in the spring of 1914.

My stay in Chihuahua brought about my gradual and voluntary separation from the faction that had formed around Carranza. The other faction—a rebellion within a rebellion—restless and impatient, represented an aspect of the Revolution with which I felt more in sympathy. This second group had already drawn together men who wanted to preserve the democratic and impersonal character of the Revolution. To be sure, I didn't see how we were going to realize our ideals. It seemed enormously difficult, improbable —as improbable for a small group, however heroic its determination, to fight to the last against personal ambition and corruption, as it would have been easy if it had represented the unanimous undertaking of a well-directed, unified Revolution. But I had seen that under Carranza's leadership the Revolution was headed for the most unbridled and unrestrained absolutism, and this was enough to turn me in any other direction in the hope of salvation.

The mere fact that the group opposed to Carranza rallied around Villa as its military leader might have been taken as evidence of the internal conflict that thwarted the Revolution in its noblest objectives; because it was impossible to think of Villa as the standard-bearer of an elevated, reconstructive movement. And even as a mere brute force, Villa had such serious limitations that dealing with him was like handling dynamite. But the only military elements on which we could count to support our ideas were those commanded by him. Felipe Angeles, without any troops of his own so to speak, had thrown his lot in with Villa; the only other important winner of battles, General Alvaro Obregón, was following the lead of the new absolutism. So for us, the future of the Constitutionalist movement was bound up in the following question: was it possible to control Villa—Villa, who was too irresponsible and instinctive even to be ambitious? Would he put his force at the service of principles that either did not exist for him or were incomprehensible to him?

This was the dilemma: either Villa would submit to the fundamental principles of the Revolution, and, if so, he and the Revolution would triumph; or Villa would follow nothing but his own blind impulses, and he and the Revolution would go down to defeat. And it was around this dilemma that the tempest of the Revolution was to revolve in the hour of triumph.

The Pact of Torreón[7]

Division of the North and Army of the Northeast, July 8, 1914

In May and June relations between Villa and Carranza unraveled. The initiative came from Carranza and Obregón who conceived a plan to undo Villa's land reform in Chihuahua and stall his drive to Mexico City. The last obstacle between Villa and the capital was Zacatecas to the south. But in May, Carranza turned Villa east, ordering him to take Saltillo. Carranza then assigned the attack on Zacatecas to local chieftain Pánfilo Natera in the hopes of forging an army between Villa and the capital. But Natera bungled the attack and Carranza ordered Villa to send reinforcements. Having caught the scent of Carranza's manipulation, Villa refused and resigned. This precipitated a near-mutiny among Villa's chiefs who compelled the first chief to restore Villa's command. Against the wishes of Carranza, Villa attacked and captured Zacatecas on June 23. Two weeks later, Villa's chieftains met their counterparts from the Army of the Northeast whose chief, Pablo González, had his own grievances with Carranza. They signed the Pact of Torreón on July 8. It reaffirmed Carranza as first chief, but sank the Plan of Guadalupe by the following: freeing Villa to run Chihuahua as he wished; naming Carranza provisional president, thereby rendering him ineligible to run in the subsequent election; naming the members of Carranza's cabinet; placing control of the presidential elections in the hands of a convention of revolutionary chiefs; and requiring the dissolution of the federal army. It also committed the Constitutionalist Army to support policies in favor of workers and peasants, including agrarian reform.

The Division of the North recognizes Señor Venustiano Carranza as First Chief of the Constitutionalist Army. General Francisco Villa will remain at the head of the Division of the North. Señor Carranza will furnish the Division of the North with all the implements required for the speedy and proper conduct of military operations leaving to its Chief freedom of action in administrative and military affairs when circumstances so demand, under the obligation to report his acts to Señor Carranza for rectification or ratification.

The Divisions of the North and of the Northeast submit to Señor Carranza the following list of persons for him to choose from, among them the members of his cabinet: Fernando Iglesias Calderón, Luis Cabrera, General Antonio I. Villarreal, Doctor Miguel Silva, Engineer Manuel Bonilla, Engineer Alberto Pani, General Eduardo Hay, General Ignacio L. Pesqueira, Attorney Miguel Díaz Lombardo, Attorney José Vasconcelos, Attorney Miguel Alessio Robles and Attorney Federico Gonzalez Garza.

On assuming, in accordance with the Plan of Guadalupe, the office of Provisional President of the Republic, the citizen First Chief of the Constitutionalist Army will call a convention, whose object will be to discuss and determine the date on which the elections shall be held, the plan of government to be put in practice by the functionaries who shall have been elected, and the other topics of national interest. The convention shall be made up of delegates of the Constitutionalist Army named in councils of military chiefs on the basis of one delegate for every thousand men in the ranks. Every delegate to the convention will be accredited as such by credentials issued by the chief of the division to which he belongs.

For the good of the triumph of the revolutionary army and to allay feeling in the State of Sonora, the suggestion is respectfully submitted to the citizen First Chief that he take such action as he may deem best to settle the conflict existing in that State without violation of its sovereignty or attack on the person of the constitutionally elected Governor, citizen José María Maytorena. Appeal shall also be made to Señor Maytorena's patriotism to induce him to resign the office of Governor of the State, a person of influence, impartial and affiliated to the Constitutionalist cause being nominated to take charge of the Government of Sonora and afford guaranties to the people whose sacred interests are in danger.

It is the First Chief's exclusive province to appoint and remove employees of the Federal Administration in the States and Territories controlled by the Constitutionalist forces and to assign to them their jurisdiction, duties, and powers.

The present conflict being a struggle of the impecunious against the abuses of the powerful and understanding that the causes of the evils that bear down the country spring from praetorianism, plutocracy and clericalism, the Divisions of the North and Northeast solemnly pledge themselves to fight until complete banishment of the ex-federal army, which shall be superseded by the Constitutionalist Army, to set up democratic institutions in our country, to bring welfare to labour, financial emancipation to the peasant by an equitable apportionment of land, and other means tending to solve the agrarian question, to correct, chastise, and hold to their responsibilities such members of the Roman Catholic clergy as may have lent moral or physical support to the usurper, Victoriano Huerta.

Corrido of Victoriano Huerta[8]

Anonymous, Morelos

Victoriano Huerta resigned one week after the Pact of Torreón and fled the country five days later. On August 15, Obregón's troops won the race to Mexico City; five days later Carranza arrived. The following corrido captures the mood in Morelos at the departure of Huerta, a mix of joy, regret, and weariness. It compares Huerta's fate to that of Carlota, the wife of Emperor Maximilian, who had futilely beseeched Napoleon III of France for aid against Mexican rebels who resisted the French Intervention of 1862–1867. But whatever relief and joy the Zapatistas felt at the departure of Huerta, it began to dissipate by August 13, when Obregón's forces replaced the federal garrisons facing Morelos.

Victoriano Huerta left for old Europe,
like Momma Carlota in search of Napoleon;

and Aureliano Blanquet too—with voices like honey,
they said: "Farewell to my faithful nation."

So they left the Fatherland in black for mourning,
weeping in its tomb for its miserable orphans;

For lying in green fields are buried faithful sons,
sent to death unjustly by Huerta's bullets.

Brave men do not flee, Señor don Victoriano;
You and don Aureliano violate this code of honour.

For courage is never hidden in the breast of a Mexican.
Only tyrants run away, afraid of the winner.

You said that in three months you would defeat Zapata
and the aristocracy hoped that you would protect them.

You said: at any cost you'll bring peace to the country,
but in the end, you marched off to another nation.

Give greetings to Félix Díaz and Mondragón too;
give them an embrace to show you are still friends.

It was your devilish work that led to this failure;
a black coup d'état for all humankind.

Back there in old Europe, in the asylum of beggars,
they give refuge to bandits, but I do not know why.

They don't know our laws, so maybe it's expected,
that they should protect such corrupt men like you.

Disgrace is our verdict; it's what you deserve—
to be exiled forever with no hope of return.

For you hideously shed the immaculate blood
of innocent people dragged from their homes.

He wanders like a ghost in the Old World
with a voice sad and brave, for his ambition is destroyed.

He's an old dope smoker, an abortion of the earth—
Pray to God he never returns to afflict the nation.

The Mexican people now feel such deep joy,
and just want to forget their long civil war.

Mexico Is Tired of Impositions[9]

Emiliano Zapata, August 23, 1914

The defeat of Huerta opened a new stage in the revolution, as the
revolutionary coalition started to dissolve into discord over the political
and social order that would replace the dictatorship. Everyone knew
that a new struggle loomed, but would it be decided on the basis of the
Plan of Guadalupe, on the Pact of Torreón, or on some other ground?
For the Zapatistas, there was no debate. They were committed to the
Plan of Ayala and would accept nothing less. By August 23, Zapata had
already resolved to prevent the succession of Carranza to the
presidency, and wrote the following letter to U.S. President Wilson to
argue his case against any move to recognize Carranza's claim.

I have read your statements in the press about the agrarian revolution that
has been developing in this Republic for four years, and have been pleasantly
surprised to find that, distance notwithstanding, you understand exactly the

causes and the aims of the revolution that has steadily taken hold in the south of Mexico, a region that, more than anywhere else, has had to endure the despoliation and extortions of large landowners.

My belief that you sympathize with the movement for agrarian emancipation, induces me to explain its facts and antecedents, so that the rest of America and the entire world might have a true account of the profound meaning of this great proletarian movement. This is necessary, for the press of Mexico City is dedicated to the interests of the rich and powerful, and therefore misrepresents this struggle with odious calumnies.

I will begin by indicating the causes of the revolution that I lead. Until the outbreak of the 1910 Revolution, Mexico was in the grip of a feudal era.

A few hundred great landowners monopolized all arable land in the Republic. From year to year they increased their domains by despoiling the people of their ejidos or communal fields, as well as taking the modest estates of smallholders. There are cities in Morelos, like Cuautla, which even lack the land necessary to dispose of their garbage, let alone to support the population. And so it is that the large landowners, with dispossession after dispossession, today with one pretext, tomorrow with another, have been absorbing all the properties that have legitimately belonged to the indigenous people since time immemorial, and who have always cultivated these lands to sustain their families.

To achieve this, the landowners used legislation adopted in their interests to seize enormous tracts of land with the pretext that they are uncultivated. That is to say, unprotected by legally correct titles.

The large landowners despoiled smallholders and became the sole owners of the entire country, with the complicity of the courts and even imprisonment or conscription into the army. And, no longer possessing land, the peasants were forced to work on these lands for very small wages and to endure mistreatment by landowners, and by their foremen and overseers, many of whom are Spanish or the offspring of Spaniards who think they can behave as in the time of Hernán Cortes. That is to say, as if they were the conquerors and the masters, while we the peons are simple slaves, still subject to the brutal law of conquest.

The relationship of the hacendado to peons is entirely the same as the feudal lord, baron, or count of the Middle Ages, with respect to his servants and vassals. The hacendado, in Mexico, controls the life of his peon as he wishes; he sends the peon to prison, if he pleases; he forbids the peon to leave the property, under the pretext of debts that the peon will never be able to pay. The big landowner is in fact undisputed master of all lives and property in his vast domains, thanks to judges who the landowner corrupts with bribes, and to the political prefects or "chiefs," who are always his allies.

This unbearable situation was [a] direct cause of the Revolution of 1910; this was a struggle to end a feudal regime, and to fight the monopoly of land in the hands of a few. But unfortunately, Francisco Madero belonged to a rich and powerful family, and was the owner of great tracts of land in the North of the Republic. Naturally, Madero quickly reached an understanding with the other landowners. He upheld Porfirian legislation—laws made by the rich to favour the rich—as an excuse to betray his promise to restore stolen lands; he refused to destroy the overwhelming monopoly exercised by the hacendados by means of expropriation with indemnification, if the possession were legitimate. Madero broke his promises, so the revolution continued, mainly in regions that suffered the worst abuses and despoliation by hacendados; that is to say, in Morelos, Guerrero, Michoacán, Puebla, Durango, Chihuahua, Zacatecas, etc. etc.

Then came the military revolt at the Ciudadela; this was an attempt by the old porfiristas and conservative elements of all shades, to recover power again. They were afraid that Madero would someday have to fulfill his promises. As a result, the campesinos became truly alarmed and their revolutionary spirit increased more than ever, because the military revolt and the murder of Madero was a challenge—a true challenge—to the 1910 revolution.

Thus the revolution spread throughout the Republic, but in light of our previous experience, we are not waiting for the final victory to begin redistributing land and expropriating the great haciendas. So it has happened in Morelos, in Guerrero, in Michoacán, in Puebla, in Tamaulipas, in Nuevo León, in Chihuahua, Sonora, Durango, in Zacatecas, and San Luis Potosí. We are glad to say that the people have made their own justice, for until now legislation has not favoured them; the present Constitution is more a hindrance than a defence or guarantee for the working people, and above all, for the peasants.

The peasants understand the need to break the moulds of old legislation. They see the Plan of Ayala as the distillation of their yearnings and an expression of the principles that must be the basis of new legislation. They have started to put this plan into practice, as a supreme law demanded by justice. Thus the revolutionaries of the Republic have restored lands to dispossessed people, re-distributed the monstrous *latifundias* [large estates], and have punished their enemies—the feudal masters, the caciques, the collaborators of the Porfirian dictatorship, and the authors and accomplices of the military revolt at the Ciudadela—by confiscating their property.

At the same time, one can be certain that peace will not come to Mexico as long as the government does not make the Plan of Ayala into a law or constitutional principle, and completely fulfill it.

This is not only a social question—the necessity of agrarian reform—but also a political question. That is to say, it is a question of naming an interim-President who will call elections and begin the process of agrarian reform.

The country is tired of impositions, and will no longer tolerate masters or chiefs who are forced upon it. The people want a say in choosing their leaders. And since we are now dealing with the formation of an interim government, emanating from and serving the revolution, it is only logical and fair that it be formed by genuine representatives of the Revolution. Leaders of the armed movement should appoint the interim-President. Thus we assert article twelve of the Plan of Ayala against the desires of Venustiano Carranza and his circle of ambitious politicians, who hope that Carranza will capture the Presidency by surprise, or better said, by striking suddenly and imposing himself.

The appointment of an interim-President by revolutionary leaders throughout the country is the only formula that will work, for they will choose a man whose antecedents and ideas give them confidence. Carranza is the owner or shareholder of large properties in the Border States and is a threat to the peasants. He would follow the same policy as Madero, with whose ideas he is perfectly identified. The only difference between the two is that Madero was a weak leader, whereas Carranza is a man very capable of imposing the strongest dictatorship. This would cause a formidable revolution, perhaps even bloodier than the previous ones.

As you can see, the Revolution of the South is a one of ideals, not revenge or retaliation. This revolution has given a formal commitment to the country and to the civilized world that it will guarantee the lives and *legitimate* interests of nationals and foreigners, and thus my commitment to you.

Carranza Made a Serious Error with the Zapatistas[10]

Francisco Villa

Francisco Villa faced the same dilemma as Zapata. As the coalition collapsed, Villa moved toward an alliance with the revolutionaries of Morelos. He disagreed with past Zapatista stands against Madero, and even more so with their previous endorsement of Pascual Orozco. But he recognized in the Zapatistas a rectitude and commitment to the rural poor that was absent in Carranza. The following excerpt is from *The Memoirs of Pancho Villa*, a semifictional account written by Martín Luis Guzmán, based on Villa's archives, including a dictated memoir.

In my opinion, Carranza was not wise in his way of occupying the capital with his armies. Being anxious to take over resources, in order to make immediate use of them for his own convenience, he arranged for only Obregón to take part in the advance. He brought neither me nor Pablo González in, nor did he even summon Emiliano Zapata and his Revolutionaries from the south, who had warred ceaselessly and now occupied much territory.

Thus the First Chief offended Pablo González who refused to accompany him on the day of his triumphal entry. He offended me and my chiefs further, when we already had grievances. As for Zapata and his men, seeing that they were treated as strangers and enemies, they developed a very deep distrust of Carranza and the Carrancista principles. The Revolutionaries of the south said to my envoys: "We are not proud, Señores; we do not claim to have won the Revolution. But we find unfriendliness in Mexico City. The Constitutionalists did not have an understanding with the other liberating armies. We consider it an act of hostility that they have replaced their advance forces with Federal troops who were our enemies. We consider the First Chief's silence suspicious. He says nothing about the political future and hasn't a word about the distribution of lands. He enjoys his power without the consent of many chiefs and has continued to punish Lucio Blanco for his agrarian reform in Tamaulipas."

Wanting, at that time, a reconciliation with the Revolutionaries of Morelos, Carranza sent the lawyer Luis Cabrera and General Antonio Villareal to see them. But Zapata insisted on strong conditions, answering, "An armistice must be signed between the armies of the north and those of the south to halt hostilities between the advance forces; Xochimilco must be delivered to use as a pledge of harmony and good will; our Plan of Ayala must be adopted by Carranza and his men since the Plan of Guadalupe cannot be relied on; a convention of Revolutionary chiefs must be assembled to name the Interim President; and, until the convention, Carranza must have one of my delegates there to advise him and take note of all his important measures."

Zapata's intelligent advisors wisely persuaded him to make these demands. In no other way could they be sure of Carranza's actions, but they went too far in holding out for all of their Plan of Ayala and not just the part which provided for the poor. Zapata had fought against Madero, thinking that the promises of the glorious Plan of San Luis would not be kept; he had recognized Pascual Orozco as his chief, without considering that Orozco was only a traitor, as he proved by throwing his aid to Huerta. These things being true, the Revolutionaries of the north could not adopt the complete Plan of Ayala, but I learned from my talks with Zapata that if Carranza had accepted his principal conditions, Zapata would not have imposed on him or on our Constitutionalist chiefs the points of the Plan of Ayala that were contrary to Señor Madero's views.

But Carranza worked here as he did when my generals and González had reached an agreement. He accepted nothing that would lessen his power as First Chief or interfere with his political plans. He answered no to everything and immediately imprisoned Zapata's emissaries, and that ruined him forever with the men of the south.

I, Pancho Villa, say that Carranza committed a serious error in his dealings with the Zapatistas, as he did through his enmity for the forces of Chihuahua and his hostility toward the government of Sonora. It seemed that he was determined to cause war among the Revolutionaries. His mistakes appear the greater if we remember that not all the enemies of our cause were defeated. Other chiefs went on struggling and inciting the inhabitants of many districts with stories to the effect that we, the Constitutionalists, were traitors to our country under orders from Washington, and criminals who were seeking to change the laws and the Constitution to serve foreign nations.

The Anti-Social Forces of the Revolution[II]

Francisco Bulnes, 1916

In this selection, Francisco Bulnes articulated the reaction of the bourgeoisie and científicos to the destruction of Huerta's dictatorship. To him, this was the final demolition of Mexican progress that had been painstakingly cultivated in the years of the Porfiriato. Bulnes clung tenaciously to social Darwinism and scientific racism, and so it was inconceivable to him that the "offscourings" of society could have accomplished victory on their own. In the end, Bulnes laid the blame for the rise of a "prehistoric regime" in Mexico on President Wilson's misguided and foolish idealism.

The revolution was composed of three elements: the determination of Sonora, or rather of the men who obtained headway there, to preserve its sovereignty and independence at any cost; the Villa faction, which represented the Madero family and which sought, with President Wilson's support, to restore it to power; and Señor Venustiano Carranza, loyal and incorruptible partisan of the interests and ambitions of Señor Venustiano Carranza. These three factions, all antagonistic to the only one with real principles—Zapata—were ignoble, anti-social and consequently unpatriotic. Demagoguism, with its deformed and poisoned mentality, charged itself with the mission of interpreting the real principles of the revolution.

At first, President Wilson resolved to leave the Mexicans to fight it out among themselves against Huerta. But Mr. Wilson was implacable. In this he was influenced by his hatred of the imaginary científicos; of the imaginary cruel landowners; of the imaginary enemies of the eight-five per cent; of the Mexican cultured classes, who refused to submit to his idealistic theories; of the patriots, who resented his interference in Mexican politics; of the imaginary foreigners who robbed the poor during the Díaz dictatorship; of all the middle classes, who refused to conform to the revolution; of all the capitalists who did not favour the program of being robbed of all their possessions; of everything in Mexico that had a conservative aspect, that represented the prestige of the past or a sentiment of tenderness of veneration for an ideal not exactly in keeping with that set down by the President of the United States for the Mexican people.

In August 1914, President Wilson's triumph was complete. Huerta had fallen. The decent landowners had fallen, replaced by bandits. The científicos, who existed only in Wilson's imagination and in the perverse will of those making game of their name, had fallen. Catholicism had fallen, as had courts, law, justice, national prosperity, respect for foreigners and for the moral power of the United States. Zapata had proclaimed the restoration of the ancient Aztec regime and radical socialism, and was the only patriotic bandit, for he never asked Wilson's protection in exchange for the slices of national sovereignty. Villa had appeared as the Mahdi of the Soudan, with his insane program of unlimited plunder and assassination, of arbitrariness and despotism, a beast or a maniac, spreading fire and destruction in his pathway. Carranza had appeared as the reactionist against Porfirism. Everything was for himself, exclusively for himself. Their revolution, the bandits, the budding statesmen, the thugs, the intellectual offscourings, the public degradation, the political corruption, the oppressed people—everything belonged to him, and was to be immediately used to inaugurate another thirty years' dictatorship, modelled after the approved pattern of 1910, with an open road to ignominy along the triumphal highway of theft. Their revolution is to be understood only in its relation to theft, and when there is no longer anything to steal the revolution will die, leaving no possession in its will for a moribund people, bereft, in the process of redemption, of every vestige of civilization.

A period of humiliation has been ushered in for President Wilson since the complete triumph of this Constitutionalism, characterized by unbridled license. The apostolic President believed that in procuring victory for the Mexican liberators, the White House would have their assistance in carrying out its experiments, enabling it to turn Mexico into a great laboratory for the working out of all sane and insane idealistic theories. But to his great surprise their one object seemed to be to relieve everyone of the great weight of all movable and immovable property, of all moral and intellectual advantages. Instead of Constitutionalism, a regime of prehistoric government has been inaugurated without other laws than the will of the chief of each band, the country having been divided into bands, nominally under the jurisdiction of different supreme authorities.

CHAPTER SEVEN
WOMEN, GENDER, AND REVOLUTION

Mexico was a patriarchal society before, during, and after the Revolution. Yet women participated in the Revolution en masse and their role challenged the limits of patriarchal structures and traditional sex stereotypes in important ways. In Porfirian Mexico, the official ideology stressed a sharp divide in sex roles, assigning the public sphere—business, labor, and politics—to men, while reserving the domestic sphere for women, reinforcing these distinctions with legal codes that subordinated women to the authority of men in most aspects of their lives. For example, men exercised legal control over their wives' property as well as their children; men also had the right to extend or deny permission for their wives to work. Needless to say, the law also circumscribed the participation of women in politics; they could not vote or run for office.

However, the dynamics of economic development in Porfirian Mexico exerted pressures on patriarchal ideals. The mass expropriation of peasants pushed rural women into the commercial economy, without alleviating the responsibility they carried for maintaining their homes. Women worked both on haciendas and in the new industrial economy; on the estates, women's labor was frequently unpaid, while in the factories women earned less than men for the same work. The resulting impoverishment of women led to an upsurge in prostitution; by 1905, 12 percent of women were registered as prostitutes in Mexico City.[1] Life prospects were certainly better for middle-class women, some of whom took advantage of the limited opportunities to enter the professions, mainly as teachers; yet these women also found themselves limited by legal constraints, as well as by the moral admonitions of intellectuals like Justo Sierra who urged women to leave public life to men.

This is the context for an expansion of feminist circles around 1900 and for the militant participation of rural women in struggles for land and women workers in the labor movement. The ten years preceding Madero's revolution saw the emergence of feminist newspapers—*Vesper*, founded by Juana Belén Gutiérrez de Mendoza in 1901, *La Mujer Mexicana*, founded by Dolores Correa Zapata, Laura Méndez de Cuenca, and Mateana Murguía in 1904, and *La Voz de la Mujer*, founded by Lauro Aguirre in El Paso, Texas, in 1907—as well as organizations that agitated for legal equality for women and the right to vote. This included the Club Femenil Amigas del Pueblo (Friends of the People Women's Club), founded in 1909 by Gutiérrez de Mendoza and Dolores Jiménez y Muro, and the Hijas de Cuauhtémoc (Daughters of Cuauhtémoc). Both of these latter organizations supported Francisco Madero's anti-reelectionist movement and subsequent rebellion against Porfirio Díaz.[2]

At the onset of the revolution against Díaz only one movement, the Partido Liberal Mexicano, incorporated an explicit demand for the equality of women and urged the participation of women in the struggle. Madero's movement had not, nor did his vision for expanded democracy lead to feminist reforms. Nevertheless, Madero's victory in 1911 did create, temporarily, more room for a public feminist discourse. That debate, which focused on demands for women's suffrage, closed down with Victoriano Huerta's cuartelazo in 1913 and subsequent dictatorship. It revived after the Constitutionalist win when two pro-feminist governors, Francisco Múgica in Tabasco and Salvador Alvarado in Yucatán, convened feminist congresses in 1915 and 1916, respectively. These events ultimately contributed to the Constitution of 1917 and a number of laws that improved the legal status of women in Mexico.[3]

All the same, as feminist scholars have pointed out, the new Constitution was uneven with respect to the equality of women. It proclaimed their formal and legal equality, but even this was limited; for example, the Constitution gave women the right to hold public office, but not the right to vote (women won the full right to vote in 1953). Likewise, the Constitution enhanced protections for women workers and mandated equal pay for equal work, but it also still required married women to seek "their husband's permission to work."[4] The results of the Constitutional Convention in 1917 reflected the gendered composition of the convention (the delegates were all men) and the gender relations of the revolutionary struggle. For in the end, the revolution was dominated by men—some to be sure, more sympathetic to the demands and interests of women, but most still wedded to one extent or the other to traditional and patriarchal ideas about gender.

Overall, women did not receive due recompense for the contribution they made to the Revolution or for their sacrifices that entailed a greater burden for women than for men. Historian Julia Tuñón Pablos points out that, "daily life was precarious for women, and abduction and rape were commonplace ... many women, especially the well-off, fled the country."[5] Most Mexican women, of course, were not wealthy and did not have the option of leaving the country. But women of the middle class, the working class, and the peasantry were not simply the victims of a violent conflict; they were also active participants who engaged the Revolution in diverse ways and on all sides of the conflict.

Soldaderas are probably the best-known role that women played in the Mexican Revolution. The term derives from the Aragonese word for a soldier's pay—soldada—which soldiers used to pay women for a variety of services while campaigning and fighting.[6] This usually included sexual relations, but almost always it meant preparing meals, carrying and loading weapons, tending to wounds, fetching water, washing laundry, and so on. Women also gave birth to and reared their children while on campaign. Soldaderas were not unique to the Revolution; they had long been a part of military life in Mexico—and not only in Mexico, but in Europe and elsewhere. Nor were they unique to revolutionary armies in Mexico; soldaderas were also integral to the federal army. Traditionally, the soldadera was a camp follower, sometimes independent, sometimes a soldier's wife or girlfriend. Soldaderas were in essence the commissary of the military, revolutionary or otherwise. Thus, a Zapatista recruitment poster in 1913 exhorted married volunteers to bring their wives to cook and load weapons; it likewise urged unmarried men to bring along unmarried women to do the same.

However, the Revolution also gave rise to another aspect of the soldadera—that of the female soldier, more often than not disguised—or at least dressed—as men and assuming masculine versions of their given names. These women were rare if compared to the numbers of women who participated in more traditional roles as soldaderas, but they were not uncommon either, except in the federal army. They fought in all the main revolutionary factions. Among the Zapatistas, described by Rosa King as "a people in arms," we find more women soldiers than elsewhere, including Colonel Amelio (Amelia) Robles and Colonel Rosa Bobadilla, the latter having fought in 168 battles. Petra Ruíz, disguised as a man, achieved the rank of lieutenant in Carranza's forces and took part in the fighting to capture Mexico City in 1914. Even the army of Francisco Villa—perhaps the commander most hostile to soldaderas—had well-known women fighters; the two best known were Pedro (Petra) Herrerra, who played a key role in capturing Torreón in 1914 and came to lead her own brigade of 1,000 women, and María Quinteras de Merás who joined Villa in 1911.[7]

★ ★ ★

Women Comrades: the Revolution Approaches![8]

Ricardo Flores Magón, 1910

The Mexican Liberal Party (PLM) was primarily concerned with organizing a revolutionary movement of workers and peasants to win a classless society in Mexico, but it also paid attention to the particular exploitation and oppression of women. Aside from the handful of feminist organizations and publications that existed prior to the Revolution, the PLM was the only political party to consistently call for equality between men and women and for regulations to protect the interests of women in the workplace. It had done so since it adopted its first political program in 1906. However, as anarchists, the PLM also rejected participation in elections as a means of achieving its aims. As a result, the PLM did not advocate for women's suffrage. The PLM was also notable for the participation of women in its leadership; among them were included Sara Estela Ramírez, Andrea Villareal, and María Talavera.[9] The PLM's stand on equality for women won support from the Hijas de Anahuac (Daughters of Anahuac), an organization of female textile workers formed by Juana Belén Gutiérrez de Mendoza. The PLM was the only revolutionary organization in 1910 to make an explicit appeal to women to support and participate in the armed struggle against the Porfirian regime. The following document, penned by Ricardo Flores Magón and published in the PLM newspaper *Regeneración*, explains the oppression of women as systemic in class-based societies and historically developed, but not as an inevitable or natural condition. The solution, Magón argued, lay in overthrowing class society.

Women Comrades:

Revolution approaches! With angered eyes and flaming hair, her trembling hands knock anxiously on the doors of our nation. Let us welcome her with serenity, for even though she carries death in her breast, she is also the herald of life and hope. She will destroy and create at the same time. Hers are the invincible fists of a people in rebellion. She does not offer roses or caresses; she offers an axe and a torch.

Interrupting the millennial feast of the contented, sedition raises her fist against the so-called ruling class. Revolution approaches! Her mission will ignite the flames in which privilege and injustice will burn. Women comrades, do not fear the revolution. You are one-half of the human species and what affects humanity affects you. If men are slaves, you are too. Bondage does not recognize sex; the infamy that degrades men degrades you also. You cannot escape the shame of oppression.

We must stand in solidarity in the struggle for freedom and happiness. Are you mothers? Are you wives? Are you sisters? Are you daughters? Your duty is to help your man, to encourage him when he vacillates, to stand by his side when he suffers, to lighten his sorrow, to laugh and to sing with him when victory smiles. You don't understand politics? This is not a question of politics; this is a matter of life or death. Man's bondage is yours and yours is more sorrowful, more sinister, and more infamous.

Are you a worker? Because you are a woman you are paid less than men, and must work harder. You suffer the impertinence of the foreman or proprietor, and if you are attractive, the bosses will make advances. Should you weaken, they would rob you of your virtue in the same cowardly manner as you are robbed of the product of your labour.

Under this regime of social injustice which corrupts humanity, the existence of women wavers in the wretchedness of a destiny which fades away either in the blackness of fatigue and hunger or in the obscurity of marriage and prostitution.

In order to fully appreciate women's part in universal suffering, it is necessary to study page by page this sombre book called Life, which like so many thorns strips away the flesh of humanity.

So ancient is women's misfortune that its origins are lost in the obscurity of legend. In the infancy of humankind, the birth of a female child was considered a disgrace to the tribe. Women tilled the land, carried firewood from the forest and water from the stream, tended the livestock, constructed shelters, wove cloth, cooked food, and cared for the sick and the young. The filthiest work was done by women. If an ox died of fatigue, women pulled the plough. When war broke out, women changed masters and continued under the lash of new owners to work as beasts of burden.

Later, under the influence of Greek civilization, women were elevated one step in the esteem of men. No longer were they beasts of burden as in the primitive clan, nor did they lead secluded lives as in oriental societies. If they belonged to a free class, their role was one of procreators of citizens for the state; if they were slaves, they provided workers for the fields.

Christianity aggravated the situation of women with its contempt for the flesh. The founding fathers of the Church vented their rage against feminine qualities. St. Augustine, St. Thomas, and others, before whose statues women now kneel, referred to women as daughters of the devil, vessels of impurity, and condemned them to the tortures of hell.

Women's position in this century varies according to their social stature, but in spite of refined customs and the progress of philosophy, women continue subordinated to men by tradition and laws. Women are treated as minors when the law places the wife under the custody of the husband. She cannot vote or be elected, and to enter into civil contracts she must own a sizeable fortune.

Throughout history women have been considered inferior to men, by law and by custom. From this derives the misfortune which she has suffered since humanity differentiated itself from lower animal forms.

Humiliated, degraded, bound by chains of tradition, indoctrinated in the affairs of heaven by clerics, but ignorant of world problems, she is suddenly caught in the grind of industrial production which requires cheap labour to sustain the profits of the voracious "princes of capital" who exploit her. She is not as prepared as men for industrial struggle, nor is she organized with the women of her class to fight alongside her brother workers against the rapacity of capitalism.

Thus, women work more than men, but are paid less, and misery, mistreatment, and insult are the bitter harvest for a life of sacrifice. So meagre are women's salaries that frequently they must prostitute themselves to meet their families' basic needs, especially when in the marketplace of marriage they do not find a husband. When it is motivated by economic security instead of love, marriage is another form of prostitution, sanctioned by the law and authorized by public officials. That is, a wife sells her body for food exactly as does a prostitute; this occurs in most marriages. And what can be said of the vast army of women who do not succeed in finding a husband? The increasing cost of life's basic necessities, the displacement of labour by machinery, the ever-decreasing price of human labour—all contributes to the burden. The compulsory draft tears strong and healthy young men from the bosom of society and lessens the number eligible for marriage. Migration of workers, caused by economic and political phenomena, also reduces the number of men capable of marriage. Alcoholism, gambling and other ills further reduce the number of available men. Consequently, the number of single women grows. Since their situation is so precarious, they swell the ranks of prostitution, accelerating the degeneration of the human race by this debasement of body and spirit.

Comrades: This is the frightful picture offered by modern society. In it you see men and women alike suffering the tyranny of a political and social environment in complete discord with the progress of civilization and the advances of philosophy. But in times of anguish, do not look to the heavens for solutions and explanations, for there lies the greatest contribution to your bondage. The solution is here on earth! That solution is rebellion.

Demand that your husbands, brothers, fathers, sons and friends pick up the gun. Spit in the face of those who refuse to pick up a weapon against oppression.

Revolution approaches!

Down with the Dictatorship: The Political-Social Plan[10]

Dolores Jiménez y Muro, March 18, 1911

Dolores Jiménez y Muro was an early feminist, drawn to the struggle for equality in the waning years of the Porfirian state. Although born to a middle-class family, she early on developed a deep empathy for the plight of Mexico's rural and urban poor, and was active in charitable work through the Friends of the People Women's Club, which she co-founded in 1909 with Juana Belén Gutiérrez de Mendoza. In 1911, Jiménez y Muro helped draft, and was the only woman signatory, of the Political-Social Plan, a revolutionary program that was adopted by a network of radicals and reformers in central and southern Mexico. While the group endorsed the Madero insurgency, it maintained an independent program that went well beyond the mild political reforms contained in the Plan of San Luis Potosí. The document was left in the care of Jiménez y Muro who distributed the document in Mexico City as a call to arms against Porfirio Díaz. Later in 1911, when the conflict developed between Madero and Zapata, Jiménez y Muro sided with the Zapatistas.

The situation that weighs on Mexicans is truly afflictive, for the rulers of Mexico have failed to quell the revolutionary movement which arose against their abuses. In order to shed the blood of more decent Mexicans, they have now suspended individual guarantees, abolishing the independent press, closing clubs, forbidding any expressions of public opinion and filling the prisons without regard for women or any other citizens who oppose tyranny.

From the beginning, these rulers were enthroned through deception, for they once proclaimed the same principle for which we are fighting today— Effective Suffrage and No Re-election. But instead of this principle, they established the most abject, abusive, and bloody dictatorship. And now, with the fraud of the last election, they stand accused of swindling the high posts they occupy, of betraying their own doctrines, and of abusing power.

In our political and social existence, there must be reforms and replacements of personnel. These are required by the needs of the contemporary generation, but are impossible to achieve at present under a plutocratic and dictatorial government.

The People are ultimately the only sovereign and supreme legislator, and we have been empowered by the people we represent—several groups, numbering more than 10,000 people in the states of Guerrero, Tlaxcala, Michoacan, Campeche, Puebla and in the Federal District, who have come together to proclaim the following plan and to invite our fellow citizens to adopt it if they agree that the nation needs reform and regeneration.

We repudiate the President and Vice-President, the senators and deputies, as well as all other elected officials, by virtue of the omissions, fraud and pressures that occurred in the last elections.

General Díaz, his Cabinet Ministers, and Sub-Secretary of the Interior Miguel Macedo—who unanimously voted to suspend guaranties—and the judges who unjustly sentenced so-called political prisoners, have violated the law and are traitors; all army chiefs will be judged according to the attitude they have taken towards the insurgents.

We recognize Francisco Madero as interim President and Supreme Chief of the Revolution.

We proclaim the Constitution of 1857 as the supreme law and uphold the principle of "Effective Suffrage and No Re-election."

The Press Law must be amended to clearly and precisely determine the instances where a person can rightly complain of defamation, as well as instances where infractions actually disrupt public order, and that properly punish the offender, if and when the act is really a crime.

The rights of suppressed municipalities must be restored.

The centralization of education must be abolished and replaced with a federative system.

The indigenous race must be protected in every way, obtaining by every means their dignity and prosperity.

All properties usurped under the current administration must be returned to their former and rightful owners.

Wages must be increased for rural and urban workers of both sexes, fixed to the rates of return on capital, as determined by a commission responsible for reviewing the data.

The hours of a work-day must not be less than eight or more than nine.

Mexican nationals must comprise no less than half of the workers employed by foreign companies in the Republic, in both subordinate and superior positions, with the same salaries, considerations and privileges granted to foreign employees.

When circumstances permit, the value of urban properties must be reviewed in order to establish fair rents, subject to additional work to create hygienic and comfortable accommodations for the working classes.

All proprietors who own more lands than they need or want to cultivate must be obliged to give uncultivated land to those who need it, receiving for their part a return of 6 per cent per year, corresponding to the fiscal value of the lands.

Monopolies of every kind must be abolished.

Down with the Dictatorship! Effective Suffrage and No Re-Election!

Reflections of a Political Prisoner[11]

Dolores Jiménez y Muro, March 3, 1914
Penitentiary of México

Following the military coup by General Victoriano Huerta, Dolores Jiménez y Muro was among the radicals rounded up and imprisoned by the regime—in her case, the result of her support for the Zapatistas in Morelos. The following document is a letter from Jiménez y Muro to General Aureliano Blanquet, one of Huerta's co-conspirators in the overthrow of Madero and Huerta's minister of war. The letter is noteworthy for a number of reasons, not the least of which is her analysis, from a feminist perspective, of the Revolution and its causes.

Señor General Aureliano Blanquet:

Señora Gutiérrez Mendoza, my friend and companion in prison, has assured you that I am ready to assist the Government in its work of pacification. She spoke truthfully, although spontaneously, and has only interpreted my desires and aspirations which are well known to her.

Yes, I am ready to help pacify our homeland, but only by peaceful means, for it is my conviction that we must avoid more bloodshed which, until now, has been the ruin of all citizens. My greatest desire is to stop up the torrent of tears and blood that have been flowing everywhere, the result of the horrors of civil war.

Señora Gutierrez Mendoza has told me that you would comment extensively and in writing on my proposals and hopes. For this I am grateful, since it satisfies my ardent desire.

To begin, my personal aspirations are nothing. I have been shut away unjustly in this prison for six months, and I am still waiting to be sentenced. If, as has so far been the case, I find no justice, I reserve the right to appeal to the court of public opinion against it and against the legal procedures that have made me a victim.

If the government accepts my services, in a manner that I am willing and able to offer, I will see my judicial process through to its end. If I leave prison to undertake a commission entrusted to me, I will return of my own accord, for my conscience demands this of me as a follower of the cause to which I remain loyal—the cause of the People and justice.

As for my general hopes, there are two. One is that you read carefully what I am about to write about the current revolution, whose root causes I have known before it started, and whose progress I have followed intimately. The other is that the Government adopts peaceful means to end it.

Before proceeding, and in order to anticipate the natural errors and prejudices of someone who does not know me, I must say that I am neither an enemy nor a personal supporter of anyone, that I am instead a passionate advocate of certain social and political doctrines, that when I am a friend, it is a personal matter, whereas in politics my only consideration is to judge people by their deeds.

In addition, you should know I am an orphan—my father and mother died when I was young—and I have always lived from my own work. I have been on my own for a long time in this world. As a result, nothing influences me other than my own judgement and conscience. Insomuch as it is in my power to decide, I have no desire for material things or to be tied down, nor to be twisted or corrupted.

With this preface, I will turn to the matter at hand, begging that you not see in my assessments, any reproaches or ill will, for I have none. It is simply necessary to speak my mind and present things as they are, to find a remedy to the truly distressing situation of the Mexican family. I am motivated by a desire to restore peace and wellbeing.

Great men of State, who might be characterized by a capacity to hold office and by a genuine concern for the governed, are very rare in a struggle that seeks to reform the political and social institutions that govern people. They are too often blinded by worries, adulation and personal interests that are not always legitimate. From this arises the need for impartial and disinterested spirits to explain, shed light on, and offer solutions to problems like those that presently concern us. So with your consent, I will offer mine.

One of the serious mistakes preventing the restoration of Peace is to dismiss this revolution as the impulse of a few ambitious men who are seeking public positions, or as the result of bandits whose sole purpose is theft.

I do not deny that there are ambitious men or bandits, but these do not exist in the proportions claimed by the press. It is rare to find a man without ambitions or who seeks nothing. One will find bandits everywhere, and they will follow any flag that allows them to commit their misdeeds with success. But Vázquez Gómez and Carranza are not merely struggling to be president, even though this would not be an unpleasant result. Nor are the people sacrificing themselves simply to let these men to govern their destinies. Nor is the goal of this struggle to appropriate other people's property, even though many do so. The revolution is the armed expression of the aspirations of the overwhelming majority. With rare exceptions, we can say they are the Mexican Nation, which yearns for its due rights and laws that guarantee equality between capital and labour.

So you see, Señor General, that despite the undeniable energy of General Huerta, that despite the great force that he has in his hands, that despite the numerous police at his disposal—which discovers plot after plot and fills the prisons with political prisoners—that despite razing villages, and all the repressive measures they have used since February 18, 1913, the revolution has grown rather than diminished.

Why is this? It is because the ideas of redemption and reform have seized every mind and inflamed every heart. They have strengthened every arm and have predisposed people to sacrifices. Rigorous measures to suppress them no longer frighten people who no longer know fear. They only exasperate, and drive them to revenge. The life-force of the blood of those who succumbed, and the tears of those who mourn, inspire many new fighters.

As proof, I'll give a brief overview of events whose truth I know my involvement as a witness and author.

After the death of my parents, I joined a philanthropic society and began to visit the slums of the destitute and to bring them bread and consolation. Since everything was given with love, they saw me as a friend and confided heartbreaking stories of misery, humiliation, and injustice—the results of theft, dispossession, and abuse, combined with unfair wages and rent for miserable homes so exorbitant that the owners of these hovels make profits of four, five and even six per cent while the homes rented to other classes bring a profit of two percent at most. And if this were not enough, their exploiters and superiors require them to maintain a humiliating servility.

After seeing the miseries of the city, I went to the countryside, where there was even greater exploitation of man by man, for in addition to low wages one must add the dispossession of land from villages and individuals.

And there among the illiterate, I heard the causes of their misery, their cries of rebellion and protest—just as I had in the city. But, no one had to explain things to them. They were already aware that they are men and not objects, that they are the sons of God and not the property of those who despoil and oppress them. And after that, I realized that the revolution was not far away, because its ideas were germinating everywhere.

Shortly afterwards I returned to Mexico City, where thousands of citizens were joining political clubs from which the revolution might arise, as it did.

During the short period of the struggle led by Madero—idolized of the people because he spoke of freedom and redemption, and because they believed that the Plan of San Luis Potosí, although deficient, would produce the reforms they desired—something happened that I should not pass over in silence.

Having discovered the revolutionary movement which was to start on November 20, 1910, citizens from various states united and formed a revolutionary committee and issued a political-social plan that recognized Madero as supreme chief of the revolution. After this they launched an armed struggle, led by Gabriel Hernández and the Mirandas (father and son).

After entering St. Augustine Taxco, Hernandez recruited 86 men. These numbers increased until he had four thousand men. Miranda happened to do the same. Meanwhile 12,000 men remained in the Federal District as a reserve, albeit without weapons. Thus, in May 1911, when Hernández and the Mirandas commissioned me to see Madero, they had 20,000 men not counting those who joined on May 24 and 25 when they demanded the immediate resignation of the dictator.

What drove these men to unite and organize if not for the ideas and aspirations I referred to? The same thing is happening today, for this revolution is a continuation of the earlier struggle.

In its first stage, Madero was the leader, because his word echoed the ideas and feelings of the people who acclaimed him an apostle, a redeemer. The second period saw arms lifted against Madero for he failed to keep his promises. Today the revolution is against General Huerta, for it sees him as an obstacle to their aspirations.

The Revolution will conclude when it has removed this obstacle, for the people of Mexico feel an irresistible need to step forward on the path of their political and social advancement and to persevere, as have the people of Turkey, Persia, China and Portugal.

This does not mean there is no remedy for the evil that afflicts us, no way to stop the civil war that threatens extermination. There is. If I have spoken with frankness that harms me as a political prisoner, it is because I believe a remedy exists, and that this remedy is in government hands. Let me explain.

The people, for whom laws and authorities have been instituted, have the right to create, repeal and amend the former, and the right to elect or dismiss the latter, when they have reason to do so. And since the government is to be for the people, it has the duty to facilitate the exercise of their rights, without bloodshed or prejudice.

Thus, the people of Mexico have resolved to reform their institutions. And thus, General Huerta need not leave his post as president, but can end the conflict by calling the revolutionaries to a convention, not to set up elections but to decide how best to bring about the aspirations of the people, to transform these into law and ensure that Congress abides by the wishes of those they represent.

If General Huerta is prepared to take this step, if he is prepared to free political prisoners who agree with this plan, and provide guarantees for everyone, then peace will be a fact, and his reputation will be enlarged and preserved in the annals of history.

As for me, you will find me ready to offer the government my intelligence, all my efforts in contributing in a small way towards obtaining a cherished peace.

The Feminist Creed[12]

Nueva Era, February 17, 1912

The following unsigned article was published in *Nueva Era*, a pro-Maderista newspaper that also advocated for the legal equality of women. The article, however, advocates a very mild brand of feminism that did not challenge basic assumptions about the nature and role of women in society; indeed the article's main argument is to defend motherhood as the paramount role for women and to criticize radical feminists—who the author calls "harmful" feminists—who were even then arguing for the elimination of barriers that kept most ostensibly male occupations and professions closed to women.

The books written by women for women cannot be viewed with disdain. Since ancient times women writers have dominated the trend of making books for their sex even more than manly ones. However, we note a new direction today. Those writers in the past were struggling to give their contemporaries advice for social life; those of today now attend primarily to inculcating a taste for the home and for the love of family life.

There is a point at which harmful feminism, which tends to separate women from their natural occupations, has done much damage. I refer to the delusional egalitarians who are advocating male occupations as careers for women.

We should not ever exaggerate doctrines that, if well emended, may be invigorating. We want women to be taught the same as men. We want women to be aware of their rights and duties, just as it should be. We want a woman to be equal to her companion before the law. These are just and legitimate aspirations. Also, it is also fair that in our society we should open the doors of all careers, arts and professions, and that women should freely enter them when they need to or if they are endowed with exceptional aptitude.

So much for my feminist credo.

But should we call at all the doors through which we wish pass? Certainly not. It is a sound wisdom that must guide us in our path, and to achieve that good judgement one needs to study, and acquire a strong and deep culture and education.

It is not only a defect of women to wish away their condition or nature. Many men who would be excellent farmers are bad writers or artists! Many a boy, who would otherwise be an honest worker, runs towards the taverns seeking a fantastic Mimi, and between the mist of snuff and drunkenness, is deceived by the poetry of Mürger!

The same is true in the feminist army. Do you know any who declare a desire to continue the modest task of preparing food and making clothing? No. It seems that with the name of "feminist" they are born with spontaneous powers. She who exclaims that "I am a feminist" will immediately add: "I am artist" or "I am intellectual." What a horror!

But there is another, even more serious, matter. When the feminist starts to believe she is persecuted, she feels hatred or defiance towards the man of competence. Sometimes, conceited in her ignorance, she comes to look down upon or to fear him. At this point, such a selfish single woman renounces marriage and the home, and dries up the source of tenderness in her soul, deprived of the most beautiful of her attributes: motherhood.

Motherhood! That mission so sad and painful to physiology; that mission so very sweet and lofty to humankind!

There is nothing higher, more sublime, more august than that rose-bush of passion that tears at your heart to give life to a rose of flesh, to divide her own being, her soul, for the continuation of this wretched humanity so beloved and so fragile.

It is not enough to have children to deserve the name of mother. It requires great culture to give life to the spirit and perform the difficult task of mothering and educating. For nothing is more necessary than the sum of knowledge on how to manage a household well. In the home, the woman has her throne. Nature endowed her with the vital functions that this post calls for. In good time, some are forced by necessity to leave the home or are driven by the mysterious force that pushes artists to leave their easels. But it is never by choice.

Those who are dazzled by feminist theories want to take the world by storm, undoubtedly unaware of how much pain they will encounter on this road and how much sweetness there is in the simple, common and happy life they abandon.

A triumph of public life occasions more bitterness than pleasure. It must be set aside as so much bramble, so many weeds that make our hands bleed.

I have heard more than one famous artist sigh for the life of those unknown women who live and die while breathing an atmosphere of sweetness and love in the home. Public triumph arouses admiration, but it also breeds hatred and passions that are small and base. There is no punishment greater than this for a heart that melts with love for mankind!

I would say to women: "Do not abandon the heaven of your home to a desire for false glory. But within the house, in art, at work, everywhere, you must seek to elevate your intellectual and moral level. Half of humanity, educators and the companion to men, must not be inferiors in knowledge and culture."

Pancho Villa and the Equality of Women[13]

John Reed, 1914

Despite the participation of women in all of the main revolutionary factions, the leaders of these factions tended to harbor quite traditional and decidedly patriarchal attitudes about women. Francisco Villa was not an exception. Indeed, Villa is often portrayed as one of the revolutionary leaders most hostile toward the involvement of women in his forces. Certainly as a military commander, Villa prized the mobility of his forces, which were mostly cavalry, and saw the soldaderas as a dead weight that slowed down his movements. Villa is also infamous for an incident in 1916 when he ordered the massacre of 60 to 90 (depending on the source) soldaderas who had been captured after a battle with Carranza's troops at Santa Rosalía. The following excerpt from U.S. journalist John Reed shows a Villa alternately startled and amused by the notion of women's suffrage.

Villa has two wives, one a patient, simple woman who was with him during all his years of outlawry, who lives in El Paso, and the other a cat-like, slender young girl, who is the mistress of his house in Chihuahua. He is perfectly open about it, though lately the educated, conventional Mexicans who have been gathering about him in ever-increasing numbers have tried to hush up the fact. Among the peons it is not only not unusual but customary to have more than one mate.

One hears a great many stories of Villa's violating women. I asked him if that were true. He pulled his moustache and stared at me for a minute with an inscrutable expression. "I never take the trouble to deny such stories," he said. "They say I am a bandit, too. Well, you know my history. But tell me; have you ever met a husband, father, or brother of any woman that I have violated?" He paused: "Or even a witness?"

It is fascinating to watch him discover new ideas. Remember that he is absolutely ignorant of the troubles and confusions and readjustments of modern civilization. "Socialism," he said once, when I wanted to know what he thought of it: "Socialism—is it a thing? I only see it in books, and I do not read much." Once I asked him if women would vote in the new Republic. He was sprawled out on his bed, with his coat unbuttoned. "Why I don't think so," he said, startled, suddenly sitting up. "What do you mean—vote? Do you mean elect a government and make laws?" I said I did and that women were already doing it in the United States. "Well," he said, scratching his head, "if they do it up there I don't see that they shouldn't do it down here." The idea seemed to amuse him enormously. He rolled it over and over in his mind, looking at me and away again. "It may be as you say," he said, "but I have never thought about it. Women seem to me to be things to protect, to love. They have no sternness of mind. They can't consider anything for its right or wrong. They are full of pity and softness. Why," he said, "a woman would not give an order to execute a traitor."

"I am not so sure of that, *mi General*," I said. "Women can be crueller and harder than men."

He stared at me, pulling his moustache. And then he began to grin. He looked slowly to where his wife was setting the table for lunch. "*Oiga*," he said, "come here. Listen. Last night I caught three traitors crossing the river to blow up the railroad. What shall I do with them? Shall I shoot them or not?"

Embarrassed, she seized his hand and kissed it. "Oh, I don't know anything about that," she said. "You know best."

"No," said Villa. "I leave it entirely to you. Those men were going to try to cut our communications between Juárez and Chihuahua. They were traitors—Federals. What shall I do? Shall I shoot them or not?"

"Oh, well, shoot them," said Mrs. Villa.

Villa chuckled delightedly. "There is something in what you say," he remarked, and for days afterward went around asking the cook and the chambermaids whom they would like to have for President of Mexico.

Elizabetta the Soldadera[14]

John Reed, 1914

Reed also wrote fascinating portraits of the soldaderas—capturing some of the ambiguities that surrounded their role—who accompanied Villa's troops, including the following excerpt where he meets a young woman—Elizabetta—who has lost her man in a recent battle. What emerges is a woman accustomed to her traditional role, but who also finds a way to assert a degree of autonomy within the limitations of her subordinate status as a soldadera.

It was not yet quite dark. I wandered down to the river bank in the vague hope of finding some of my *compadres*[15] who were still reported missing after the battle. And it was there that I first saw Elizabetta.

There was nothing remarkable about her. I think I noticed her chiefly because she was one of the few women in that wretched company. She was a very dark-skinned Indian girl, about twenty-five years old, with the squat figure of her drudging race, pleasant features, hair hanging forward over her shoulders in two long plaits, and big, shining teeth when she smiled. I never did find out whether she had been just a peon woman working around La Cadena when the attack had come, or whether she was a *vieja*[16]—a camp follower of the army.

Now she was trudging stolidly along in the dust behind Captain Felix Romero's horse—and had trudged so for thirty miles. He never spoke to her, never looked back, but rode on unconcernedly. Sometimes he would get tired of carrying his rifle and hand it back to her to carry, with a careless "Here! Take this!" I found out later that when they returned to La Cadena after the battle to bury the dead he had found her, apparently out of her mind; and that, needing a woman, he had ordered her to follow him. Which she did, unquestioningly, after the custom of her sex and country.

Captain Felix let his horse drink. Elizabetta halted, too, knelt and plunged her face into the water.

"Come on," ordered the Captain. "*Andale!*"[17] She rose without a word and waded through the stream. In the same order they climbed the near bank, and there the Captain dismounted, held out his hand for the rifle she carried, and said, "Get me my supper!" then he strolled away toward the houses where the rest of the soldiers sat.

Elizabetta fell upon her knees and gathered twigs for her fire. Soon there was a little pile burning. She called a small boy in the harsh, whining voice that all Mexican women have, "*Aie! Chamaco!* Fetch me a little water and corn that I may feed my man!" and, rising upon her knees above the red glow of the flames, she shook down her long, straight black hair. She wore a sort of blouse of faded light blue rough cloth. There was dried blood on the breast of it.

"What a battle, señorita!" I said to her.

Her teeth flashed as she smiled, and yet there was a puzzling vacancy about her expression. Indians have mask-like faces. Under it I could see that she was desperately tired and even a little hysterical. But she spoke tranquilly enough.

"Perfectly," she said. "Are you the gringo who ran so many miles with the *colorados*[18] after you shooting?" and she laughed—catching her breath in the middle of it as it hurt.

The *chamaco* shambled up with an earthen jar of water and an armful of corn-ears that he tumbled at her feet. Elizabetta unwound from her shawl the heavy little stone trough that Mexican women carry, and began mechanically husking the corn into it.

"I do not remember seeing you at La Cadena," I said. "Were you there long?"

"Too long," she answered simply, without raising her head. And then suddenly, "Oh, but this war is no game for women!" she cried.

Don Felix looked up out of the dark, with a cigarette in his mouth.

"My dinner," he growled. "Is it *pronto?*" [19]

"*Luego, luego!*" [20] she answered. He went away again.

"Listen, señor, whoever you are!" said Elizabetta swiftly, looking up to me. "My lover was killed yesterday in the battle. This man is my man, but, by God and all the saints, I can't sleep with him this night. Let me stay then with you!"

There wasn't a trace of coquetry in her voice. This blundering, childish spirit had found itself in a situation it couldn't bear, and had chosen the instinctive way out. I doubt if she even knew herself why the thought of this new man so revolted her, with her lover scarcely cold in the ground. I was nothing to her, nor she to me. That was all that mattered.

I assented, and together we left the fire, the Captain's neglected corn spilling from the stone trough. And then we met him a few feet into the darkness.

"My dinner!" he said impatiently. His voice changed. "Where are you going?"

"I'm going with this señor," Elizabetta answered nervously. "I'm going to stay with him . . ."

"You . . ." began Don Felix, gulping. "You are my woman. *Oiga*, señor, this is my woman here!"

"Yes," I said. "She is your woman. I have nothing to do with her. But she is tired and not well, and I have offered her my bed for the night."

"This is very bad, señor!" exclaimed the Captain, in a tightening voice. "You are the guest of this Tropa and the Colonel's friend, but this is my woman and I want her . . ."

"Oh!" Elizabetta cried out. "Until the next time señor!" She caught my arm and pulled me on.

We had all been living in a nightmare of battle and death—all of us. I think everybody was a little dazed and excited. I know I was.

By this time the peons and soldiers had begun to gather round us, and as we went on the Captain's voice rose as he retailed his injustice to the crowd.

"I shall appeal to the Colonel," he was saying. "I shall tell the Colonel!" he passed us, going toward the Colonel's cuartel, with averted, mumbling face.

"*Oiga, mi Coronel!*" he cried. "This gringo has taken away my woman. It is the grossest insult!"

"Well," returned the Colonel calmly, "if they both want to go, I guess there isn't anything we can do about it, eh?"

The news traveled like light. A throng of small boys followed us close behind, shouting the joyful indelicacies they shout behind rustic wedding parties. We passed the ledge where the soldiers and the wounded sat, grinning and making rough, genial remarks as at a marriage. It was not coarse or suggestive, their banter; it was frank and happy. They were honestly glad for us.

Without the least embarrassment, Elizabetta lay down beside me on the bed. Her hand reached for mine. She snuggled against my body for the comforting human warmth of it, murmured, "Until morning," and went to sleep.

When I awoke in the morning she was gone. Elizabetta was squatted over a little fire near the corner of the house, patting tortillas for the Captain's breakfast. She smiled as I came up, and politely asked me if I had slept well. She was quite contented now; you knew from the way she sang over her work.

Presently the Captain came up in a surly manner and nodded briefly to me.

"I hope it's ready now," he grunted, taking the torillas she gave him. "You take a long time to cook a little breakfast. *Carramba!* Why is there no coffee?" he moved off, munching. "Get ready," he flung back over his shoulder. "We go north in an hour."

"Are you going?" I asked curiously. Elizabetta looked at me with wide-open eyes.

"Of course I am going. *Seguro!*[21] Is he not my man?" She looked after him admiringly. She was no longer revolted.

"He is my man," she said. "He is very handsome, and very brave. Why, in the battle the other day . . ."

Elizabetta had forgotten her lover.

A Diplomat's Wife in Mexico[22]

Edith O'Shaughnessy

Edith O'Shaughnessy was married to Nelson O'Shaughnessy, the Chargé D'Affaires of the U.S. embassy in Mexico City. O'Shaughnessy was in Mexico from 1910 until the U.S. occupation of Veracruz in April 1914, after which the U.S. diplomatic mission was closed. The following excerpts are compiled from two journals she published afterwards, *Diplomatic Days* and *A Diplomat's Wife in Mexico*. Like U.S. ambassador Henry Lane Wilson and the rest of the embassy staff, Edith O'Shaughnessy shared a conservative political perspective on the

Mexican Revolution. She was favorably impressed with Porfirio Díaz and sympathetic toward Victoriano Huerta; conversely, she saw Francisco Madero as a hopeless and inept dreamer, while in Francisco Villa and Emiliano Zapata she perceived an atavistic threat to civilization. O'Shaughnessy's observations are laced with prejudice against the indigenous nature of Mexico, and she was clearly skeptical about the possibilities for civilization in that country, but she nevertheless felt great empathy for the fate of women during the Revolution.

May 20, 1911

I saw some Mexican suffragettes the other day whom I wish their American sisters could have gazed upon. They were armed with bandoliers full of ammunition crossed over their breasts, and it did look like bullets rather than ballots among the sisterhood here.

I stay at home a good deal. It is so pleasant—and after so many years of the concurrences, of the displacements, the hastes and excitements of the great world, how I love this full leisure! I have been looking into the history of Mexico since Independence—to try to get some sort of a "line" on governmental psychology. So much bloodshed has always attended a change of government here. The long reign of Díaz was preceded by all sorts of upheavals, in which any one who had to do with government lost his life.

However, all this concerned Mexicans alone. But now, with disorders menacing huge foreign interests, a new element of discord and complication comes in. Díaz seems at last pushed to the wall, and with him many foreign interests, which I understand are vital to the life of the country. He is supposed to have promised his resignation, if his conscience lets him. He fears anarchy, and, of course, he knows his people very, very well.

June 9, 1911

People holding property are worried about the ever-increasing banditry all over the country, murders of people on isolated haciendas, and general dislocation of business and lawlessness. A swift sliding down into the old pre-Díaz brigandage is feared. The slopes are so attractive to the dissatisfied and uncontrolled. Has any one ever witnessed such an anomaly as we witnessed here? The heads of a solid, recognized government turning over their offices to a relatively few armed opponents.

August 17, 1911

All quiet in Mexico City, but we understand that a battle is taking place at Cuernavaca between Zapata, our "foremost" brigand, with three thousand troops, and the Federals. Those who know tell me that Zapata is atavistic in type, desirous of Mexico for the Indians, á la a celebrated Indian chief of the Sierras de Alica, Manuel Lozada. "Mexico for the Indians" really means a sponging out of everything between us and Montezuma.

November 6, 1911

Well, Madero is President of Mexico, and what difficulties lie before him! I could not but ask myself, as I looked about the vast assemblage at the inauguration, and heard the roar of the Indian throngs outside, what have they had to prepare themselves for political liberty after our pattern? But then, you know, I have always had a natural inclination for the strong hand and one head. Many of these millions have nothing to lose, and hope, mixed with desire, is rampant during the periods of upheaval. Some sort of new day is rising in Mexico, but Madero would seem to be president simply because he is a successful revolutionary leader. It seems the normal thing, the inevitable, preordained way for men to come into power, but, that being the case, they ought to take it a little more quietly. For a pure Aryan like myself it's startling, it's disconcerting to a degree!

January 27, 1912

Most amusing lunch here today. We got on to the eternal land question. Madero walked to the presidency on the plank of the distribution of land, which he promptly and inevitably kicked out from under him—it didn't, couldn't hold. What the Indian loves is his adobe hut running over with children and surrounded by just enough land, planted with corn, beans, and peppers, not to starve on, when worked intermittently, as fancy or the rainfall indicate. The Indians seem, under these conditions, a thousand times happier than our submerged tenth. Anybody who has been to Mexico knows that the Indian has little or no qualification to permit being changed into a scientific farmer by the touch of the wand. And as for slogans! They're all right to get into office with, but try tilling the soil with them!

April 25, 1912

The newspapers have had large headlines regarding the Zapatistas, for "the Attila of the South" is moving on Cuernavaca, and it seems but a question of time before the lovely town falls into his hands. In all this the women and children seem the pity of it. At home or afield, they are continually caught up into mysterious traps of destiny. Even here in my house there are, from time to time, curious disappearances.

Josefina, the silent, consumptive Indian seamstress who comes to sew and mend, has one of those vanishing sorts of lives. She has wonderful hands, and can copy with her slender, tapering fingers the most complicated French clothes. In fact, if one were able to get the stuffs here, one couldn't tell the copy from the original, cut and all. She has just been copying that rather intricate Jeanne Hallé purple-and-black blouse. Except for the inside waistband, whose origin is nameless, like Josefina, you can scarcely tell them apart, not a sixteenth of a centimeter's difference in length, breadth or width.

She sits in the sun by an open window, and has egg and sherry at eleven and before she goes home, but the sands of her life are slipping fast. She lives in a room with three other consumptive sisters. The eldest went out one night to get some oil for their lamp. It is now ten days, and she has not returned. Is she working in the powder-mills, or what? Who will care, and who could if he would inform himself of her fate—just gone out into the night. One can only battle so far with Indian situations. After a certain point everything seems to slip away into mystery, racial and individual.

Does not constitutional democracy seem a snare and a delusion if two-thirds of the population are composed of such? It brings a smile of despair to the face. My very good Indian washer-woman, not long ago, left me. The usual excuse of an aunt or a grandmother, or some one being ill or dead, was not used. She just stood there with her three children, clutching the ends of her *rebozo*, that the last, fat little baby was rolled up in, and repeated that she must return at once to her pueblo whose Indian name I didn't catch. She had a sort of an antique, troubled look. I asked Celia if she knew what the matter was. She answered the *"Pués quién sabe, Señora!* [Well, who knows, Señora.]"

Talking about housework, I wish some of the airy stipendiaries of other climes, or even the women of those sections of my native land where they don't have "help," could really know what it is here, where half the female energies of the nation are engaged in the grinding of corn. They don't do it occasionally, but every day, and hour after hour, or the nation would starve.

It's one of the most appalling things in Mexico, this grinding of the mother literally between the upper and nether stones. How can a nation advance when the greater part of the women pass their lives grinding corn, making tortillas, and bearing children? There is no time or strength left to sketch in the merest outline of home-making, let alone a personal life, or any of the rudiments of citizenship.

October 11, 1913

Now I must hie me down-stairs and tackle a few of *my* "affairs of the interior." The house is so big that, even with many servants, it doesn't seem "manned," and bells are answered very intermittently. One or more of the servants can always be found at the gates of the garden, greeting the passers-by—a little Indian habit, and incurable. What I need is a European *maître d'hôtel* to thunder at them from his Aryan heights as the Wilsons had. There are some good Aztec specimens left over from their administration, whom I shall keep on.

December 14, 1913

Villa has just set up a somewhat uncertain dictatorship in Chihuahua, in which state he, so to speak, graduated in banditry. He began his public killing career *not* too badly, according to the story, by shooting a man for seducing his sister. It was probably the best act of his life. He is now in the prime of his life and "ready for anything." Even in Díaz days, Villa was a proscribed bandit; but with a few followers, well-mounted and knowing every trail and water-hole in the country, he was uncatchable. He subsequently went over to Madero. The women flee the towns that he and his men enter. I suppose there is no crime that he has not committed; brutality toward wounded, sick, and prisoners and women. With it all, he may be the heaven-born general that some assert, but God help Mexico if he is!

January 1, 1914

Three hundred Morelos peasant women were taken from their families and sent to Quintana Roo, the most unhealthful of the Mexican states, lying south of Yucatan, where it is customary to send men only. The women had been convoyed there with some idea of forming a colony with the unfortunate men deported to that region for army service. On their arrival there was a mutiny and a scramble for the women by the soldiers. Such disorder prevailed that the officials shipped the women back to Vera Cruz and dumped them on the beach. Almost every woman had a baby, but there was no food, no clothing, no one responsible for them in any way. They were merely thrown there, separated from their families by hundreds of miles. It was one of those tragedies that countless Indian generations have enacted.

January 4, 1914

Two train-loads of Federal soldiers, well-armed, have just pulled out of the station, where women were weeping and holding up baskets of food to them as they hung out of the windows. They were laughing and joking as befits warriors. Poor wretches! I couldn't help my eyes filling with tears at the sight of them and the women, with their babes completely concealed and tightly bound to their backs or breasts by the inevitable *rebozo*. One feels hopelessly sad at the thought the world of chaos those little heads will, in their time, peep out upon.

A thick and heartbreaking book could be written upon the *soldadera*—the heroic woman who accompanies the army, carrying, in addition to her baby, any other mortal possession, such as a kettle, basket, goat, blanket, parrot, fruit, and the like. These women are the only visible commissariat for the soldiers; they accompany them in their marches; they forage for them and they cook for them; they nurse them, bury them; they receive their money *when* it is paid. All this they do and keep up with the march of the army, besides rendering any other service the male may happen to require. It is appalling what self-abnegation is involved in this life. And they keep it up until, like poor beasts, they uncomplainingly drop in their tracks—to arise, I hope, in Heaven.

The Corrido of the Soldadera

The ubiquitous presence of the soldadera in the federal and revolutionary armies generated numerous ballads. The best known is perhaps

"Adelita," but there were many others besides. A handful of these ballads deal with the exploits of fighting women, but most concern the soldadera as a "camp follower." The following two ballads are from the same cycle, but the first is recounted from the perspective of the soldadera, while the second is from the perspective of a male soldier.

La Soldadera (female version)[23]

Anonymous

I am a soldadera and I have my Juan; he is my first one and everyone knows it. When he is drunk, everybody respects him; and when he is sober, they all imitate him.

As the Sergeant of the company, they keep him inside all day long. They do not want him out on the street, since they do not want to guard him.

The Second Lieutenant told me one day, that I would be his assistant, But what I will do in exchange I do not know, for he did not explain.

Since that day, night by night, I am happy to travel in the coaches, for the captains and even the majors are very gallant and offer me flowers.

I make them happy because my Juan will someday be promoted to Captain.

In the trenches and the line of fire, I am the queen and I go there with courage.
I am a soldadera and I have my Juan; he is my first one and everyone knows it.

La Soldadera (male version)[24]

Anonymous

I have my Juana, my Juana comes with me, and the campaign is going to begin.
Your eyes will be my only shelter and they know how to kill the enemy.

My Juana, can you hear the trumpets; how they vibrantly call us together? The manes of the horses are flying and prayers are filling my heart.

With pride, I will follow my flag and I assure you that I will succeed, if cartridge belt is full and if my soldadera cheers me on.

If I go into the battle and if your sapper is killed, recover my soul, look for my ribbon, while you kill the wicked enemy.

But when victory has been decided and if my battalion has won,
look for my body and if I am alive, put your heart into my wound.

But if the bullets are accurate, just my soul and courage will remain.
Make some skirts or whatever you want with the flags of the invader.

And when victory is determined, afterwards, do what you want.
Make some earrings with their medals, and see if they give you pleasure.

CHAPTER EIGHT
THE REVOLUTIONARY CIVIL WAR

The defeat of General Victoriano Huerta and his government in July and August of 1914 did not bring peace to Mexico. The struggle had been waged by a loose alliance of two armies that had little in common beyond their opposition to the Huertista regime. Almost immediately, the victorious revolutionaries divided into hostile factions to wage a civil war from 1914 to 1920 to decide what type of state and society would emerge from the Revolution. The Zapatista Liberating Army of the South, which was based on peasant communities in Morelos and neighboring states in central Mexico, followed the Plan of Ayala, which promised to divide up the haciendas and restore lands to these communities. This was anathema to the first chief of the Constitutionalist Army, Venustiano Carranza, a Porfirian-era hacendado and liberal politician. His Plan of Guadalupe promised only to reestablish constitutional government to Mexico, without making fundamental changes to the economy or to the social order. It was inevitable that conflict would erupt between Carranza and Zapata. However, such pressures were also at work even within Carranza's Constitutionalist Army, itself a coalition of diverse class and political interests. The most serious tensions revolved around the differences between Carranza and Francisco Villa, a conflict that nearly produced an open split in the spring of 1914. Disagreements over land reform lay at the heart of their dispute, for Villa had confiscated haciendas in Chihuahua and other areas under his control, promising to redistribute land to his soldiers when they defeated Huerta. The rivalry between Villa and Carranza was further complicated by the divided loyalties of populists and middle-class revolutionaries in the north—intellectuals, smallholders, and provincial elites, many of whom were veterans of the anti-reelectionist movements and then Maderistas in 1910. Some—like the Maderos in Coahuila or José María Maytorena, the governor of Sonora —were nearly as conservative as Carranza, but aligned with Villa in pursuit of their own ambitions, seeing in him a counterweight to the first chief. Others, including most Constitutionalist military chieftains, were liberals of a reformist cut and were willing to make concessions to workers and peasants if this helped them to supplant the old ruling classes. A handful of chiefs were more radical, embracing socialist notions, and were sprinkled throughout the ranks of the Constitutionalist armies.

After a period of maneuvering, and a failed attempt at revolutionary reconciliation in the autumn of 1914, the civil war began in earnest by December, pitting the forces of Villa and Zapata against Carranza and the Constitutionalist troops led by Generals Alvaro Obregón and Pablo González. The issue was settled on the field of battle in favor of the Carrancistas—as Carranza's partisans were known—but not before the military chieftains made a final attempt to preserve the unity of the revolutionaries. In August, Obregón and the United States pressed

Carranza to hold a convention to form a new government. For Obregón, this was a double gambit to strengthen his own position vis-à-vis Carranza and to buy time to strengthen his forces before engaging Villa in combat; as for Washington, it wanted to stabilize politics in Mexico at a moment when hostilities were beginning in World War I. The Revolutionary Military Convention convened in October in the city of Aguascalientes where delegates adopted the Plan of Ayala, deposed Carranza, and elected General Eulalio Gutiérrez as provisional president. But Carranza repudiated the Convention and ordered his supporters to withdraw. He proclaimed a Constitutionalist government and moved his capital to Veracruz. Meanwhile, Villa and Zapata occupied Mexico City and installed the Conventionist government of President Gutiérrez.

As it turned out, the Conventionist government was short-lived, fatally weakened by the policy of Gutiérrez who tried to use the military capacity of Villa and Zapata in order to strengthen his hand in negotiating a settlement with Carranza. When Villa and Zapata resisted, Gutiérrez and some of his key ministers decided, in the words of Martín Luis Guzmán, "to help our declared enemies, Carranza's followers, defeat our official supporters, Villa and Zapata," to the point that "we were functioning more as Obregón's allies than as theirs." [1] In mid-January 1915, Gutiérrez fled Mexico City when it became known that he had secretly offered to join Obregón against Villa and Zapata. Two weeks later, Villa and his forces moved north to pursue Gutiérrez and his troops and to engage Constitutionalist forces in Jalisco and in the northeast. Meanwhile, the Zapatistas pulled back into Morelos where they hosted the remnants of the Conventionist government in Cuernavaca and began to implement a sweeping agrarian reform in their state.

When Obregón reentered Mexico City at the end of January 1915, the prospects for the Constitutionalists had improved. U.S. military forces ended their occupation of Veracruz on November 23, 1914, and left Carranza with a stockpile of ammunition and control over the customs revenue collected at the port. Meanwhile, the Constitutionalist military chiefs had convinced their first chief to bolster the appeal of their movement by promising land reform and labor rights. Pressed by Obregón, Carranza negotiated a deal with the Casa del Obrero Mundial; in exchange for decrees to improve the conditions of workers, the leaders of the Casa agreed to raise recruits for Obregón as he prepared for war with Villa. The decisive series battles were in the Bajío, a region to the north of Mexico City, first in April and then in June 1915. Both times, Obregón shattered Villa's army. For Villa, political disaster followed on the heels of military defeat. On October 9, 1915, the United States recognized Carranza and the Constitutionalists as the de facto government in Mexico, and choked off Villa's access to weapons and munitions from the United States. By December, the Villista movement lost control of Chihuahua. Meanwhile, the Zapatistas were contained in Morelos, fending off Constitutionalist attacks by Pablo González even as they carried out the most sweeping program of land reform in Mexico's history. Both Villa and Zapata reverted to guerrilla campaigns, which they sustained for another four years. Meanwhile the Carrancistas began the process of building a new Mexican state.

★ ★ ★

United We Can Fulfill Revolutionary Aspirations[2]

General Antonio I. Villareal, October 14, 1914

The idea of a revolutionary convention was first proposed in the Pact of Torreón, signed by Francisco Villa and Pablo González in July 1914, in order to avert a split prior to the defeat of Huerta. The idea resurfaced in August, when the danger of civil war was imminent. The main impetus came from Obregón who hoped to reap the reward of political power by neutralizing both Villa and Carranza. Carranza was reluctant, but his military chiefs welcomed the plan, seeking "a rapprochement with Villa that would not entail a break with Carranza."[3] The Revolutionary Military Convention met in the city of Aguascalientes, from October to November. Participation was limited to military chiefs, meaning that civilian figures like Carranza were excluded. Nor did Villa or Zapata attend; they opted to send personal representatives. There were 152 delegates, but only 39 were Villistas, while 26 were Zapatistas.[4] The Constitutionalists had an absolute majority. Yet, the Convention moved to the left of Carranza—indicated by the unanimous adoption of the Plan of Ayala—for the Constitutionalists split into two factions. The first group was a minority, was led by Pablo González, and included mostly chiefs from the Army of the Northeast who hoped to win the Convention for Carranza. The other was a larger group of radicals and reformers who followed Obregón, and who emerged as a "third force" that sought the removal of Carranza and Villa from the revolutionary leadership. This group dominated and nearly won the Convention when delegates elected Obregón's nominee for interim president, General Eulalio Gutiérrez, but they stumbled over the refusal of Carranza to recognize the decisions of the Convention. This was decisive, for the Convention secured Villa's agreement to relinquish his command on the condition that Carranza also resign as first chief. Obregón needed Villa out of the picture in order to remove Governor

José María Maytorena and consolidate his power base in Sonora. Faced with a choice of either Villa or Carranza, Obregón and most of the "third force" abandoned the Convention and sided with the first chief.

The following speech by Antonio I. Villareal, who presided over the Convention, conveys the optimism and political perspective of Obregón's faction when the convention began its deliberations. Villareal started his revolutionary career as a founding member of the Mexican Liberal Party (PLM), but broke with the Magonistas at the start of Madero's revolution in 1910. After Huerta's coup, Villareal became a general in the Division of the Northeast under the command of Pablo González, but identified with Obregón's faction at the Convention. Villareal returned to Carranza when he repudiated the Convention.

Having sworn and signed an oath of honour before the Mexican flag, and having taken the transcendental act of uniting to fulfill what we decide here, we solemnly declare this Convention established and declare with even greater solemnity that it is Sovereign.

Whether we succeed or not, we are making a sincere effort to unify the country.

Contending factions no longer have a pretext to tear apart our country, which has been covered with mourning and misery for four years, waiting for the freedom we promised and have not yet delivered.

The outcome of this gathering will be transcendental and our country will enjoy the benefits of our work here. Although foreigners doubt that Mexicans can live as cultured men, this convention can restore our reputation as citizens who know how to be free in the midst of peace.

The reputation of Mexicans will improve with the news that all members of the Constitutionalist Army, that all those active in the revolutionary movement, are ready to discuss, agree, and change ideas like thoughtful people. But the best outcome will not be an improved reputation or the enrichment of potentates—but the wellbeing of the needy who find it impossible to sustain themselves or satisfy their most urgent needs owing to the lamentable situation of our country, the appalling depreciation of our currency, and the lack of work.

Today, we are declared sovereign for we represent the lifeblood of the country, because we represent combatants who have been worthy at every stage of the revolution, who have made truly selfless sacrifices to a higher cause.

In declaring this Convention to be Sovereign, in declaring it the highest power of the Republic, we can now restore peace, suspend hostilities, end the bloodshed among brothers, embrace one another with warm love, end the savagery, and become civilized patriots and guardians of our national destiny.

Warfare is criminal if unjustified by the demands of progress, if it fails to deliver freedom, if it does not improve lives and offer economic wellbeing to those who suffer from hunger. Wars are criminal if they only satisfy personal ambitions, if they are ignited by personalism, if they only produce outrages and base passions. If at this moment, when we are gathered together in a principled communion, we end up provoking war, we will all be criminals.

Let us say to Zapata, redeemer of the peasant, apostle of their emancipation, let us tell him: there are many here who embrace you, that many hearts here beat in unison with the Southerners, that our aspirations are twinned with yours, that strong arms are willing to work with energy, for a great tyranny has fallen, and it is now possible to re-divide the lands and make each campesino a free man and happy citizen.

Let us say to Maytorena and [General Benjamín] Hill: it is time to end the struggles in Sonora that are based only on the desire to impose or seize power. It is time to say: men of Sonora, end the killing; work together to return to the Yaquis and Mayos the lands stolen by the científicos.[5]

And we say to Carranza and Villa: the revolution was not carried out to make any man President of the Republic; the revolution was carried out to end hunger in Mexico.

Above these considerations is another: the future of the nation. As our freedoms were about to drown in a fratricidal war, we see our libertarian aspirations sinking at this time of reconciliation for the stars and stripes still float over Veracruz.

If we end the Revolution peacefully now that Huerta's dictatorship has collapsed, if we agree that we need schools and employment more than we need guns, if we can work together for the national welfare, then all the good intentions, expressed a thousand times by the United States government, will be fulfilled and we will be able to say that Mexico is truly free and independent.

That is why we must achieve harmony at this Convention. We must ensure that a meaningful peace comes to our country, and that we save the country from the threat in Veracruz. United, we can fulfill revolutionary aspirations, achieve true freedom, carry out the reforms we have preached, and make our experience fruitful.

Now is time to dedicate ourselves to the indispensable task of re-establishing self-government. We must annihilate our real enemy: reactionaries who wait for the moment of our disagreement and weakness to return to power once more in Mexico. We must kill the enemy with truth to ensure that freedom rules. Our enemy is rich and powerful, while we are poor. We must snatch from the enemy the resources it needs for a new reactionary revolution. We must seize their properties and leave them impotent.

Our enemy is privilege, sustained from the pulpit by vice-ridden antichristian clericalism and associated with militarism and cuartelazos. We have seen it fall in shame. We have seen it dispersed, for without cuartelazos, without support from the upper classes, and without organization, it is incapable of facing an army of armed citizens.

We must seize the riches of the powerful. Just as the Reform Laws of 1857 nationalized clerical property, so can we nationalize the property of the privileged classes.

It has been done already. But it has not been done in an orderly way, nor has it increased the wealth of the Republic. We must do this in an orderly and organized way and we must do so wisely, for with these riches we can pay our war debts and ensure the economic future of the country.

We must also seize the illegally-acquired assets of the clergy. The clergy has the right to own churches, but no right to own convents and beautiful buildings dedicated to what they call education, which is nothing more than a perversion of education.

However, the Revolution must not attack freedom of conscience or freedom of worship. In this agitated time it is justified to punish clergy who aligned with Huerta, to punish the Catholicism that supported Huerta. But as good liberals, we must respect all religion without allowing our children to be poisoned. It is more important to forbid clerical education than it is to forbid religion. We must allow prayers and preaching, as long as they do not teach lies.

We must annihilate our three main enemies: privilege, clericalism and militarism. We must discuss and act with energy to keep the friar in his church and the soldier in his barracks, while the citizen—the true god of the Republic—is everywhere.

We must address fears about the army that will be born. We must attend to its awakening and take care with its organization, always bearing in mind that we are armed citizens who want an army to protect our freedoms, not one of cuartelazos and tyrannies.

We must work with all the strength of our conscience, so that we do not promote praetorianism, so that we do not form an army that aspires to dominate or govern. In a republic, the majority vote must rule—and not armed men.

This Revolution is more than political and is eminently social; it has been fostered by the pain and hunger of serfs. It will not be complete until slavery —as existed in the Yucatán and the South—has disappeared, until we no longer have sweatshops paying the wages of hunger, until citizens no longer suffer from unemployment because they cannot find work.

We must end peonage, we must increase wages, and we must reduce the hours of work, so that the peon and the worker can be citizens. They have a right to eat well, dress well, and live in a good house for they were not created to be pariahs, not to feel the lash on their backs, and not to be damned the moment they were born, but to live a civilized life!

We also do away with personalism, to acknowledge that the governed have a say in solving problems. We must do so in harmony, brandishing the weapon of reason, and deciding our affairs. Only when we are deprived of these rights, only when we are struck with the lash of tyrants, only when we are prohibited from meeting, discussing, speaking, or choosing our leaders— only then do we have the right to grasp the liberating rifle and become armed citizens again.

Let us have the courage to proclaim that it is preferable to see all caudillos die in order to preserve the welfare and freedom of the homeland. Instead of shouting "vivas" for the caudillos, we will shout: "Viva la Revolution!"

Pact of Xochimilco[6]

Emiliano Zapata and Francisco Villa, December 4, 1914

Zapata and Villa met face-to-face for the first time on December 4, 1914, at a schoolhouse in Xochimilco, a village just south of Mexico City (neither one of them had attended the Revolutionary Military Convention, sending their personal representatives instead). Several other key Zapatistas and Villistas were also present. The meeting, which represented the high tide of the peasant insurgency during the Mexican Revolution, was recorded by a stenographer and is reproduced in the excerpt below. Immediately after, in a private conference, Villa and Zapata settled the details of a military campaign against the Carrancistas, and drew up a list of enemies to arrest and execute when their armies occupied Mexico City two days later. The dialogue between Villa and Zapata illustrates their common commitment to land reform and a shared hostility not only for Carranza but for the wealthy classes in general. Their attitude toward government also foreshadows the conflict that soon strained and broke their relationship with Conventionist President Eulalio Gutiérrez. Neither Villa nor Zapata was willing to hold political power in their own hands; yet, if they were resigned to fighting while more "cultured" men governed, they were equally reluctant to give politicians a free hand any longer. The Conventionist government relied on the peasant supporters of Villa and Zapata for its social basis and political legitimacy, but the tradition of peasant resistance to central government—now greatly magnified in the context of the revolution—frustrated Gutiérrez and other middle-class and petit-bourgeois politicians who sought a negotiated settlement with Obregón. Only six weeks after the meeting in Xochimilco, Gutiérrez abandoned Mexico City and the Conventionist government was on the verge of collapse. Equally short-lived was any effective military coordination between Villa and Zapata; this was in part the result of Villa's inability or unwillingness to provide the Zapatistas with promised munitions and trains, but it also had much to do with the desire of both chiefs to maintain independence of command over their own troops and to tend first to affairs in their own home regions. For both Villa and

Zapata, this became paramount after the flight of Gutiérrez; neither could conceive of permanently garrisoning Mexico City without ensuring the security of the rear in Chihuahua and Morelos, respectively. Thus, both armies withdrew from the capital in late January, allowing Obregón to reenter it unopposed on January 28, 1915.

General Villa: I was always concerned that things would be forgotten, things I believed in when I entered this revolution. As for Carranza, he has behaved shamelessly, and I understood that he was trying to take control of the Republic. I was just waiting.

General Zapata: It's like my comrades have always said, just as I have always said: Carranza is a swine.

Francisco Villa: They are men who have always slept on soft pillows. How can they be friends to people who have spent their entire lives suffering?

Emiliano Zapata: To the contrary, they are accustomed to being the scourge of the people.

Francisco Villa: With men like these we won't have progress or welfare or the division of land, but a tyranny. Because, you know, when a tyranny is intelligent, it will dominate. But the tyranny of these men will be a stupid tyranny and that will be death for the country. I know Carranza will turn the Republic into anarchy.

Manuel Palafox [Zapata's personal secretary]: What they did in Mexico City has no precedent; if barbarians had entered the city, they would have behaved better than them.

Francisco Villa: It is a barbarity.

Emiliano Zapata: In every village that they pass through . . .

Francisco Villa: Yes, they destroy and that is their way. There is no better way to discredit them, than to make them known for what they are. They had prestige before, but now . . . These men have no feelings of patriotism.

Palafox: They have no feelings of any kind.

Francisco Villa: I thought they would fight us when I started marching from the North, but no, they did not fight.

Emiliano Zapata: Here they established themselves in strength, and . . . you have already seen it.

Alfredo Serratos [a Zapatista advisor]: The first thing that Carranza said was that if you did not submit to him, he had 120,000 men to send against the South.

Francisco Villa: We ended up fighting so that they could get to Mexico City first. The only army that fought was ours [referring to the advance southward]. They never did a thing for us, even though they had garrisons of a thousand men. Those who fought very hard were the Huertistas; we had battles where there were more than five thousand dead.

Emiliano Zapata: In Zacatecas?

Francisco Villa: In Torreón also. There the fighting was very heavy. As many as 18,000 men fought. In the Laguna region we fought for twenty-seven days. Pablo González promised to stop the Federals, but he let eleven trains through. Still, we had a run of good luck and took Saltillo and other points, and in case González has forgotten, we'll take him too. (Laughter).

Emiliano Zapata: I figured that they were waiting and concentrating strength in Queretaro.

Francisco Villa: I was expecting that around the Bajio there would be about 600 or 700 dead, but nothing: it was clear running.

Alfredo Serratos: In the Huasteca it was the same thing.

Francisco Villa: [General Francisco] Murguía recently entered a village there.

Alfredo Serratos: Zitácuaro.

Francisco Villa: Right, I think so. He surprised the garrison by saying that they were Conventionist troops. Then he murdered something like thirty officers and chiefs and some of the troops. But I sent forces against him from various other places. (Pause.) Well, we're going to arrange the fate of Mexico here, and do what we need to do. I do not want public office because I do not know how to deal with it. Let's see if we can find people who can. We'll just make sure to appoint people who won't make any trouble for us.

Emiliano Zapata: I'll have to warn our friends to be very careful. If they aren't, the machete will fall on them. (Laughter.) Well, I don't think we'll be fooled. It's been enough to rein them in, to keep a close eye on them, to guide them like shepherds.

Francisco Villa: I know very well that we uneducated men have to fight the war, and that cultured men have to be in the government; but afterwards they won't give us any more trouble.

Emiliano Zapata: The men who work the hardest are always the ones who are least able to enjoy city sidewalks. Every time I walk over these sidewalks, I feel like I'm going to fall down.

Francisco Villa: This ranch is too big for us. It's better to be outside of it. There's nothing more for me to arrange, except go North for the campaign. We have a lot to do there. The people are going to fight very hard.

Emiliano Zapata: They are going to regroup in their old stomping grounds.

Francisco Villa: They are going to try and burn me, but I think I'll beat them. They can be sure I'll lead the campaign in the North, and we'll take every place we come to. We'll end this like the bulls and horses of Tepehuanes [a region in Durango].

Emiliano Zapata: But how long can they stay in the mountains and the hills? How? They don't know the hills.

Francisco Villa: I think Carranza will, but I don't see patriotism in him. The Convention proposed the withdrawal of me and Carranza, and I said: that's good but I better talk with General Zapata first. I want to settle our business, for there have been some little gossips trying to divide us. I hope that we divide up the lands of the rich. God forgive me! Is anyone with me? (ironically).

Voices: The people are, the people are.

Francisco Villa (continuing): Well, the people want their small bit of land.

Emiliano Zapata: They have so much love for the land. They still don't believe it when they're told: "This land is yours." They think it's a dream. But when they see that others are harvesting the land, they say: "I'm going to ask for my land too, and I will sow it." This is the love that people have for the land. For this the people have stayed firm.

Francisco Villa: They will see that the people are in charge, and they will see who their friends are.

Emiliano Zapata: The people know that Carranza wants to take away the land. The people know they have to defend themselves. He will have to kill them before they leave the land.

Francisco Villa: Our people have never had justice or freedom. The rich have all the best lands, while the poor people are fleeced, working from dawn to dusk. I think that from now on, there will be a better life. Otherwise, we'll refuse to put down our Maussers [rifles]. In the capital I have 40,000 little Maussers and 77 cannons and about 16,000,000 cartridges, because when I saw that Carranza was a bandit, I decided to buy ammunition, and said: I'll win with God's will and with the men of the South, because I never abandoned them, and stayed in touch all the time.

Emiliano Zapata: They're all sons of bitches . . . as soon as they see a little place, right away they want to take it. That is why I broke with all those sons of bitches. I won't give up. The times have changed a little, with or without Carranza. They are all a bunch of shameless scoundrels. They belong in the past.

Francisco Villa: I don't like to flatter anyone, but you know, I have been thinking about you for a long time.

Emiliano Zapata: It's the same with us. Those who went North to see you—these lads, [Gildardo] Magaña and others—they told you my hopes. I said: Villa is the only one I trust. The war will continue because we can't solve anything here on our own, and I will continue here until I die, I and all those who are with me . . .

(They were served cognac. General Villa asked for water.)

Francisco Villa: Well, I have finally found real men of the people.

Emiliano Zapata: I'm glad I found a man who knows how to fight.

Francisco Villa: Do you know how long I've been fighting? I started to fight the government twenty-two years ago.

Emiliano Zapata: Well, me too, since I was eighteen years old.

Francisco Villa (offering General Zapata his glass of water): Do you want water, General?

Emiliano Zapata (politely): No, you drink it.

Francisco Villa: After 1910, I thought the científicos were defeated, but Orozco rebelled and I realized that that was a científico uprising. I felt it in my soul.

Emiliano Zapata: That was a disappointing time. But it's a pity that Orozco didn't come here. I would have killed him as well as his father. But I said: this is what a coward does, so send your father! So, now your father will pay. So I executed him, because I have a duty to kill traitors.

General Villa stood up and said: Comrades: these are the words of an uncultured man, but my heartfelt sentiments dictate that you hear words that are only about our homeland. This is what is in my heart. A long time ago we were enslaved by tyranny. I am a son of humble people, and the people are watching to see if we lead them on the road to happiness. You can be certain that Francisco Villa will never betray people who have suffered slavery. I am the first to say I do not want public office, just the happiness of my homeland, so that no Mexicans will be ashamed of us. As for all these big landowners, I support the Plan of Ayala, to recover these lands and give them back to the people who have been enslaved by the landowners. As a man of the people, I pledge never to betray you, never to betray your desire to end the suffering of the people. When I see the destiny of my country assured, I will be the first to retire. You will see that we are honest, that we truly are men of the people, men of principle. I come, Señores, to embrace you.

Additions to the Plan of Guadalupe[7]

Venustiano Carranza, December 12, 1914

As the Conventionist government established itself in Mexico City, and as Villa and Zapata prepared their campaigns, the Carrancistas were likewise planning their return to the fight. The main outlines of their strategy are evident in the following document, a revised version of the Plan of Guadalupe. Carranza's strategy was to divide and conquer; to this end, he focused first on isolating and defeating Villa. As a result, the revised Plan avoided any mention—critical or otherwise—of Gutiérrez and his government, other than to blame the outcome of the Revolutionary Military Convention on Villista machinations and threats. Carranza hoped to drive a political wedge between Villa and Gutiérrez by leaving the door open for reconciliation with his Conventionist counterpart. Similarly, Carranza sidestepped any reference to Zapata, other than blaming the downfall of Madero on "the forces [i.e., the Zapatistas] that support General Villa." At the same time, and at the urging of his chiefs, Carranza attempted to cultivate popular support—and to lure Conventionist leaders back into the Constitutionalist fold—by promising reforms similar to those adopted by the Military Convention. Among these were measures to return land to peasants and to improve the conditions of the working class. The revised Plan had one other notable aspect; it marked the beginning of a vigorous and virulent Constitutionalist propaganda campaign that branded Villa as a "reactionary" who was operating in league with conservative forces, in Mexico and abroad, that intended to demolish the revolution.

On February 19, 1913, General Victoriano Huerta arrested the President and Vice-President of the Republic and usurped the Public Power. He later took the lives of these legitimate officials, thereby interrupting constitutional order and leaving the Republic without a legal government.

The undersigned, as Constitutional Governor of Coahuila, pledged to respect and enforce the Constitution and, in fulfilling this duty, was obliged to take up arms to fight the usurpation perpetrated by Huerta and restore constitutional order in Mexico.

This duty was also imposed by a decree of the Legislature of Coahuila, which ordered him to categorically repudiate the usurped government of Huerta and to fight it by force of arms until it was completely overthrown.

By virtue of this, the undersigned called Mexican patriots to arms and formed the Plan of Guadalupe on March 26, 1913, which has served as the banner and the statute of the Constitutionalist Revolution.

To combat the Huertista usurpation, military groups were formed. The Divisions of the Northwest, Northeast, East, Central and South operated in perfect harmony under the First Chief, to achieve this end. The same did not happen with the Division of the North, under General Francisco Villa who, from the start, had a tendency to act on his own disregarding orders from the headquarters of the Constitutional Revolution, to such a degree that the First Chief does not know, to this day, the means by which this General financed his campaign, nor the amount of these funds, or how they were used.

Once the triumphant Revolution arrived in the capital, it tried to properly organize a Provisional Government, meet the demands of public opinion, satisfy the urgent social demands of the people, and respond to the difficulties that the reactionaries had prepared in the Division of the North in the hopes of thwarting the Constitutionalist Army.

The First Chief, eager to organize the Provisional Government in accordance with the ideas of the fighting men of the Constitutionalist Revolution, convened an assembly of Generals, Governors and military chiefs in Mexico City, to agree on a government program, to indicate the reforms essential to reviving the social and political life of the nation, and to set the manner and time-frame for restoring constitutional order.

This had to be postponed because the Generals, Governors, and Chiefs attending the Military Convention in Mexico City considered it appropriate to have representation from all the armed movements who took part in the fight against the Huertista usurpation. Some of them had refrained from attending the convention in Mexico City on the pretext that they lacked guarantees and because General Francisco Villa had started his rebellion against the First Chief. For this reason they wanted to move the convention to the city of Aguascalientes, which they judged to be an appropriate and neutral location for the Military Convention to continue its work.

The members of the Convention agreed to this after confirming the undersigned as First Chief of the Constitutionalist Revolution and head of the executive branch, which he then formally surrendered to prove that he is not motivated by personal ambition. His true desire was to avoid division among the revolutionaries that might derail the fruits of the triumphant Revolution.

The undersigned did not put any obstacles before the Military Convention in Aguascalientes, even though I was convinced that, far from achieving reconciliation, the convention would create more profound differences between the Chief of the Division of the North and the Constitutionalist Army. However I did not want it to be thought that I was deliberately excluding the Division of the North from discussing momentous issues. Nor did I wish to be seen refusing a last effort at compromise. I also thought it was for the good of Revolution to expose the real purposes of Villa in an obvious way, and to show the error of those who had faith in the sincerity and patriotism of General Villa and the men around him.

The work of the Convention had just started when the delegates discovered the unrestrained machinations of Villista agents who played the main role in putting into motion a system of threats and pressure against those who had the spirit of independence and honour to resist the attempt by Villa to control the Convention.

On the other hand, many chiefs attending the Convention failed to perceive the true mission of the convention, and due to their inexperience in political matters, were deceived by the malice of Villista agents, and were inadvertently dragged into supporting the manoeuvres of the Division of the North, without addressing the cause of the people, or outlining the program of the pre-constitutional government.

To avoid a struggle of a personal nature and more bloodshed, the First Chief did everything possible for reconciliation, even offering to withdraw from power in order to establish a government that could implement the social and political reforms required by the country. It was not possible to satisfy Villa's hunger for power, notwithstanding the successive concessions by the First Chief. In view of the clear-cut attitude of the many Constitutionalist chiefs who repudiated the agreements of the Convention and who re-affirmed adherence to the Plan of Guadalupe, the First Chief now accepts the fight started by the reactionary General Francisco Villa.

The forces that support General Villa are the same ones who prevented President Madero from carrying out his program and are responsible for the political situation that led to his downfall. Moreover, statements made by the chief of the Division of the North—that he wants to restore constitutional order before carrying out reforms—leave us with a clear understanding that General Villa has a purely reactionary character that is opposed to the Constitutionalist movement. He intends to frustrate the triumph of the Revolution, and prevent the formation of a pre-constitutional Government that will enact the reforms which the country has been struggling for over the last four years.

It is my duty to continue the Revolution started in 1913, and to continue fighting against these new enemies of the Mexican people.

The Plan of Guadalupe must therefore remain in force and continue as our banner until we have defeated the enemy and restored the Constitutional rule.

It is also necessary that the people and the Constitutionalist Army know the military goals to be achieved: the annihilation of the reaction led by General Villa.

Therefore, the Plan of Guadalupe is in force until the triumph of the Revolution, and Citizen Venustiano Carranza will serve as First Chief of the Constitutionalist Revolution and as the head of executive branch, until the enemy is defeated and peace restored.

The First Chief will draw up and enact all laws and measures to meet the needs of the country, including: a regime that guarantees equality; agrarian laws that favour the smallholders; dissolution of large estates; the restitution of lands to the people who were despoiled; equitable tax laws for rural peons, workers, miners, and the proletarian classes in general; and municipal autonomy as a constitutional institution.

Manifesto Dismissing Villa, Zapata, and Carranza[8]

Eulalio Gutiérrez, Conventionist President, January 13, 1915

Prior to the Revolutionary Military Convention, Eulalio Gutiérrez had been a minor independent General in San Luis Potosí, allied with the Constitutionalists. At the Convention, he identified with Obregón's faction and was elected interim president of Mexico. However, the failure of the Convention to preserve unity severely hobbled his administration, for the political base upon which he depended was precisely the group—the "third force"—that abandoned the Convention in the wake of Carranza's refusal to resign. With civil war approaching, Gutiérrez still hoped to restore the unity of Obregón's "third force" but was, in the meantime, compelled to rely on the very forces—Villa and Zapata—that his faction had hoped to sideline. Meanwhile Villa and Zapata were loyal to the Conventionist government but harbored their own suspicions about Gutiérrez and resisted his attempts to control their movements. They believed that civil war was now inevitable and were not prepared to surrender control of their forces to a president they feared might abandon them. When hostilities renewed in December, Gutiérrez began to secretly contact Obregonista commanders to propose an alliance that would fight both Villa and Carranza; meanwhile minister of war, José Isabel Robles, was systematically denying Villa and Zapata the troop trains, munitions, and supplies they needed for their campaigns. This created friction between Villa and Zapata and weakened their alliance by making it difficult to keep the military promises they made in the Pact of Xochimilco. But it also heightened their doubts about Gutiérrez. In late December, when Villa heard that the president might defect, he promptly placed Gutiérrez under house arrest. The final break came in January 1915 when Villista General Felipe Angeles defeated Antonio Villareal in Saltillo; Angeles discovered a letter from Gutiérrez that confirmed

Villa's fears. Warned that Villa had ordered his execution, President Gutiérrez fled Mexico City on January with 10,000 loyal troops and headed north to Nuevo León. The day before leaving the capital, Gutiérrez issued the following manifesto denouncing Villa, Zapata, and Carranza.

The Constitutionalist Revolution believed it had consummated its triumph when the usurper Huerta fled the country and General Alvaro Obregón occupied Mexico City. However, the military victory was not the end of the social struggle. All the difficulties since then have appeared because Venustiano Carranza refused to incorporate national aspirations into a definitive political program; because he refused to specify a date when he would step down as First Chief, or when elections would be held. He also refused to give guarantees and freedoms for delegates to meet in the capital in a national convention to deal with problems that urgently require resolution.

Facing these circumstances, and protesting against them, were the military chiefs, including those from the Division of the North, the most distinguished force during the military campaign. Faced with the threat of rebellion against Carranza, a group of leaders, anxious to restore harmony, convened the Military Convention which met in the neutral territory in Aguascalientes and was attended by the majority of armed forces.

One of the first tasks of the Assembly was to form a Government. At that time, the country was divided into three military zones: the Northwest, North and Northeast. The first and the latter supported Carranza while the North demanded his resignation.

The Convention considered that the interest of the country was not to have one man in command. It decided to dissolve the Army Corps to protect our institutions, to ensure compliance with the goals of the Revolution, and to avoid a new military caudillo. It agreed that Francisco Villa, Alvaro Obregón and Pablo González, would resign their commands and transfer their forces to the Ministry of War, and that Venustiano Carranza would resign as First Chief. It also decided that General Zapata would resign command of his forces when he submitted to the authority of the Convention.

The entire country welcomed these measures, hoping that they would save them from the militarism that Mexico has endured throughout its painful history.

The Convention of Aguascalientes then elected the President by a majority vote, and I was honored with that designation. Unfortunately, many chiefs retained a personal commitment to Carranza, and began to express their disagreement with the Convention, including my election as President. They openly ignored the Convention and the new government.

Despite war preparations by Carranza's supporters—in contrast to the Division of the North—we remained committed to unity, and held several conferences with Carranza, General Pablo González and others. But we did not find any support for my Government from forces other than my own, some other chiefs, and those of the Division of the North.

I then called Generals Alvaro Obregón, Pablo González and Antonio Villarreal to Aguascalientes in order to win their support for the Government of the Convention. Had this happened, we would have avoided the clash between the Division of North and other Constitutionalist forces, and the subsequent dominance of General Villa. Unfortunately, these Generals refused and instead declared that they would fight my government until we dismissed General Villa. If these gentlemen had remained faithful, instead of aligning once more with Carranza, the campaign against them would have been unnecessary and so would have the appointment of General Villa as chief of operations.

In view of the military situation created by the split—which allowed Carranza to continue calling himself First Chief—I was obliged to enforce the agreements of the Convention and to appoint General Villa as head of the Convention forces. General Villa began to advance with his forces and it has been impossible since then to contain him. In his eagerness to fight, he disobeyed orders to suspend his march. He occupied León and continued into Mexico City.

One day after the aforementioned General proclaimed loyalty to my government, General Guillermo García Aragón, vice-chairman of the Convention of Aguascalientes, was arrested by General Villa, at the request of General Zapata, who had personal issues with Aragón, according to what I know from speaking with General Zapata. I ordered General Villa to release Aragón and he promised to obey. But he turned the prisoner over to General Zapata, who executed him without any form of trial. Completely lacking the forces that would obey an order to arrest an individual who has thousands of men under his command, I had to remain inactive in the face of this crime.

Another member of the Convention, one distinguished for his civility and talent, was Colonel David Berlanga, who was also killed after being seized by forces of General Villa.

Faced with these attacks, the Council of Ministers met to discuss what measures to take. Although we found ourselves impotent and threatened, we made it known to General Villa that we would punish those guilty of these murders. General Villa replied that those executed were traitors; he then left for Guadalajara where he committed further attacks. Meanwhile Zapata calmed down and we decided to postpone punishments until the Government had greater authority. However, some members of the Convention were alarmed and wanted to transfer to San Luis Potosí, where there were sufficient forces to protect them.

When General Villa learned of this, he dared to issue warrants for the arrest and execution of Convention members who are supposed to enjoy government privileges and are the source of authority. In view of these orders, the delegates left the area controlled by General Villa.

During the long period that Morelos has been under the control of General Zapata, no social reforms have been implemented. Instead, the government is a fierce military dictatorship. There have been no elections or municipal freedoms and they have forgotten their promise to restore stolen lands and divide the large estates. Instead there is a system that protects large landowners in exchange for monthly payments to General Zapata. This is contrary to the public interest; the only justification for forced loans is that the money be invested in public needs through the National Treasury and distributed according to laws issued for this purpose.

All of this contradicts what is fair and honest in the Revolution of Morelos. We recognise that much is good and legitimate in the Southern movement. But in order that the people know which side is inclined towards truth and just, we need to determine, once and for all, the differences that exist between the Revolution in Morelos and the Zapatista warlords who manipulate it. No one resents these disastrous results more than the South. The people there have infused the movement with their regenerative spirit, but they suffer under the yoke of a dictatorship and a personalist authority that masks the most restless enemies of democracy. Time will offer a painful confirmation of these fears if there is not an appropriate remedy. I am not hostile to the legitimate demands of the South and I will continue to offer the most selfless efforts to help it achieve its noble purposes. However, it is otherwise with the administration of General Villa.

Without consulting the government, General Villa has appointed governors and military commanders in every state he passes through, thereby usurping the authority of the Interior Ministry. General Villa is also meddling in our international relations; in his conferences with the American press and in meetings with representatives from the U.S. government, he makes declarations, pledges and promises that are not in his power to make as a General and a soldier.

Ever since General Villa returned to the capital, this city has experienced renewed kidnappings and murders. There are daily home invasions, attacks on property and life, and spreading horror and alarm in society in Mexico City.

General Villa became aware that I intended to move elsewhere in the Republic, to a place where my government could exercise its functions and freely protest the above-mentioned acts. As a result, on December 27, General Villa came to my home, pistol in hand, with eight or ten armed men, including Rodolfo Fierro and Tomás Urbina, and two thousand cavalry who surrounded my house and replaced the guards who defended it.

Villa then insulted me and made various accusations against me, among others that my Government was weak for not executing members of the Convention. But I am a long-time revolutionary, if not as celebrated as Generals

Villa and Zapata. My supporters and I have an understanding of the Revolution that is entirely different from theirs; thus we cannot conceive of aligning ourselves with robbery and murder. We believe that when the Revolution kills, it must do so publicly and based on the strictest justice; that when the Revolution seizes property, it must do so under general laws and for the national good and never for the personal benefit of chiefs who impose forced loans, and take property away from those who they declare to be enemies of the cause.

The country does not benefit if this revolution does not channel all its tremendous energy into an honest direction. A just Government might destroy the large estates—but not to perpetuate burdens as in Morelos, or through arbitrary encroachments as happened in Chihuahua. The Government cannot establish itself firmly and make changes, except through laws that once and for all regulate property rights, prevent the hoarding of land, and protect smallholders against any threats.

Moreover, political freedoms are being trampled on more than ever before in our history. This popular movement will fail if we do not abandon the dictatorial practices of false warlords. We must remember that Mexico fought for both bread and freedom, and that all citizens must be able to play their part in forming a government that will respect and guarantee the rights of everyone, with laws that apply to everyone and provide a firm foundation for prosperity and progress. It is time once more to put Mexicans to the test of civility. They may choose to follow the caudillos of the North and the South, they may choose to follow Carranza, or they may choose to follow the liberal and democratic government that was born at the Convention. The Revolution has traveled a difficult road but has done little because it has divided into factions and degenerated into personalism. Those following Zapata, Villa, and Carranza are bad revolutionaries, for they are loyal to personalities and not to principles.

I hesitated to take this resolution, for it may lead to more bloodshed. Ultimately, I have resolved to take a path that is honourable. Therefore I ask Mexicans to support the decision of the National Government in demanding that Generals Francisco Villa and Emiliano Zapata resign their respective commands, that Señor Carranza resign and that the military leaders who support him withdraw their support, and that all commanders and armed forces only obey orders emanating directly or indirectly from the Ministry of War.

Pact between the Casa del Obrero Mundial and the Constitutionalists[9]

February 17, 1915

In a bid to broaden the base of peasant and working-class support for the Constitutionalists, Obregón and his faction had prevailed upon the first chief to promise agrarian reform; Obregón did likewise with respect to organized labor after reentering Mexico City at the end of January 1915. Within three weeks, his policies had helped to broker a deal between the Casa del Obrero Mundial and the Constitutionalists in which the Casa pledged to support Carranza's government and to recruit 5,000 workers to volunteer for Obregón's army—along with a nursing corps of women workers—in exchange for union recognition and government support for workers in negotiations and strikes against employers. The Casa soldiers became known as the Red Battalion, while the nurses were the Acrata Health Group. The deal was surprising given the Casa's historical reticence to endorse armed struggle or engage in any form of bourgeois politics, and a large minority of Casa members opposed it. However, the ground had been laid in Mexico City on February 6, when Obregón supported the Casa's Electricians' Union, whose members were on strike against the Mexican Telephone and Telegraph; when the company refused to recognize the union or negotiate, Obregón expropriated the company and turned its management over to the union. The crucial debates in the Casa occurred in the days following this expropriation, and it turned the tide in favor of those who argued that the labor movement had to give concrete support to the Constitutionalist Revolution if it expected to claim its rights afterwards. As a result, four Red Battalions fought for Obregón in his decisive battles against Villa in April and June. The next document contains the text of the deal between the Casa and the Constitutionalists, and was published in Mexico City immediately afterwards; the subsequent document is an editorial printed in the Casa press, justifying the pact and urging fellow workers aligned with Villa or Zapata to abandon their affiliation and join the Red Battalions.

Comrades:

Everyone knows what the House of the World Worker campaigned for until February 10, 1915, when its members met for an extensive and thoughtful discussion and agreed to suspend union organizing and to enter into a different phase of activity. This was done in view of the pressing need to promote and intensify a revolution which, in its ideals, is closest to our unanimous goal of economic and social improvement, a goal that has guided the groups resisting the oppression of capitalism in different villages, towns and cities in the Republic.

We have always condemned the involvement of workers in armed movements, an attitude derived from many years of painful experience in supporting caudillos who, by manipulating the ingenuous credulity of the people, recruited followers who were willing to sacrifice their lives for an illusory cause. We have always argued from the podium, in leaflets and in our newspapers, that only the collective effort of workers deployed within trade unions could slowly but surely achieve their desired freedom. We have always fought against the prejudices that exist at the root of any revolutionary action, prejudices that will never transform a society dominated by those who consume everything but produce nothing. But given the tremendous destruction of lives by weapons and hunger, which falls directly onto the serfs exploited in the fields, factories and workshops, it is necessary to enter, with resolution and conviction, once and for all, the struggle against the common enemy: the bourgeoisie, whose immediate allies are professional militarism and the clergy.

We have had enough of exhortations demanding that we remain ineffective in the ranks of neutrality. We have had enough suppressed yearnings, of useless demonstrations that only leave us weak and in a desperate and iniquitous state of affairs. In a word, we have had enough of formulas and doctrines that do not help at the present moment, except to assist the reactionaries in obstructing the flow of progress. We must be the first to harness and provide overwhelming impetus to the revolution. We have an opportunity to throw down the gauntlet to our infamous executioners, to collaborate in words and deeds on the side of the Revolution, a revolution that has not compromised with reactionary machinations, that has punished them instead, and has reclaimed the rights that the multitude has eternally sacrificed.

The House of the World Worker is not calling for the formation of groups of unconscious workers to be militarized and serve blindly in a fight that offers no benefits other than the glory of a few bold leaders who send everyone to the slaughterhouse in order to satisfy their own excessive ambitions. We do not want abject followers who misunderstand true courage and who simply obey the commands of their fanatical chiefs. No! We are calling for the cooperation of all our brothers in order to save the interests of the community of workers. We are confident that you will, at all times, rise to the task of this redemptive mission, for our revolutionary participation has been secured by a special agreement between a delegation of the revolutionary committee appointed for this purpose and the First Chief of the Constitutionalists, citizen Venustiano Carranza.

The document below outlines the way in which we will join the revolution. We will always fight together, with weapons or without them. We will toil in the villages, towns and cities to raise the morale of workers who support our decision, helping them understand that the Constitutionalists are the future of workers' organizations of the people in general. We will organize local revolutionary committees and one central committee close to the Constitutionalist government. We will comply with the social program of the Revolution with regard to proletarians in the countryside and in the cities. We will resume our work as a labour organization when circumstances permit throughout Mexico.

Pact between the Constitutionalist Revolution and the House of the World Worker

The workers of the Casa will adhere to the Constitutionalist government, headed by citizen Venustiano Carranza, on the basis of the following clauses which govern relations between the government and the workers.

1. The Constitutionalist Government reiterates its resolution, expressed by decree on December 12, 1914, to improve, by appropriate legislation, the status of workers, and to issue, during the fight, all laws that are necessary to fulfill that resolution.

2. In order to accelerate the triumph of Constitutionalist Revolution and intensify its commitment to social reforms, the workers of the Casa, while seeking to avoid the unnecessary shedding of blood, will uphold the decision to work for the triumph of the Revolution by taking up weapons and providing garrisons in villages, towns and cities that are held by the Constitutionalist government, and also to combat the reactionaries.

3. To carry out the previous two clauses, the Constitutionalist Government will support, with the solicitude it has so far employed, the just claims of workers in conflicts that arise between them and employers over honouring the terms of the work contract.

4. In the villages, towns and cities already occupied by the Constitutionalist Army, and in order to expedite the needs of the campaign, workers will be organized in agreement with the military commander of each location, providing security and keeping order. In the event of a withdrawal, the Constitutionalist Government, through the respective military commander, will warn workers of this decision and provide every opportunity for them to relocate to places occupied by Constitutionalist forces.

5. The workers of the Casa will compile lists of names in each one of the villages, towns and cities where they are organized, and of course in Mexico City, of all comrades who agree to comply with the conditions provided in the second clause. The lists will be sent immediately to the headquarters of the First Chief of the Constitutionalist Army, so that it is aware of how many workers are willing to take up arms.

6. The workers of the Casa will conduct active propaganda to win the sympathy of all workers in the Republic for the Constitutionalist revolution, showing them that joining the Revolution will lead to improvements for the working classes, goals which they now pursue through their organizations.

7. The workers will establish revolutionary centers and committees in all places they wish. In addition to propaganda, the committees ensure organization in support of the Constitutionalist cause.

8. Male workers, who take up arms in the Constitutionalist Army, and female workers who care for the wounded, will be known as the "Reds" whether they are organized in companies, battalions, regiments, brigades or divisions.

To the Armed Serfs[10]

Felipe Sánchez Martínez, May 28, 1915

Whenever I am reflecting or dreaming, I feel a deep conviction that we, as Red Libertarians, have an inescapable duty—great and sublime, in these times of trial—to participate with ardour, fortitude, with enthusiasm, with virility and stoicism, in the regenerating work of this war. My nerves are on edge, but I restrain my spirit for it cannot contemplate so much injustice in the destiny of the people. There are moments in which the tumultuous din of combat enters my feverish brain, and I want to be there, to be worthy of joining those with whom I have shared pleasant hours of work along with very hard struggles for our emancipation. I want to face the dangers of combat, this master of our cause. It is blessed!

Never mind the reactionaries and the imbeciles, never mind those who are neutral or indifferent, never mind the enemies of our just cause— Francisco Villa and Emiliano Zapata. We pay them no mind because the people will realize that they are the destroyers of their freedoms. Thus, the Casa is making common cause with the Constitutionalists, for among them are men who will heal the bleeding wounds of the Mexican working people; we could not remain with our arms folded in the face of such irrefutable facts and such eloquent evidence.

Hence our mission: to stir the hearts, brains, spirit and energy of our lost brothers—those who still lack consciousness, or have been forced or deceived into fighting, not for their welfare, but for the ambitions of others— in order to crush the common enemy. Until now the enemy has not only been at the front. No! We also find the enemy among us and in our rear.

There are those who have not yet succumbed to the blows hurled by the just anger of the people; they laugh as they watch the destruction of our race. Let us not regret that we did not exterminate them, for today we have the cauterizing instruments in our hands, and we must apply it, not to heal our enemies, but to burn them.

We believe in the broad agenda of the Revolution, in the comrades in the campaign, and in the dedicated army. We know where we are going and why we fight: but how sad it is to realize that there are comrades in the other camp who, like us, pursue the same ideals—that is to say: the welfare of the proletariat in the countryside, in industry and in the arts. What a paradox that something so sublime has been converted into a huge catastrophe! Comrades, you must realise that this will lead to our collective destruction! We must not allow this! With love and strength of character, we must aid this Revolution in its diverse manifestations, we must face the dangers arising from it, and we must go to the enemy camps to win the hearts of our fellow comrades and help them understand that their attitude obstructs the triumph of the cause we are all pursuing.

Comrades, stop a moment! Be aware that I am speaking to you as someone who struggles like you, who burns with the same desires of free men and who is today caught within the embers of fire and blood; but that within this sphere of Mephistopheles of intrigues and traitors, that from within this place is the small radius of the Casa which encompasses our aspirations for better days, it knows why it is participating in the armed struggle.

Do you know why? Four years of constant struggle! It is too short a time to fully awaken the consciousness of workers in the Republic, to spread the seed of unity among workers. These constant efforts were silenced with prisons and repression, even to the point of taking the lives of our champions. They can kill a person, but they can never kill the idea. The blood spilled early on failed to stop us. To the contrary, it drove our desires to new heights, desires well defined and broadcast widely by our tribune, our newspaper, by every means at our fingertips.

As our newspaper has said, the moment has now arrived when we must move from theory to practise. What better opportunity can we have than the open field before us? Some will take weapons in hand, while others will educate and raise the spirits of the workers on the land and in the workshops, helping them understand the need to unite and organize. What better aspiration is there? What better freedom can the revolution bring, if not this? We have a duty to advance the people's just aspirations, and even to die for this. To be worthy, a bloody revolution must give rise to all that is fair, reasonable, and human. Otherwise the Revolution is evil!

CHAPTER NINE

VILLA AND THE PUNITIVE EXPEDITION

Following the coup against Francisco Madero in 1913, U.S. President Woodrow Wilson repeatedly intervened to isolate the government of General Victoriano Huerta: the United States refused to recognize the new regime and withdrew its ambassador in August 1913; it applied an arms embargo that favored the Constitutionalist revolutionaries; and then, in April 1914, it sent an expeditionary force to occupy the port of Veracruz, thereby denying Huerta access to his most important source of customs revenue, as well as complicating his ability to import arms and munitions from abroad. All the while, and with the help of Argentina, Brazil, and Chile—the so-called ABC countries—Wilson sought to broker an end to the armed conflict and influence the choice of a new president. While Wilson's policy was not decisive in defeating Huerta, it did play an important role in shaping the course of events. It would continue to do so during the revolutionary civil war.

In the spring of 1914, when the defeat of Huerta seemed assured, the question of recognizing a new government was again on the agenda of the U.S. State Department, but it was complicated by the split between Villa and Carranza. Washington therefore tacitly supported Obregón's efforts to preserve unity at the Military Convention in the autumn of 1914. However, the Convention's failure produced a dilemma for Wilson in the form of two competing governments: the Conventionists and the Constitutionalists. For months, the U.S. government debated which side to support. One view preferred the conservatism of Carranza over the peasant radicalism embodied in the Villista-Zapatista alliance. A contrary view pointed out that Villa had been the revolutionary leader with the friendliest attitude towards the United States. The latter view prevailed in Washington until the collapse of Eulalio Gutiérrez's Conventionist Government. U.S. support for Villa declined when it became clear in the spring and summer of 1915 that the Constitutionalists would win the armed conflict, but the history of Carranza's economic nationalism remained an issue. The solution for Washington was to manipulate Villa's remaining military capacity—much reduced but still potent—as a lever to pry concessions from Carranza (particularly access to oil reserves and mineral resources) in exchange for recognizing his government. In August, Washington proposed to mediate a settlement to the civil war, along with the participation of six "neutral" Latin American countries: Argentina, Bolivia, Brazil, Chile, Guatemala, and Uruguay. Villa and Zapata accepted Washington's offer, but Carranza—buoyed by General Obregón's decisive victories over Villa—flatly refused. In October, Washington accepted the inevitable and convinced its Latin American partners—but not without cajoling—to recommend the recognition of Carranza's administration as the de facto government of Mexico.[1]

This was a crippling blow to Villa. It simultaneously bolstered the legitimacy of Carranza's government and choked off Villa's access to

weapons and ammunition from the United States. It also gave Alvaro
Obregón an edge in military mobility; when Villa besieged the
Constitutionalist garrison in Agua Prieta, Sonora, on November 1, he
discovered that Obregón had managed to send reinforcements by
railway across the United States. This also imperilled the Zapatistas, for
the reduction of Villa's military capacity brought the day closer when
Zapata and his forces might have to stand alone against the full weight
of the Constitutionalist Army. Responding to what he saw as a betrayal
by Washington, Villa reversed his earlier practice of respecting—and
even protecting—U.S. properties and economic interests in Mexico.
Certainly Villa was in a vengeful mood, but there was a deeper purpose
to his strategy than just retribution; it was calculated to provoke a crisis
between Carranza and Washington and thereby strengthen his own
position. He began by seizing the properties of U.S. companies in his
area of operation, but events took a violent turn in January 1916 when
Villista General Pablo López stopped a train at Santa Isabel and killed
17 U.S. mining engineers employed by the Cusihuiriachic Mining
Company. A few weeks later, Villa decided to destabilize the frontier
with raids on U.S. border towns. Villa made his first and only raid on
March 9, leading about 500 men in an attack on the town of Columbus,
New Mexico. The fighting killed more than 100 Villistas and 18 U.S.
civilians and soldiers before the garrison drove Villa back across
the border.

Villa's attack on Columbus was a gamble that paid him short-term
dividends but ultimately failed to shift the balance in the civil war.
Without waiting for permission from Carranza, Washington sent a
"punitive expedition" after Villa. Commanded by General John J. Pershing, the expedition numbered 10,000 troops, including cavalry,
mechanized units, and airplanes. It entered Mexico on March 15, 1916,
and remained for 11 months, pushing nearly 400 miles into Chihuahua
before reaching Parral, near the state line with Durango. The expedition
did engage with some of Villa's forces but failed in its mission to capture
Villa himself. Meanwhile, its extended presence in Mexico gave rise to
fears of an ulterior motive on Washington's part and strained relations
between Mexico and the United States to the breaking point, particularly when Carranza's troops confronted and defeated the 10th U.S.
Cavalry at the town of Carrizal on June 21. The expedition also heightened Mexican nationalism to such an extent that it revived Villa's
popularity and helped him to expand his army once more to
10,000 troops, enabling him to raid and temporarily hold urban centers
like Chihuahua City and Saltillo in the autumn of 1916. However, none
of this destabilized the Constitutionalist government, which continued
building the framework for a new nation-state; on December 1,
Carranza inaugurated a constitutional convention in Querétaro, a

gathering that produced a new and radical Constitution on February 5, 1917. That same day, the Pershing Expedition completed its withdrawal from Mexico.

★ ★ ★

The Consequences of Recognition: Santa Isabel and Columbus[2]

Manuel Calero, 1916

Prior to Madero's revolution, Manuel Calero had been a científico politician in the Mexican Congress during the rule of Porfirio Díaz and a son-in-law to Justo Sierra, the Porfirian minister of education. Calero had been intimate enough with the president that Díaz once offered him the post of vice president. Calero then served in the cabinet of Francisco De la Barra, and made the transition to Madero's first cabinet in 1911, serving first as the foreign minister and then as Madero's ambassador to the United States. After Huerta's coup, Calero remained in the United States where, in 1916, he severely criticized the foreign policy of President Woodrow Wilson. Although sharing Carranza's worldview, Calero was antagonistic towards the first chief and did not support the Constitutionalist revolution; nor did he have any sympathy for the movements led by Villa and Zapata. Nevertheless, Calero was an ardent nationalist, and in the excerpt below, blamed Wilson for a foreign policy that only aggravated and prolonged the conflict in Mexico. Villa's raid on Columbus, in Calero's view, was the direct and logical result of Wilson's own policy. As for the Pershing Expedition, Calero accused Wilson of hypocrisy and violating international law.

The policy of President Wilson had been crowned by two positive successes: the elimination of Huerta and the triumph of the "Constitutionalists." To obtain these results, the President sacrificed in Vera Cruz the lives of some twenty of his countrymen and spent millions of dollars. But these sacrifices were puny compared with the enormous losses which the triumph of the "Constitutionalists" occasioned, losses in lives, in property and honour. The quota of American citizens in this disaster is not insignificant.

And all this for what? The President has explained: "To serve Mankind, to serve the Mexicans, to help Mexico save herself and serve her people." What has the President of the United States to do with the quarrels of Mexicans? It is simple common sense that the American Government was not instituted to act outside its territory in the service of humanity or Mexicans, but in the service of Americans in a foreign country and their legitimate interests. The author censures the President only to emphasize the absurdity of promoting the welfare of Mexicans with results so completely negative that never has Mexico been poorer, hungrier and more oppressed by an anarchical and criminal faction.

With the triumph of the Constitutionalists, the object for which President Wilson took Vera Cruz was attained—the expulsion of Huerta. When Carranza occupied the capital, Vera Cruz should have been delivered by the American Government. The explanation of the stay of the American troops in Vera Cruz was the rupture between Villa and Carranza. Villa demanded that the plan of the revolution be complied with, which was the return to constitutional government, while Carranza wanted to remain "First Chief" with unlimited powers.

It was explicable that Wilson decided not to abandon the base he occupied in Mexican territory, when a second civil war was threatening between the men for whose sake Vera Cruz had been occupied. Wilson then sent Paul Fuller to Mexico as his agent, a learned and honourable man, acquainted with the country and who spoke Spanish with perfection. Fuller's report justified the attitude of Villa. For the first time the bandit had reason on his side. Fuller's report condemned Carranza who he declared was devoured by personal ambition.

This was natural and logical. Carranza could not transform himself into an apostle of liberty and a reformer. He had passed twenty-five years serving the man who today he calls the Tyrant of Mexico, Porfirio Díaz. Carranza was a senator under Díaz and never did anything except to approve the recommendations of that tyrant. And in two years as Governor of Coahuila, Carranza promoted nothing which would reveal him as a reformer, nor did he do anything for the political, moral or economic advancement of the people. This is the true Carranza, who together with Villa received the aid of the United States in seizing the Government of Mexico.

It was explicable that President Wilson should hesitate to evacuate Vera Cruz. It would not "have served Mexicans" if he abandoned them in the midst of a frightful anarchy. But Congressional elections were approaching in the United States and it was necessary to present a triumph of "watchful waiting." Thus the President announced on September 15, 1914, that Vera Cruz would be evacuated. The evacuation happened two months later when Carranza, a fugitive from Villa, arrived at the Gulf coast and would have abandoned the country. President Wilson saved him by delivering Vera Cruz to him. The possession of this important port permitted Carranza to rehabilitate himself, and General Obregón to initiate a campaign against Villa. Civil war was again kindled with savage fury.

In the face of this struggle and the ruin it brought for the Mexican people, President Wilson intervened again. With innocent good faith, the President directed a solemn admonition to the leaders of the divided Constitutionalism: "I call upon the leaders of the factions of Mexico to act together and promptly for the relief and redemption of their prostrate country." Carranza and Villa, by way of reply, impressed upon the struggle a greater ferocity. When the results became adverse to Villa, the latter stated his desire to comply with the admonition. Carranza declared that he was not disposed to compromise with his enemies or to allow President Wilson to meddle with the internal affairs of Mexico.

Wilson called to his aid six countries of Latin America. The diplomats of Brazil, Chile, Argentina, Bolivia, Uruguay and Guatemala, were invited to a conference on the internal affairs of Mexico. A joint note from the seven countries to the factions in Mexico invited them to resolve their differences in a peaceful manner and to organize a common Government. Carranza remained inflexible and refused the invitation. The other factions accepted it.

To the surprise of everybody, the Government of the United States at this moment changed its attitude and recognized Carranza as the de facto government. This involved a stupendous contradiction of the principles Wilson had proclaimed—that he would not accept a government not in conformity with the constitution of Mexico. Secretary Lane asserts that the recognition of Carranza was recommended by the six countries of Latin America, and that the United States yielded to their recommendations. We must say that this is not correct. The opinion of the conference was divided, and only one of the Latin American representatives was a champion of Carranza. It was the efforts of the American Government which determined the conference to recognize Carranza.

Carranza is trying to govern Mexico, not as provisional President, but simply as "First Chief," like a "Sheik" who rules despotically over a tribe of Bedouins.

The act of recognizing Carranza was not inspired by "serving humanity," but by another more business-like purpose. It was necessary to present the American Congress with a modification of the ridiculed policy of "watchful waiting." It was also important to make the public believe that the President had produced a Government in Mexico. The President had the frankness to confess that he was making a new experiment. The new experiment resulted in a new fiasco. The problem Wilson tried to solve with the recognition of Carranza was complicated by Francisco Villa. The President declared war on him, and Villa took up the glove.

It is worthwhile to relate the history of relations between the Government of the United States and the famous Mexican bandit. The revolution which Carranza headed acquired military importance thanks to the soldierly qualities of Francisco Villa. The bandit was transformed into a general, and began to be officially designated with this title by the American Government. Astute and ambitious, he comprehended that it was important to gain the good-will of the United States and exploit the unfavourable impression which Carranza caused in Washington. Villa was always compliant and lost no opportunity to flatter President Wilson and Secretary [William Jennings] Bryan.

This resulted in a preference by the United States for Villa. This was not due to a transformation in the criminal spirit of Villa, but Carranza was so incapable that Washington believed Mexico must place its hopes in the bandit-general. "The one-time bandit has become a military genius; why not a peacemaker and statesman?" said the newspaper most friendly to the Administration (*The New York World*, June 22, 1914). On August 4, 1915, Senator James Hamilton Lewis, the "Democratic whip of the Senate," asserted that the President was on the point of recognizing Villa. The United States sent the Chief of Staff of the Army [General Hugh L. Scott] to Villa as a special ambassador in August, 1915.

Villa had dictated a series of confiscatory decrees and was trying to obtain a large cash advance from mining companies. Washington resolved to protect American companies affected by these iniquitous decrees. But instead of taking an attitude against him, it resolved to treat him as an equal and imposed upon General Scott the humiliating mission of appeasing the brigand. Villa considered the American general his "colleague" and received him with honours. Honours were reciprocated the following day when the Mexican "general" went to El Paso to visit General Scott. The trip was fruitful for Villa who revoked some of his decrees. But the spirit of the bandit was inflated with pride.

Such were the relations between Washington and Villa when the Department of State sent the invitation to Carranza, Villa and the other chiefs of factions, to reconcile their differences and to form a common government. Villa accepted with good will and named his delegates. Villa still dominated an important portion of north and could not be rationally considered an insignificant factor in Mexico. A few weeks later, to the surprise of Villa and everybody, the United States recognized Carranza. The wild beast felt humiliation in its cruel intensity. Why was he repudiated unceremoniously, and his rival Carranza recognized as ruler of Mexico?

However odious was the personality of Villa, the conduct of Washington was illogical. It was also imprudent. Villa represented a force which would surely be turned against his former protector. President Wilson must have comprehended this and decided to help Carranza crush Villa. The first thing he did was to establish an arms embargo to the ports of the frontier which Villa held in his possession. The second was to permit Carranza to use the United States for operations against Villa. When Villa arrived to capture the frontier town of Agua Prieta, he found the Carranza garrison reinforced with fresh troops that had been sent rapidly through the United States on American railroads at the same time that Villa's forces were moving slowly and laboriously through Chihuahua and Sonora.

Villa felt lost. Villa troops began to desert. His generals went over to Carranza or sought refuge in the United States. The indignation of the bandit knew no limits and he swore vengeance. He thought to avenge himself upon President Wilson by sacrificing the lives of innocent, peaceful Americans and assaulting a camp of American troops. The eighteen victims at Santa Isabel and those at Columbus are victims immolated upon the altar of the imprudent friendship of Wilson for Carranza.

How to satisfy public opinion, justly outraged by the Columbus "raid"? If a party of Canadian bandits sacked a settlement in North Dakota, Wilson would not have sent a punitive expedition. If an American bandit had sacked a settlement in Manitoba, the Canadian government would not have sent a punitive expedition. This would have been an attack on the sovereignty of the respective countries. The people of the United States would never consent to this. Nor would they tolerate a column of ten thousand Canadian soldiers that stationed itself indefinitely on U.S. soil in a camp one hundred and fifty miles south of the border.

According to the United States, Mexico has a *recognized* government. It is the fault of Washington if it declared a government, what is simply an instrument of tyranny, disorganized and impotent. The honour and self-respect of the American government indicated its duty after Columbus. That duty was to exact from Carranza the pursuit of the malefactors, and their arrest and delivery to the United States, or to break relations with the "de facto government" and dispatch the punitive expedition, leaving Carranza with the choice of declaring war if he did not accept the expedition.

But it was a violation of international law to despatch a punitive expedition without the consent of the "de facto government" or breaking relations with it.

The day after the "raid" the President of the United States said: "An adequate force will be sent in pursuit of Villa with the object of capturing him and putting a stop to his forays." The resolution added with cruel sarcasm that the punitive expedition would be conducted with scrupulous respect for the sovereignty of Mexico. President Wilson said that the punitive expedition was sent in agreement with the "de facto government." But when the President dispatched the punitive expedition, Carranza had not been consulted or even notified.

If the expedition was an attack from the point of view of international law, it was useless from a practical standpoint. General Pershing was to capture Villa. But Villa, six months later, is laughing at his pursuers and harassing Carrancistas with impunity. It is surprising that a man as intelligent as President Wilson would not realize that with the advantage of six or eight days that Villa had—the time it took Pershing to prepare himself—it would be impossible to overtake a bandit who is audacious, astute, acquainted as no one else with complicated topography of the region, who is accustomed to live as a fugitive, and who can count on the sympathy of the local population.

Very soon the difficulties of the undertaking began to appear. Carranza had never consented to the expedition, but did not have the force to repel it. In consequence, he limited himself to placing every kind of difficulty in its way, and to these, the American government submitted. The expedition was marching between two lines of railroad, but was not permitted to use them. Carranza prohibited it from entering towns, and it did not enter. It continued to advance until it was opposed by the Carrancista force in Parral. At this point Washington should have recognized with valour and honour the position in which it had been placed, and should have ordered General Pershing back to the United States. If the expedition was useless, why insist upon it? If the expedition was useful and legitimate, why not carry forward? But Mr. Wilson chose a middle course. He did not withdraw the column nor did he permit it to go forward. The only possible explanation of this contradictory position is the personal political interests of Wilson.

Carranza did what he could to obtain the withdrawal of the expedition, whose continuation in Mexico is an offence to the patriotic sentiments of Mexicans. Forced by this, Carranza notified Washington of his intention to resist any attempt of the column to advance. The result was the combat of Carrizal, in which a small American column was destroyed.

Withdraw U.S. Troops from Mexican Territory[3]

Cándido Aguilar, May 22, 1916

Just two days before the Pershing Expedition entered Mexico, Carranza appointed General Cándido Aguilar as his foreign minister. One of his first responsibilities was to handle the fallout from the Columbus raid and to obtain Pershing's withdrawal from Mexico. The Constitutionalist government objected to the intervention, but did not see fit to demand its withdrawal until May 12, when a squadron of the 13th U.S. cavalry was driven from Parral by its pro-Villa inhabitants and the local garrison of Carracista troops. Two weeks later negotiations began in Ciudad Juárez between representatives of the U.S. and Mexican governments. The Mexican side insisted on an unconditional and immediate withdrawal, while the U.S. side demanded guarantees against any further raids across the border and, failing that, open-ended permission to cross the border in pursuit of raiders. To reinforce these demands, Washington prohibited the export of arms and munitions to the Mexican government. The talks were suspended on May 11 without having reached an agreement. Two weeks later, more U.S. troops crossed the boundary line in pursuit of border bandits who had raided into Texas, prompting the following letter of protest by Aguilar to his U.S. counterpart, Secretary of State Robert Lansing. Aguilar also pointed out that the presence of the punitive expedition, combined with the embargo on arms exports, was undermining Constitutionalist efforts to pacify Mexico—thereby frustrating the central goal of U.S. policies in Mexico.

The Mexican Government has just learned that more U.S. troops have entered Mexico and are near El Pino, sixty miles south of the line. The crossing of more troops without the consent of the Mexican Government endangers good relations between the United States and Mexico. This Government considers the above action as a violation of the sovereignty of Mexico, and requests that Washington re-consider its policy towards Mexico.

After the incursion at Columbus by Francisco Villa, the Mexican Government, sincerely deplored the occurrence, and proposed that the Governments of the United States and Mexico enter into an agreement for the pursuit of bandits. The Government of the United States considered that the good disposition of the Mexican Government was sufficient to authorize the crossing of the boundary without awaiting a formal agreement, and ordered a column of American forces into Mexican territory in pursuit of Villa and his band. The United States Government made emphatic declarations that it was acting with good faith and that its only purpose was to pursue and capture or destroy the Villa band that had assaulted Columbus; that this action did not mean an invasion or any intention to impair Mexican sovereignty, and that as soon as a practical result was obtained the troops would withdraw.

However, the Mexican Government was not informed that U.S. troops crossed the frontier until March 17. This Government then addressed the Government of the United States to state that, until an agreement was reached between both countries, the United States Government was not authorized to send the expedition. Washington expressed regret that a misinterpretation had occurred, that this had been done under the impression that the previous exchange of messages implied the consent of the Mexican Government. The United States Government also explained the necessity of quick action, and that it was disposed to receive any suggestions that the Mexican Government might make in regard to an agreement covering the operations of troops on either side of the boundary. Both Governments began to discuss an agreement, and the Mexican Government insisted that troops be limited to a zone of operations within foreign territory, and that the duration of time, the number of soldiers, and class of arms carried, be fixed. The United States, while agreeing, stated that these conditions would not apply to the Columbus expedition.

As a result, the Mexican Government asked the United States Government to withdraw its troops, since their stay was not based on any agreement, and the expedition was unnecessary, as the Villa bandits had been dispersed and reduced to impotency. The United States Government delayed, and took no action to withdraw its troops. However the military commanders of both countries met to review the situation and to arrive at a satisfactory solution. For Mexico this was the withdrawal of American troops.

Generals Hugh Scott and Frederick Funston represented the U.S. Government, while General Alvaro Obregón, Secretary of War and Marine, represented Mexico. A draft memorandum was submitted in which General Scott declared that the destruction and dispersion of the Villa band was complete and that the United States Government would withdraw troops if the Mexican Government would guard the frontier against incursions similar to Columbus. The Mexican Government refused that agreement, because the evacuation of its territory is a matter entirely affecting the sovereignty of the country, which should not be subject to the discretion of the American Government.

General Scott, General Funston, and General Obregón were discussing this when, on May 5, a band of outlaws assaulted a U.S. garrison at Glenn Springs, and returned across the Rio Grande into Mexican territory via Boquillas. Fearing that the United States Government would send new troops into Mexico, the Mexican Government instructed General Obregón to notify the United States that their soldiers would not be allowed into Mexico, and that military commanders had been ordered to prevent it. Generals Scott and Funston assured General Obregón that no troops had been ordered to cross the frontier, and that no more American soldiers would enter our territory. General Scott reiterated this in a later conversation with Juan Amador, Sub-Secretary for Foreign Affairs.

Fearing that various bands of outlaws organized or armed near the frontier might repeat their incursions, and hoping for effective military cooperation between American and Mexican forces, this Government suggested a military plan to distribute troops along the frontier to keep an effective watch over the whole region to avoid a recurrence of similar assaults. In this, the Mexican Government showed good faith and a frank willingness to cooperate with the Government of the United States to avoid further friction between the two countries. This plan was proposed to prevent any new difficulty and with the idea of arriving later at an agreement for the reciprocal crossing of troops. The conference between Generals Scott, Funston, and Obregón adjourned on May 11 without agreement on the unconditional withdrawal of U.S. troops. All the assurances by Generals Scott and Funston led us to suppose that the Glenn Springs incident would not bring about new difficulties.

However, the Mexican Government has just learned that 400 men of the Eighth Regiment of the United States Army crossed the line in the direction of Boquillas and are near El Pino. This was brought to the attention of Mexican authorities by the commander of the U.S. troops, who informed the Mexican military commander at Esmeraldo that he crossed the frontier in pursuit of the outlaws who attacked Glenn Springs, in accordance with an agreement between the United States and Mexican Governments regarding the crossing of troops. The Mexican Government cannot assume that an error has been made a second time by the United States Government in ordering its troops to cross without the consent of the Government of Mexico. It fails to understand how a commander of troops of the United States Army can enter Mexican territory without authority from his superiors.

The explanation given by the United States Government in regard to the crossing of troops after Columbus has never been satisfactory. But the new invasion is no longer an isolated fact and convinces the Mexican Government that something more than a mere error is involved. The Mexican Government cannot consider this last incident as anything but an invasion by United States forces. We request that the United States Government order the immediate withdrawal of these new forces and to abstain completely from sending any other expedition of a similar character.

The Mexican Government understands its obligation to protect the frontier, but this obligation is not exclusively its own, and it expects the United States Government to appreciate our difficulties, since U.S. troops themselves are unable to effectively protect the frontier on the American side. The Mexican Government has made every effort to protect the frontier without disregarding the considerable task of pacification in the rest of the country, and the U.S. Government should understand that any lamentable incursions into U.S. territory by irresponsible outlaws should be a case for financial reparation and a reason to adopt a combined defence, but never a cause for U.S. authorities to invade our territory. The incursion of outlaws into U.S. territory is deplorable, but in no way can the Mexican Government be made responsible for them, as it is doing everything possible to prevent them. However, the crossing of U.S. troops into Mexican territory, against the will of the Mexican Government, is an act for which the U.S. Government is responsible.

The Mexican Government believes the time has come to insist that the United States Government abstain from sending new troops. The Mexican Government will have to consider this as an invasion, and will defend itself against any U.S. troops found within Mexico. With reference to the troops in Chihuahua on account of Columbus, the Mexican Government is compelled to insist on their withdrawal. The Mexican Government understands that it may be left no other recourse than to defend its territory by arms, but it understands at the same time its duty to avoid armed conflict between both countries. The Mexican Government requests the United States Government to give a more categorical explanation of its real intentions toward Mexico.

With respect to Mexico, the United States Government has stated on various occasions that it has no intention to intervene in its internal affairs and that it wishes to let our country decide by itself its difficult problems of political and social transformation. On account of the Columbus expedition, the United States Government has made the declaration that it does not intend to interfere in the affairs of Mexico or invade it, that it does not desire to acquire a single inch of its territory, and that it will in no way impair its sovereignty. Washington and its representatives have also declared that it is not the will of the American people to go into war with Mexico. Summing up the above, and judging by official declarations, there appears an honest purpose on the part of the United States Government not to start a conflict with Mexico. But the Mexican Government regrets that the acts of the U.S. military are in conflict with these statements. The United States Government stated that the punitive expedition from Columbus would withdraw when the Villa outlaws had been destroyed or dispersed. More than two months have elapsed since this expedition entered Mexico; Generals Scott and Funston declared that Villa's band has been dispersed, but U.S. troops are still in Mexico.

The United States Government stated that its purpose in sending troops into Mexico was to defend the frontier against probable incursions. This statement conflicts with the attitude by the United States Government in which it expects to have frequent occasion to cross the frontier, indicating its willingness to enter Mexico beyond what the necessities of defence require. According to President Wilson, the Columbus punitive expedition had no purpose than to punish outlaws who committed the outrage, and it was organized under the supposition that the Mexican Government had consented. This expedition, however, has had a character of clear distrust toward Mexico and cannot be considered anything but an invasion without the consent, knowledge, and cooperation of Mexican authorities.

It is a known fact that the Columbus expedition crossed the frontier without the consent of the Mexican Government. The United States military authorities launched this expedition without awaiting consent from Mexico, and even after they were informed of this, they continued, causing more troops to cross the line without informing Mexico. The U.S. military authorities have maintained complete secrecy regarding their movements. The Columbus expedition has happened in a spirit of distrust towards our authorities. This lack of advice and agreement was the cause of the clash which occurred in Parral between United States forces and Mexican citizens.

The protests of friendly cooperation by the United States authorities are not in keeping with the use of infantry and artillery to be employed against regular Mexican forces. If the Columbus expedition had taken place with the consent of the Mexican Government, the use of artillery and infantry would have been considered an insult because of the supposition that we might attack U.S. forces. There has been a great discrepancy between the protests of sincere cooperation and the actual attitude of the expedition, which clearly indicates that it was a hostile expedition and a real invasion. It cannot be explained otherwise that General Scott insisted that the United States forces would not withdraw if any other incident occurred. The conclusion is that the Columbus expedition entered into Mexico promising to withdraw when it destroyed Villa, but that its real purpose was to be an instrument to guarantee the protection of the frontier.

The United States Government justly desires that the frontier be protected. If the frontier was properly protected against incursions from Mexico there would be no reason for the existing difficulty. The United States Government knows the difficulties involved, for notwithstanding its own immense resources, the U.S. Government itself cannot render effective protection along a line of more than 2,000 kilometres.

The United States Government prefers to keep its troops inactive and idle within Mexico, instead of withdrawing them along the frontier in cooperation with Mexican authorities who would do likewise. By doing this, the United States Government gives room to believe that its true intention is to keep troops in Mexico in anticipation of future operations. The United States Government has declared its desire to help the Constitutionalist Government complete the pacification of Mexico. But the attitude of the United States Government is incongruous for it does not render any assistance to pacify Mexico, but places obstacles in front of this task.

The support given at one time to Villa by General Scott and the State Department was the principal cause for the prolongation of civil war in Mexico for many months. The continuous aid from American Catholic clergy to the Mexican Catholic clergy, which is working against the Constitutionalist Government, and the activity of the interventionist press and business men in the U.S. are an indication that the United States Government is unable or unwilling to prevent acts of conspiracy against the Constitutionalist Government.

The United States Government constantly demands that the Mexican Government effectively protect the frontiers, but bands of rebels against this Government are armed and organized on the U.S. side under the tolerance of American authorities. Mexican emigrants plot and organize incursions from the U.S. side, because they know that any new difficulty between Mexico and the United States will prolong the stay of American troops; they are trying to increase conflict and friction. Meanwhile, the United States Government has detained shipments of arms and ammunition purchased by the Mexican Government in the United States, which could be used to hasten pacification and protect the frontier. The embargo on war material to the Mexican Government can have no other interpretation than that the U.S. is trying to keep out arms and ammunition that might be used against U.S. troops by Mexican forces. The American Government has the right to take this precaution, but it ought not to say that it is endeavouring to cooperate with the Mexican Government.

The United States Government either desires to help the Mexican Government re-establish peace—if so it should not prevent the export of arms—or its true purpose is to prepare for future war with Mexico. If this is the case, it should say so.

The Mexican Government does not wish war with the United States but, if this happens, it will be a consequence of a deliberate purpose by the United States. The Mexican people and Government are absolutely sure that the American people do not wish war with Mexico. There are, nevertheless, strong American interests and strong Mexican interests labouring to secure a conflict between the two countries. The Mexican Government firmly desires to preserve peace with the United States, but it is indispensable that the U.S. Government frankly explain its true purposes toward Mexico.

The Mexican Government formally invites the Government of the United States to end the uncertainty between the two countries and to support its declarations of amity with real and affective action that will convince the Mexican people of its sincerity. This action cannot be other than the immediate withdrawal of the United States troops now in Mexican territory.

The Bandits Have Been Protected by Carranza[4]

U.S. Secretary of State Robert Lansing, June 20, 1916

Lansing replied to Aguilar four weeks later, at the very moment when relations between Mexico and the United States were reaching their nadir. The Constitutionalists had upped their military presence in Chihuahua to 10,000 troops. Meanwhile, U.S. President Wilson militarized the northern side of the border with 100,000 militia troops, just two days before authorizing Lansing's reply, reproduced below. Although the U.S. State Department accepted Aguilar's complaint that Pershing had crossed the border without permission from Mexico, it justified this breach on the necessity for a hot pursuit in order to capture Villa. Lansing then accused the Mexican government of torpedoing the negotiations in Juárez over withdrawal, of protecting "bandits" like Villa, and even of sanctioning the participation of government troops in attacks on U.S. properties and businesses inside Mexico. The next day, on June 21, Carrancista troops confronted and defeated a patrol of the 10th U.S. Cavalry at Carrizal, taking several prisoners. Three days later, tensions heightened when U.S. President Wilson threatened to send an even larger military force into Mexico, perhaps expanding the pursuit of Villa into a wider conflict with Carranza as well. Neither side wanted to see any further deterioration of relations; within two weeks both agreed to resume negotiations.

Sir: I have read your communication delivered on May 22, 1916, on the subject of American troops in Mexican territory, and express surprise and regret at the discourteous tone and temper of de facto Government of Mexico.

The United States Government has viewed with deep concern and increasing disappointment the progress of the revolution in Mexico. Continuous bloodshed and disorders have marked its progress. For three years the Mexican Republic has been torn with civil strife. The lives of Americans have been sacrificed. Vast properties developed by American capital and enterprise have been destroyed or rendered non-productive. Bandits have been permitted to roam at will through territory contiguous to the United States and seize, without punishment or effective attempt at punishment, the property of Americans, while the lives of citizens of the United States in Mexican territory have been taken, in some cases barbarously, and the murderers have neither been apprehended nor brought to justice.

It would be difficult to find in the annals of the history of Mexico conditions more deplorable than those which existed there in these years of civil war. It would be tedious to recount instance after instance, outrage after outrage, atrocity after atrocity, to illustrate the nature and extent of the lawlessness and violence which have prevailed. During the past nine months in particular, the frontier of the United States along the lower Rio Grande has been thrown into constant apprehension and turmoil because of incursions into U.S. territory and depredations and murders on U.S. soil by Mexican bandits, who have taken the lives and destroyed the property of American citizens, sometimes carrying American citizens across the international boundary with the booty.

American garrisons have been attacked at night, American soldiers killed, their equipment and horses stolen. American ranches have been raided, property stolen and destroyed, and American trains wrecked and plundered. In these attacks Carrancista adherents and even Carrancista soldiers took part in the looting, burning, and killing. Not only were these murders characterized by ruthless brutality, but uncivilized acts of mutilation were perpetrated. Emphatic requests were made to General Carranza to stop these reprehensible acts in an area which he has long claimed to have under his authority. The indifference of the de facto Government has gone so far that some of these bandit leaders have received the protection, encouragement, and aid of that Government.

This Government has repeatedly asked the de facto Government to safeguard American citizens and interests in Tamaulipas, Nuevo Leon, Coahuila, Chihuahua, and Sonora, and in States to the south. For example, on January 3, troops were requested to punish the outlaws who looted the Cusi mining property in Chihuahua, but no results came from this request. The following week the bandit Villa, with 200 men, was operating between Rubio and Santa Ysabel, a fact well known to Carrancista authorities. Meanwhile a party of Americans started by train from Chihuahua to visit the Cusi mines, having received assurances from Carrancista authorities that the country was safe, and that a guard was not necessary. The Americans had safe conducts from the de facto Government. On January 10, the train was stopped by Villa bandits, and eighteen of the Americans were stripped of their clothing and shot in cold blood, in the "Santa Ysabel massacre."

General Carranza told the Department of State that he had issued orders for the immediate pursuit, capture, and punishment of those responsible for this atrocious crime, and appealed to this Government and to the American people to consider the difficulties of according protection along the railroad where the massacre occurred. Assurances were also given, presumably under instructions from the de facto Government, that the murderers would be brought to justice, and that steps would also be taken to remedy lawless conditions in Durango. It is true that Villa, Castro, and Lopez were publicly declared to be outlaws and subject to apprehension and execution, but so far only a single man connected with this massacre has been brought to justice by Mexican authorities.

Within a month after this, Villa was within twenty miles of Cusihuiriachic and publicly stated his purpose to destroy American lives and property. Despite repeated demands for protection of Americans, Villa carried on his operations, approaching closer and closer to the border. He was not intercepted, his movements were not impeded by troops of the de facto Government, and no attempt was made to frustrate his hostile designs against Americans. While Villa and his band were moving toward the frontier near Columbus, not a single Mexican soldier was seen in this vicinity.

Yet Mexican authorities were fully cognizant of his movements, for on March 6, General Gavira advised U.S. military authorities of the outlaw's approach, so that they might be prepared to prevent him from crossing the boundary. Villa's unhindered activities culminated in the cold-blooded attack on American soldiers and citizens in Columbus on March 9. After murdering, burning, and plundering, Villa and his bandits, fleeing south, passed within sight of the Carrancista military post at Casas Grandes, but no effort was made to stop him by the officers and garrison of the de facto Government stationed there.

In the face of these depredations, the perpetrators of which General Carranza was unable or unwilling to apprehend and punish, the United States had no recourse other than to disperse the Mexican outlaws systematically raiding across the international boundary. The marauders in the attack on Columbus were driven across the border by American cavalry, and as soon as a sufficient force could be collected, were pursued into Mexico in an effort to capture or destroy them.

Without cooperation or assistance on the part of the de facto Government, despite repeated requests by the United States, American forces pursued the lawless bands as far as Parral, where the pursuit was halted by the hostility of Mexicans, presumed to be loyal to the de facto Government, who arrayed themselves on the side of outlawry and became in effect the protectors of Villa and his band.

In this manner and for these reasons have the American forces entered Mexican territory. Knowing the circumstances set forth, the de facto Government cannot be blind to the necessity which compelled this Government to act, and yet it has seen fit to recite groundless sentiments of hostility and to impute, to this Government, ulterior motives for the continued presence of American troops on Mexican soil.

It is charged that these troops crossed the frontier without the consent of the de facto Government. Obviously, there was no opportunity to reach an agreement (other than that of March 10–13, now repudiated by General Carranza) prior to the entrance of an expedition into Mexico if the expedition was to be effective. Subsequent events and correspondence have demonstrated that General Carranza would not have entered into any agreement providing for the capture and destruction of the Villa bands.

While the American troops were moving rapidly southward in pursuit of the raiders, it was the form and nature of the agreement that occupied the attention of General Carranza—the number of limitations that could be imposed upon the American forces to impede their progress—rather than the obstacles that could prevent the escape of the outlaws. It was General Carranza who suspended negotiations for an agreement. Shortly after this, the conference between Generals Scott, Funston, and Obregon began at El Paso, where they signed on May 2 a memorandum regarding the withdrawal of American troops.

As an indication of the alleged bad faith of the American Government, you state that General Scott declared in this memorandum that the destruction and dispersion of the Villa band "had been accomplished," but that American forces are not withdrawn from Mexico. It is only necessary to read the memorandum, which is in English, to ascertain that this is a misstatement, for the memorandum states that "the punitive expeditionary forces have destroyed or dispersed many of the lawless elements and bandits or have driven them far into the interior of the Republic of Mexico," and that the United States forces were "carrying on a vigorous pursuit of small numbers of bandits or as may have escaped."

The context of your note gives the impression that the object of the expedition being accomplished, the United States had agreed in the memorandum to begin the withdrawal of its troops. The memorandum shows, however, that it was not only on account of the partial dispersion of the bandits that it was decided to withdraw American forces, but also on account of assurances that Mexican forces were "being augmented and strengthened to prevent any disorders occurring in Mexico that would endanger American territory," and that they would "diligently pursue, capture, or destroy any lawless bands of bandits that may still exist in northern Mexico," and that it would "make a proper distribution of its forces to prevent the possibility of invasion of American territory from Mexico." It was because of these assurances and General Scott's confidence that they would be carried out that he said that American forces would be "gradually withdrawn." It is to be noted that, while the United States Government was willing to ratify this agreement, General Carranza refused because it imposed improper conditions upon Mexico.

Notwithstanding the assurances in the memorandum, it is well known that the forces of the de facto Government have not carried on a vigorous pursuit of the remaining bandits, and that no proper distribution of forces to prevent the invasion of American territory has been made. I am reluctant to be forced to the conclusion that the de facto Government, in spite of the crimes committed and the sinister designs of Villa, does not intend or desire that these outlaws should be captured, destroyed, or dispersed by American troops or, at the request of this Government, by Mexican troops.

Mexico for the Mexicans![5]

Francisco Villa, October 1916

Villa returned to the offensive in the autumn of 1916, after having lain low since Columbus, rebuilding his strength. His forces raided Chihuahua City in November and then Torreón in December, signalling a revival of Villismo that lasted until 1919 before expending its second wind. The Zapatistas also revived and went on the offensive to once more drive the Constitutionalist forces, commanded by Pablo González, out of Morelos. In announcing his renewed military operations, Villa published the following manifesto, which now recast the civil war as a patriotic struggle to defeat both the invading United States and Carranza. The statement had a highly nationalistic tone, castigating Carranza for failing to defend Mexico against U.S. aggression. It offered a program of economic nationalism to Mexicans, promising to expropriate all foreign-owned estates, mining operations, and railway companies. However, as much as the U.S. intervention had rekindled the fortunes of Villismo and Zapatismo, their movements could no longer spark nationwide resistance to Carranza and their impact remained purely local. For one thing, the negotiations over the punitive expedition finally led to a decision to withdraw in early January, taking the steam out of any appeal to resist the invaders. For another, the recent experience with the intervention, coupled with the Villista and Zapatista resurgence, helped to radicalize the delegates to the Constitutional Convention in Querétaro. Their deliberations produced the Constitution of 1917, a document that was far more radical than anything Carranza had expected; among other things, it nationalized control over Mexico's resources, mandated the expropriation of haciendas and agrarian reform, and guaranteed the right of workers to form unions and strike. This was in effect a national program for Mexico, promulgated by a national government enjoying international recognition, and it proved increasingly attractive to many—perhaps even most—Mexicans, now exhausted by seven years of warfare.

Fellow Citizens: All peoples of the earth are capable of the greatest sacrifices when they see their national integrity threatened and when their rights as freemen are trampled under foot. We have a fine example of this in the titanic European conflict, and particular in heroic Belgium which, conscious of being one of the most civilized nations in Europe, went into this devastating war without the remotest hope of victory but with the consciousness of duty fulfilled, and succumbed when the greater part of its sons had fired their last cartridge in order not to have their beloved country encroached upon with impunity by the invader.

Our own beloved country has arrived at one of those moments when, in order to oppose the unjustified invasion by our eternal enemies, the barbarians of the North, we ought to unite on behalf of the beloved country which gave us birth. Unfortunately there can be no unification for, while our country has patriotic and self-denying sons, it also has Carrancistas, who now govern the country which, impoverished, defenceless and manacled, was surrendered to the invader when there is no fortress to defend its already weakened frontiers.

As an irrefutable proof of this there has been there, March, in the Galeana District the American army commanded by Pershing engaged in constructing cement highways from the Rio Grande to the Valley of San Buenaventura, which is the base of operations of the abhorred Yankee, with the tolerance of the Constitutionalist Government, which would like to establish ammunition factories in order to saturate the fertile fields of our country with the blood of its sons and facilitate the entrance of its allies and protectors into the interior of the Republic.

Therefore, dear countrymen, the task which we must perform as Mexicans is great and arduous. I call on you to take up arms to overthrow the most corrupt Government that we have had, these office holders who, through their extreme radicalism and in order to perpetuate themselves in power and enrich themselves shamelessly, have covered themselves with ignominy, going so far in their sordid conduct as to criminally disregard the cries of our troubled country.

Do not doubt that victory will crown our efforts, for just causes always triumph. But if destiny is adverse to us, we shall fall with our faces to the sky, like the ancient gladiators. We shall fall with the crash of a volcano in eruption. We shall collapse like the masses of granite under the impulse of seismic tremors. We shall disappear proudly and haughtily, shouting in a chorus: "Beloved Country, thy sons swear they will expire on thy altars."

Intentionally and with the best of good faith I remained inactive with my forces in the hope of seeing the so-called Constitutionalist Government repel the invasion and attempt the unification of the Mexican people. The bitterest disappointment was not long in coming for, from endeavouring to oust the invaders, they exploited the gravity of international relations for personal benefit and to the absolute detriment of honour. Thus we have seen how forces that were armed for no other reason than to defend the territory were deceived and submitted perfidiously and maliciously. Thus we have seen how patriots, who were eating the bitter bread of exile, crossed the boundary to enlist in the national defence, and how many of them were interned in the penitentiary in Chihuahua as a reward for their abnegation and patriotism.

As I do not see the slightest hope of a change of conduct on the part of the men in power in the country, I have the honour to state to the Mexican People that, from this time on, I shall push military operations as far as possible in order to overthrow the traitors and place at the head of the Government the citizen who, through his recognized honour and civic virtues, shall cause Mexico to figure in the catalogue of civilized and free peoples, which is the place legitimately belonging to her; for which purpose the following plan will be put into force from this date on, it being subject to additions and amendments and being applicable throughout the area controlled by the revolution:

The disposition of the Revolutionary Government shall be to call the people to election for President of the Republic, making use of free suffrage without restrictions of any kind, in order that the people may conscientiously elect the Chief Magistrate of the nation, the military vote being included in the elections. Those guilty of misconduct at the elections will be punished by the death penalty. Not one of the armed leaders or military officers shall be permitted to run for President.

Elections shall also be called for the Congress, in accordance with instructions that will be distributed in due time in order that voters be apprised of the importance of these elections. In this connection, the public should select persons of well known culture and humble birth who will be capable of understanding the needs of society, especially of that numerous class who are suffering in penury and poverty: the proletariat. Military men shall likewise be precluded from these offices. It is of vital importance that members of Congress should be honourable persons who concern themselves for the welfare and progress of their constituents. They must not mix up in affairs beyond their jurisdiction, such as labours on behalf of concessions, etc., which may redound to their benefit to the detriment of the public, under penalty of being shot, and when this painful example is set, the state they represent shall be notified in order that the vacancy may be filled by the substitute.

The defects of the laws governing the country being well known owing to the modifications or revisions which they have been undergoing in recent years, the President shall adhere to the reform laws in governing the country. The revised Carrancista codes shall be annulled and the original ones put into force, for they have merely served to satisfy the ambitions of a certain number of persons.

From this date on the Revolutionary Army declares void the acts of the so-called Constitutionalist Government, in the way of loans, concessions, etc., with the exception of those which, on moral grounds and out of respect to society, are inviolable, such as marriages and other acts affecting civil status. As the revolution needs resources of its own and outsiders for reconstruction, it will not answer for any debt, though it be claimed by foreigners who have, most of them, trebled their fortunes here. Therefore it is just and logical that they should now suffer the consequences inherent to any country at war.

From the date of this statement no foreigner shall be allowed to acquire real estate except those who have been naturalized 25 years ago and have resided continually in this country. In the meantime, all interests of foreigners shall be confiscated on behalf of the nation. In future an essential prerequisite for acquiring real estate shall be to become naturalized. Since the North Americans are in large part responsible for the national disaster and that, for absolutely illegitimate purposes they have stirred up fratricidal war in our country, amply proven by their unwarranted stay on our soil, they are hereby disqualified, the same as Chinese subjects, from acquiring for any real estate.

The railroad lines, together with their equipment, shall be confiscated and become the absolute property of the Mexican Government. Mining property in this country and owned by foreigners shall likewise be confiscated and become national property. In order to encourage Mexican manufacturers and the development of industry in the country, all kinds of mercantile operations with the United States shall be suspended, it being hoped by this measure to awaken greater diligence in the Mexican workman as well as his ingenuity in seeking the greatest improvement in our national products. Telegraph and railroad communications shall be cut off to within 18 leagues of the frontiers in the United States. This stretch of territory shall be garrisoned by the rural forces of the Republic.

It is an urgent and patriotic necessity that military leaders operating in the various States require the Mexican people to militarize rapidly to be prepared as soon as possible for any emergency in the probable and long struggle with the invader. They are urged to proceed with the activity and energy in this direction. Every Mexican who refuses to take part in the conflict at this time of trial, in which national autonomy is jeopardized, shall be declared a traitor and his property confiscated without claim for restitution.

The military leaders shall act in accordance with the strictest morality in order to demand of their subordinates a good and beneficial military training which shall reflect brilliance and renown upon the Revolutionary army. Any act in contravention to this provision shall be punished by the death penalty, without distinction as to military rank.

In order to punish all those who make a bad use of power and in order to prevent future evils, we shall request the extradition of Venustiano Carranza, his advisers and accomplices, in case they go abroad; and in case such Government should refuse our just demand, the subjects of the country in which they have sought refuge shall be without the guarantees which the laws grant to good citizens.

Fellow countrymen: Thus you now know my greatest desire, which I believe will be yours, for it is a question of exterminating the most odious and shameful tyranny that the land of Cuauhtemoc has ever had. To war against the traitors, crying: Mexico for the Mexicans.

Columbus and the Punitive Expedition in Popular Culture

In spite of everything else, the audacity of the Columbus raid and the failure of the punitive expedition transformed Villa into a hero of Mexican nationalism, at least in popular culture. Not long after the withdrawal of Pershing's forces, numerous ballads sprang up in Mexico, principally but not only in the North, that portrayed Villa rather than Carranza as the winner in this episode of the Mexican Revolution. It was particularly satisfying for Mexicans who remembered the history of Mexico's relationship with the United States as a long series of humiliations, outrages, and frustration—from the disaster of the 1846 "Yankee Invasion" that led to the loss of half of Mexico to the United States, to the role that the Arizona Rangers played in the repression at Cananea in 1906, not to mention the part played by Henry Lane Wilson in the overthrow of Madero and the subsequent U.S. occupation of Veracruz. One apocryphal tale about the punitive expedition captures much of the popular feeling: as U.S. troops approached a small village in Chihuahua, a Carrancista officer stopped a Mexican who was fleeing and asked if he was a Villista; the man replied: "Today all Mexicans should be Villistas." The officer gave him a horse and let him escape. The two corridos below, although they are wildly inaccurate and highly imaginative, nevertheless convey the sense of national pride that many Mexicans invested in Villa during and after the punitive expedition.

Corrido of Columbus[6]

Anonymous

When we entered the town of Columbus, all the gringos just turned tail and ran.

And our leader, Francisco Villa, shouted: "Mexicans, attack the barracks!"

Pancho Villa, the brave guerrilla, and his soldiers at the bottom of the canyon,
were fighting to the very last bullet in defence of our nation.

The gringos think they can finish us off, just a handful of Villistas.
They have a thousand rifles and cannons, but they will lose them in the mountains.

What did the North Americans think; that combat is only a dance?
Now they are retreating back to their country, their heads hanging down in shame.

Mister Wilson, Carranza and his gang, they just wanted to grab everything.
But our leader Pancho Villa is alive, and he's going to take it all back.

Goodbye to Mexico, for Carranza let the Americans cross the border,
with ten thousand soldiers and five hundred airplanes, to chase Pancho Villa
and kill him!

But Francisco Villa is no longer on horseback and neither are his men;
Francisco Villa has his own airplanes, and he flies them with comfort!

The Pursuit of Villa[7]

Anonymous

In our country, beloved Mexico, Carranza was the governor
who let twelve thousand Americans in, to punish Pancho Villa

Ay! Carranza told them gravely: "If you are brave and want to chase him,
I will let you; you have my permission to learn how to die."

And so they pursued him without ever seeing him, and had to retreat,
very sad and dejected, for they could not catch Pancho Villa.

The soldiers came from Texas, and the poor boys began to tremble;
after eight hours of marching they were tired and wanted to go home.

As the soldiers were fainting from the heat of the sun,
Pancho Villa just mocked them with feelings of pity

Pancho Villa is no longer on horseback and neither are his men
Pancho Villa owns airplanes which he flies in great comfort.

When they thought Villa dead, they cried out with such joy:
"Now, dear comrades, we can go back to Texas with honour!"

But Villa was alive and they never will catch him;
if they want to see him, they can find him in Parral.

When they began the pursuit, Pancho Villa was disguised,
like an American soldier, and so were all of his men.

Villa made an American flag to fool the American pilots;
And took them as prisoners when they landed their planes.

Pancho Villa told the prisoners that he had saved them, for
in Carrizal six hundred were killed, thanks to Don Venustiano.

Ay! Carranza told them sternly: "if you are brave and want to pursue him
I'll give you my permission, if you want to learn to die."

What did these Americans think? That combat was like a dance?
With shames on their faces, they retreated again to their country.

Now they know that they will die in Mexico, and they will die like that
each day;
With a single Mexican soldier waving our flag in his hands

When the gringos entered Chihuahua, they thought they would give us a
scare;
They thought this was Nicaragua,[8] but now they are too afraid to return.

CHAPTER TEN
THE END OF THE REVOLUTION?

In the aftermath of the punitive expedition, and the adoption of the Constitution of 1917, the armed phase of the Mexican Revolution entered its denouement. The ability of the Villistas and Zapatistas to sustain their resistance to the Constitutionalist government, although tenacious, steadily waned—especially in the aftermath of an epidemic of the Spanish influenza that cut a devastating swath through Mexico from October 1918 to the end of January 1919, killing perhaps half-a-million people. While pacification was still paramount for the Constitutionalist government, the central focus of social and political struggles was shifting away from the armed conflict with Villa and Zapata and toward ending the persistent tension between Carranza's political conservatism and the social reformism embodied in the Constitution of 1917. In a rerun of the Revolutionary Military Convention, the 200 delegates at the constitutional convention in Querétaro had divided into two opposing factions: once again, the minority were Carranza loyalists who supported the first chief's desire to slightly amend the 1857 Constitution to strengthen presidential powers; the majority rallied behind Alvaro Obregón—now the minister of war—and resurrected the political program of the ill-fated "third force" that had almost carried the Military Convention at Aguascalientes. Not that the Obregonistas were all that radical per se—the overwhelming majority were bourgeois or middle class and only a tiny handful considered themselves to be socialists. Nevertheless, they and Obregón had concluded that it was necessary to consolidate Constitutionalist rule by making major radical concessions to the interests of workers and peasants.

In March 1917, Carranza finally became a constitutionally elected president, but his policies increasingly ran counter to the spirit and the letter of the new Constitution. As early as 1916, Carranza moved to crush the Casa del Obrero Mundial and other unions when his army no longer needed the services of the Red Battalions. He remained hostile to organized labor after 1917, and refused to enforce constitutional provisions for the eight-hour day and a minimum wage. This later redounded to the benefit of Obregón who wasted no time in establishing his patronage over the Confederación Regional Obrera Mexicana (Regional Confederation of Mexican Workers, or CROM), which was formed in May 1918. Carranza also flouted the Constitution's mandate for agrarian reform; rather than liquidating the haciendas and returning land to peasants, Carranza actually returned confiscated properties to Porfirian-era landowners. However, the Constitution limited Carranza's presidency to one term, and with the presidential elections scheduled for July 1920, the political struggle focused on choosing a successor. By January 1919, both Alvaro Obregón and Pablo González were busy preparing the ground for their as-yet unannounced presidential campaigns. In the midst of the resulting turmoil—the splitting apart of the Constitutionalist coalition, combined with worker and peasant unrest—both Villa and Zapata made a final bid to ride the cresting wave of discontent with Carranza.

★ ★ ★

The Criminal Ambition of Venustiano Carranza[1]

Emiliano Zapata, January 1, 1919

By 1919, Zapatista fortunes were declining. The forces of Pablo González were waging a ruthless scorched-earth campaign in Morelos that exceeded even those waged earlier by Generals Huerta and Robles under Madero. In addition, the population of the state was devastated by warfare, periodic famine, and the Spanish influenza; over the course of the Revolution, the population of Morelos has decreased by at least 25 percent. In desperation, Zapata sought to reach out and form any possible alliances that might sustain the struggle against Carranza, hoping to exploit the differences that were then rising to fore among Obregón, González, and Carranza. This is the logic underlying the following manifesto issued by Zapata on New Year's Day, 1919. In it, Zapata called for all revolutionaries to unite against Carranza's "exclusionary" policies and to condemn his refusal to implement to social reform provisions of the Constitution. Zapata also picked up the theme first mooted by Villa in 1916, which characterized Carranza as a traitor to Mexico's national interests. In this manifesto, Zapata accused the Mexican President of having sold out Mexico to the interests of German militarism during World War I, just concluded. This charge was unfounded; Carranza had permitted German espionage—including his minister of communications—and propaganda on Mexican soil, but he otherwise maintained neutrality in the world war and twice refused German proposals for a formal alliance.

The criminal ambition of Venustiano Carranza continues to grow. As if there were not enough difficulties already, new and large conflicts now threaten the Republic from within as well as from without. His domestic policies are intransigent and exclusionary, while his foreign policies are perfidious and misleading. Both are filled with double-dealing and hypocrisy. He is false in everything and disloyal to everyone. Today Carranza has attracted the hatred of his compatriots, even those who originally supported him. He has also earned bitterness and animosities from foreign nations.

His policy has been characterized by insolence and by the systematic exclusion of any group or personality that is not willing to be as an instrument for his tortuous designs. Ever since convening and then ignoring the Revolutionary Convention in 1914, Carranza has elevated himself with unparalleled boldness above the interests of the revolution and the nation. Ever since the Convention, his autocratic and exclusionary tendencies have expanded to a scandalous proportion.

He has declared all his adversaries to be outside the law to, deprived them of the right to vote and to stand in elections; this has applied not only to reactionary elements, but also to those who served the Convention, including Villismo and the Revolution of the South. Ignoring public opinion and the popular will, he seeks to govern only with his own circle and does not even comply with their wishes. He has gradually reduced and narrowed the circle of his own supporters and his friends.

Countless revolutionaries have separated themselves from Carranza, convinced that he is false and has betrayed the Revolution. Many have taken up arms, following the example of Francisco Coss, Eulalio and Luis Gutiérrez, Luis Caballero, Eugenio Gómez and many other chiefs who have been outraged by Carranza's behaviour and have rebelled against him.

But there is more. If these facts do not speak for themselves and with enough eloquence, Carranza has endeavoured to widen the chasm between him and genuinely revolutionary opinion. Still fresh in everyone's memory are the debates of the Carrancista Congress when the opposition, represented by the Constitutional Liberal Party, tried to curb the attacks of Carranza and compel him to adopt reforms desired by the people. Carranza became so obstinate that he declared war on his opponents rather than conform to the demand of revolutionary opinion. He attacked them so relentlessly in the press that the Constitutional Liberal Party and its members finally turned their back on and renounced any effort to strengthen the work of government. Today the members of that party are proscribed, its candidates for Congress are everywhere crushed by the official slates, and so-called popular representation has been reduced to a confusing and bland conglomerate of the dictator's unconditional friends.

With their support Carranza hopes to complete his work of ambition and arrogant conceit. He is reforming the new Constitution of 1917 to make it more to his taste. He is removing everything that he dislikes and will continue like this until a constitution that once had a radical vision is reduced to a set of precepts that only serve as the basis for the autocracy and reaction of Carranza. It has already been proposed that the right of workers to strike be limited. It has already been suggested that henceforth no draft laws will be discussed by Congress after the mandatory deadline that he set. With these and future innovations, created at the mere whim of Carranza, what will remain of the Constitution of 1917?

This is why Carranza is becoming isolated, why there is such a growing distance between him and those who were once his supporters. Instead of seeking settlements with the opposing factions, with opposition parties, or military groups who profess different views, he has rejected all of them.

He believes that only he knows how to think, that only he has this gift, that only he can solve the agrarian problem, the problems of workers, political problems, and international issues. For him there are no other legitimate parties or factions, no other intellectual center or opinion to be heard. What he says is the supreme truth, and what he decides must prevail over all other interests, all other parties, all other convictions held by citizens of the Republic.

With a pedantic and exclusionary approach, Carranza has succeeded in ruining the country, and he has tarnished Mexico before foreign powers. He chose to be intransigent against the justice, reason and law represented by the allies in the war in Europe, and conducted himself in an arrogant and Machiavellian way. While claiming to be neutral, he protected the interests of Kaiserism. He protected the agents of Teutonic espionage. He placed all radio and telegraph installations in the country under German control. He unleashed furious newspaper propaganda against the allies. He received big loans from German banks. And to complete his work he tried to inflame and excite public opinion against our country's powerful northern neighbours, imitating his predecessor Victoriano Huerta.

This is how Carranza maintained neutrality and complied with his international responsibility during the greatest conflict in world history! In this conflict, Carranza openly sided against law and on the part of imperialism, against democracy and in favour of a military government, against the people's freedoms. He supported the Kaiser who symbolized the aristocratic hierarchies and the decrepit political parties who constituted a threat to the freedoms of Europe and the world. While maintaining neutrality, he conspired against justice, together with a man—the Kaiser of Germany—who was the scourge of its people, a great people who knew how to shake the yoke of an insufferable megalomaniac at the earliest opportunity.

Carranza's obstruction of the goals and interests of the allied powers was evident in all his actions. He attacked French and British capital, and looted banks with deposits from the nationals of these countries. With regard to oil, he issued laws that pleased the German ambassador, and that tried to deny this essential raw material to the industries and fleets of England and its allies. If, after all this, conflicts arise and difficulties mount for our country, nobody but Carranza will be to blame. For this reason, we denounce him, before the nation and before history. Carranza, and only Carranza, will have to answer for his intrigues, his falsehoods, his double-dealing and his felonies.

All honest revolutionaries, all respectable Mexicans, must now sound the alarm. Today more than ever we must unite against the source of our national misfortune. Today as never before, we must put a stop to a shameful situation whereby the whims of one man substitutes for the will of all Mexicans. Once we have overthrown the tyrant, we will again be masters of our destiny and genuinely assume our responsibilities in the eyes of the world. We can no longer tolerate a usurper who has only ever represented the interests of a clique, but never those of the Republic.

The gravity of the current historic moment requires all conscious revolutionaries to maintain a calm and composed conduct. Let us not [be] surprised or misled by the official lies of the press. Let us act with the prudence and the fortitude that the Republic needs. Let us preserve the cohesion and unity that will allow us to tackle any situation however difficult it may be. May that vile schemer fall soon, so that tomorrow we might appear before the cultured countries of the world, without the mark of shame on our foreheads, and with full awareness of righteousness and justice.

The Assassination of Emiliano Zapata

Less than four months later Emiliano Zapata was dead, the victim of an act of betrayal and assassination that shocked not only the Zapatistas, but even high members of the Constitutionalist government. The plot was hatched by General Pablo González, some believe in collaboration with Carranza. In March, Zapata discovered that González was embroiled in a conflict with one of his subordinates, Colonel Jesús Guajardo. As had happened often during the Revolution, Zapata hoped to suborn Guajardo and convince him to switch sides; he therefore proposed this in a letter to the Colonel. González instructed Guajardo to play along, in the hopes of trapping and killing Zapata. Guajardo lured Zapata to the Chinameca Hacienda on April 10, where the ambush killed Zapata and a small number of his personal escort. The leadership passed to Gildardo Magaña, but the death of Zapata demoralized his movement and prompted a search to find the way out of the civil war, without losing everything that the peasant rebels had achieved in Morelos. As it turned out, the exit from the labyrinth appeared in the form of an Obregonista rebellion against Carranza one year later, in April 1920.

The next three documents address the killing of Zapata. The first two are the earliest known reports of the ambush. The first is by Salvador Reyes, Zapata's personal secretary, who survived the ambush and sent his account to Magaña later that day. The second is Guajardo's version, sent to Pablo González five days after the fact. The final document is from a Mexican American newspaper, *El Heraldo Mexicano* (*The Mexican Herald*) published in Los Angeles, California, which expresses the grief and shock felt by many Mexicans abroad; the author, Ramón Puente, blames Carranza for the killing and compares him to Shakespeare's MacBeth who is prepared to commit murder in pursuit of his political ambitions.

Zapata Was Treacherously Murdered[2]

Salvador Reyes Avilés, April 10, 1919

It is with profound sorrow that I must inform you that today, at half past one p.m., Citizen General-in-Chief, Emiliano Zapata was treacherously murdered by the troops of Colonel Jesús Guajardo. They carried out this premeditated and cowardly act at the Hacienda of San Juan Chinameca. So that you are properly informed about this tragic event I will recount the following details:

As you know, we had learned about the deep discord between Pablo González and Jesús Guajardo. As a result, General Zapata wrote to the latter with an invitation to join the revolutionary movement.

Guajardo replied to this letter: "I am ready to work alongside you, as long as you give sufficient guarantees for me and my soldiers." Citizen General-in-Chief Zapata immediately answered Guajardo and offered every kind of assurances and congratulated him for being "a man of his word and a gentleman, who will honour his promises to the letter." The negotiations continued in this way, by correspondence.

That very day, in order to definitively arrange things, the Citizen General-in-Chief sent Citizen Colonel Feliciano Palacios to Guajardo's camp in San Juan Chinameca. He remained with Guajardo until yesterday at four in the morning, when Guajardo headed to Jonacatepec. Palacios wrote two letters to the Chief, copies of which are attached to this. Here I must mention a fact that made Citizen General-in-Chief Zapata confident in the "sincerity" of Guajardo.

The rumours were circulating publicly that Guajardo was negotiating to join with Citizen General Zapata. These rumours were so widespread that some villagers asked the Citizen General-in-Chief to punish some traitors who were responsible for looting, rapes, murders and robberies. These were committed by Victoriano Bárcenes and his men who were then under the command of Guajardo.

In view of this justified request Citizen General Zapata ordered Guajardo to arrest Bárcenes and 59 of his soldiers, under the command of General Margarito Ocampo and "Colonel" Guillermo López. They were all disarmed by Guajardo at a place called "Mancornadero." This was yesterday while Guajardo was in Jonacatepec.

Upon learning this we went to Pastor Station, and from there Palacios wrote to Guajardo, by order of the Chief, to say that we would meet in Tepalcingo. General Zapata planned go with thirty men and asked Guajardo to do likewise. The Chief ordered the rest of his men to withdraw and headed to Tepalcingo with thirty men, where we waited for Guajardo. Guajardo arrived at four pm, but not with thirty soldiers. He had sixty cavalry and a machine gun.

It was there that we saw for the first time the man who, the next day, would be the murderer of our General-in-Chief, who with all the nobility of his soul received him with opened arms. He smiled and said: "My Colonel Guajardo, I congratulate you with all my heart!" At 10 pm, we left Tepalcingo and headed for Chinameca, where Guajardo arrived with his column. It was nearly eight in the morning at Chinameca.

The Chief then ordered his people (150 men had joined us in Tepalcingo) to wait in the courtyard. Meanwhile he, Guajardo, Colonels Castrejón, Casals y Camano, and Colonel Palacios, went to discuss the coming campaign. A few moments later rumours began to spread that the enemy was approaching. So the Chief ordered Colonel José Rodríguez of his escort to take some men and scout towards Santa Rita. Then Guajardo said to the Chief: "General, if you head towards Piedras Encimada, I will head towards the plain." The Chief agreed and took thirty men to the point indicated. Getting ready to march, Guajardo mustered his men, and returned saying: "My General, I am at you orders. Will you take Infantry or Cavalry?"

"The plain has a lot of fences; you take the infantry" replied General Zapata. At Piedras Encimadas we explored the countryside but, seeing no enemy movement, we returned to Chinameca. It was approximately half past twelve. The Chief sent Colonel Palacios to Guajardo, to ask about the promised delivery of five thousand cartridges.

Then "Captain" Ignacio Castillo and a sergeant presented themselves, and in the name of Guajardo invited the Chief to enter the Hacienda, where "Guajardo and Palacios were arranging things." We waited another half an hour with Castillo, and after repeated invitations, the Chief agreed. "We're going to see the Colonel; no more than ten men are going with me," he ordered, mounting the sorrel horse that Guajardo had given him the previous day.

He approached the door of the house of the Hacienda. As ordered, we ten men followed, leaving the others to rest confidently under the shade of the trees with their carbines at rest. The guard formed and seemed ready to do our Chief honours. The bugle sounded the call of honour three times, and as it played the last note our General-in-Chief arrived at the threshold of the door. Then in the most perfidious, most cowardly, and most villainous manner, at point blank range, and without giving him time to draw his pistols, the soldiers who were presenting arms fired their rifles twice and our unforgettable General Zapata fell, never to rise again!

His faithful assistant Agustín Cortes died at the same time. Palacios also must have been killed inside the Hacienda. The surprise was terrible. Soldiers of the traitor Guajardo were high up in the parapets, in the plain, in the gully, and everywhere (about a thousand men) and they discharged their weapons against us. Very soon resistance was futile. On the one hand, we were a handful of men shocked by the loss of our Chief, and on the other hand, the enemy soldiers took advantage of our natural confusion to attack us fiercely. That was the tragedy. So it happened. Guajardo betrayed the nobility of our General-in-Chief. So Emiliano Zapata died.

Official Report on the Assassination of Zapata[3]

Colonel Jesús Guajardo, April 15, 1919

Commander:

I am honoured to report on the operations carried out during April 8 to 10 of this month.

April 8: Having received instructions from Citizen General-in-Chief of the Army Corps of Operations in the South, Pablo Gonzalez, I left with my escort heading towards Chinameca at 8:15 am, arriving at Moyotepec at 11 am the same day. There I waited for an escort of fifty men commanded by a second captain. I left that point and reached Chinameca at 3 pm. I then proceeded to communicate with Emiliano Zapata through the so-called General Feliciano Palacios, secretary of the aforementioned Zapata, who spent a few days with our detachment, finalizing arrangements to incorporate me and my men, unknown to the Supreme Government, receiving later instructions.

April 9: At one o'clock this morning, leading my men, mounted, fully armed and well-supplied with ammunition, we left the Chinameca Hacienda heading to Huichila Station, arriving there at 7 am, where we foddered the horses and received instructions for the attack on Jonacatepec. We headed there at 9 am and arrived within a kilometre of that place at 12:45 pm, where, as agreed, I met the men waiting for me, led by Citizen Captain Salgado, of the 66th Regiment. We then proceeded to attack and capture the plaza, fighting for half an hour, losing two men of the troop who died in the battle.

At 4 pm, I left Jonacatepec to meet Emiliano Zapata for the first time in front of the Pastor Station, bringing approximately 600 men. I was well received by the southern ringleader, who expressed his desire to meet my officers. This was done immediately. I was invited to move out to Tepalcingo, where Zapata accepted my forces. We spent the night there, where there was a force of Zapatistas of close to 1300.

At 8 am, Zapata, with a force of approximately four hundred men, came to inform me that Constitutionalist forces numbering three thousand were advancing to attack us. He gave orders to some of his forces to fight them and ordered to me to stay in my place. Meanwhile Emiliano and his escort occupied Piedra Encimada in order to repel an attack.

At this time the so-called Generals Castrejón, Zeferino Ortega, Lucio Bastida, Gil Muñoz and Jesús Capistrán arrived, bringing with them forces close to 2500 men.

At 1:30 pm, I was at the Hacienda with Castrejón, Palacios, Bastida and another general whose name I do not remember, who came to call for Emiliano Zapata. Citizen Captain Salgado also arrived at this time.

At 2 pm, Zapata arrived with 100 to enter the Hacienda. I had arranged in advance to have the guard at the entrance give him honours, with orders to fire on the ringleader at the second call of honour, while the rest of the force was organized and ready to fight his men. The result was that at 2:10 pm he appeared before the guard who opened fire and killed Emiliano Zapata himself, Zeferino Ortega, and Gil Muñoz as well as other generals and troops who could not be identified. The casualties, dead and wounded, were approximately 30 men.

At the same time, I personally shot Palacios, while Castrejón y Bastida was also killed on the spot. I note that Citizen Captain Salgado, who had been at my side left at the precise time of discharge, returning moments later. There was already a mounted force that pursued the enemy in different directions to completely disperse them, leaving large numbers of dead and wounded, including the so-called General Capistrán.

An hour later, the bugler sounded Bota Silla with the aim delivering the corpse of Zapata. Half an hour later, at 4 pm, I left the Hacienda with my force, heading towards Cuautla, where we arrived at 9:10 pm, delivering the corpse to Citizen General-in-Chief of the Army Corps of Operations in the South, Pablo González, as proof that I fulfilled the order I was given 60 hours earlier.

This day, we lost 16 men.

I am honoured, my General, to present my obedience and respect.

The Death of Zapata[4]

Dr. Ramón Puente, May 19, 1919

Carranza must be content, for killing Zapata must mean to him, more or less, what it meant for Huerta to have murdered Madero. It is the eternal mistake of all tyrants who believe that their enemies are men, not the ideas that these men embody. Zapata, much more than a man, represented and will continue to represent the unstoppable strength of an idea.

The death of this fighter does mean the disappearance of a great enemy of Carranza, an enemy who was as much his rival as Francisco Madero and Francisco Villa. But Zapatismo is not finished, and will yet rise from the ashes of its apostle and martyr. A new champion will appear before Carranza, like the shadow of Banquo at Macbeth's banquet, the character in Shakespeare's tragedy who symbolizes the homicidal madness of political ambition.

Carranza, with a cold heart, but with a conscience dripping in blood—and which "cannot be cleaned with oceans of water"—has seen many revolutionaries fall, men who dreamed of a better Mexico in good faith and without political ambition—such men as Calixto Contreras the good, Orestes Pereyra the honest, and Zapata the visionary. They were simple men who took to heart the cause of the humble classes to which they belonged and who were ready to sacrifice their lives for a moral and transcendental ideal.

The revolution was of the people and for the people, but Carranza, when he came to the revolution, never understood this. He wanted the Presidency of the Republic, with such a voracious ambition that he used every means to achieve it. He has tolerated the excesses of revolutionaries, and has pretended to be a reformer with principles that he has never had, either in his mind or in his soul. He has only managed to be a dagger wielded against many good men and the source of hatreds that have divided those who should be brothers.

Zapata is dead—and the deaths of giants are always a joy to dwarves—but his blood is rich with the demand for justice. The time of redemption for the proletarians is approaching, for those who yearn for land usurped by large landowners. Zapata was one [of] the first to struggle for this ideal and everyone heard his call. Villa also may disappear, but his revolutionary strength is also great and tenacious, and he will not be forgotten either. On the other hand, Carranza will go to his grave stained with blood, and History will one day ask in anger, just as God asked the son of Adam: Cain, Cain! What have you done to your brother?

The Revolt of Agua Prieta

The closing chapter in the armed phase of the Mexican Revolution began in early 1920 as Obregón and González launched their respective campaigns for the presidential elections in July. It ended with separate rebellions in April by the two candidates against an attempt by Carranza to impose his own handpicked successor, Ignacio Bonillas, on Mexico. From the start, it was obvious that the presidential campaign might well end in violence, for Carranza wanted a president who would continue his conservative policies, while Obregón's campaign attracted the support of those who wanted fulfillment of the 1917 Constitution. As for González, his politics were closer to Carranza, but he hoped to split the difference between Bonilla and Obregón in order to win the election.

There is little doubt that Obregón would have been the front-runner. Among other things, Obregón had the support of organized labor, and he negotiated an accommodation with the surviving Zapatistas in Morelos. As a result, Carranza tried to remove Obregón from contention, calculating that Bonilla's prospects for victory were more certain in a runoff against González. In addition to an attempt to manipulate the electoral procedures in the various states, Carranza expanded the scope of military control exercised in the north by loyal commanders like General Miguel Diéguez. At the end of March, Carranza ordered the arrest of Obregón, for sedition. On April 5, Obregón denied the charges at a court-martial in Mexico City, and then fled the capital for Guerrero, assisted by his newfound Zapatista allies.

Ten days later, Sonora Governor Adolfo De la Huerta rebelled against Carranza, and then issued the Plan of Agua Prieta on April 22, which called for the removal of Carranza, and named De la Huerta as interim president until elections could be held for a new president. Meanwhile, Carranza angled for an alliance with Pablo González in order to counter the Obregonista rebellion; the failure of this tactic turned on their inability to negotiate a compromise candidate for president. As a result, González mounted his own independent military coup on April 30, even as support for the revolt of Agua Prieta gathered momentum and quickly overwhelmed the Gonzalista coup. Then, on May 7, Carranza fled Mexico City, making for Veracruz in the hopes of resisting the rebels from there, but he never made it. On May 21, members of his bodyguard murdered Carranza while he slept in his camp in Tlaxcalantongo, Puebla.

On May 24, the Mexican Congress elected De la Huerta provisional president by a vote of 224 to 28. Elections for a new president were held on September 5, easily won by Alvaro Obregón.

The next two documents are manifestos issued by Obregón and Carranza as the rebellion broke out against the government. The first is Obregón's statement, issued from Guerrero, which accused Carranza of trying to impose a handpicked successor on the Mexican people. Carranza's statement denies the imposition, and accuses Obregón of having planned an armed rebellion from the very start.

Why It Is Necessary to Take Up Arms[5]

Alvaro Obregón, April 30, 1920

In my Manifesto to the Nation, issued from Villa de Nogales, Sonora, on June 1, 1919, I agreed to include my name as a candidate for the Presidency of the Republic. I did so feeling certain that the political struggle would develop with absolute adherence to the law. I also believed that the current President—who led the bloody revolution of 1913 and who continued the struggle of 1910 when the Apostle of Democracy, Francisco Madero upheld the basic principle of freedom of suffrage—would ensure the strictest neutrality in order to permit the people of the Republic to freely and spontaneously elect their representatives.

However, we have faced a painful reality in experiencing all manner of attacks inspired by the President himself. These have been carried out willingly by his many subalterns who, as the saying goes, are honoured to wear the lackey's uniform.

The current President has forgotten the duties of his high investiture of supreme authority, has violated all moral principles to convert himself into the leader of a political faction, and has placed all the resources of the nation —which were entrusted to his care—in order to serve his own ambitions. He has used the wealth of the public Treasury as a weapon of bribery to pay off the venal press. He has tried to make the National Army into an instrument of his political will, and has intrigued against and slandered members of the Army who remained conscious of their honour as soldiers and their dignity as citizens, and who refused to perform acts that stain their honour and swords.

The political passions of this President have stripped away his respect for lawful authority, and he has made a series of attacks against independent candidates and their supporters. His actions have revealed a divisive and vulgar ambition that stains the path of duty and lawfulness by seeking to impose a successor on the country who will sustain his policies and serve as a tool for the unfathomable ambitions of him and his circle of friends.

This same President, the ex-officio Chief of the Bonillista party—realizing that an overwhelming majority of citizens have rejected his brutal imposition with dignity and civility—has now provoked an armed conflict, hoping to achieve by violence what he could not achieve within the law. Led by the State of Sonora, the authorities and the sons of that State have responded to this provocation with a dignity that has earned the praise of all good sons of the Fatherland.

This same President, stung by the humiliation and contempt produced by the attitude of Sonora, believed that he could control events by establishing different policies for different states, by slandering the independent candidate, and by imposing the strictest surveillance upon him.

Under such conditions, it became impossible to continue the political campaign and it was necessary once more to take up weapons and to take back our rights.

In view of the above facts I suspended the political struggle and, following my old habit of serving the country when its institutions are in danger, I found myself a soldier once again. And at the head of the Great Liberal Party, whose various denominations have supported my candidacy in the political struggle, I placed myself at the orders of the citizen Governor of Sonora, supporting his decisions and cooperating with him until we have deposed those in high power: the executive, for the acts listed above, and the other two—the judiciary and the legislature—for of their complicity in supporting his attacks.

I do not hope to achieve power through the path of violence. I solemnly declare that I will remain absolutely subordinate to the citizen Governor of

Sonora who, with dignity and civility, is fighting to recover the legacy of our rights, a legacy that the people conquered in a bloody ten-year struggle, and which were about to disappear thanks to the criminal behaviour of a man who has betrayed you.

The Subversive Activities of Obregón and González[6]

Venustiano Carranza, May 5, 1920

The sensitive military and political situation spreading across the country requires a frank and accurate account of its origins and the measures taken to deal with it.

I address my fellow citizens in my capacity as President, a post that imposes on me the duty to enforce the law and to preserve order, and as the Chief of the Party that carried out Constitutionalist Revolution, and who bears the responsibility to uphold the principles for which we struggled for ten years. The Revolution of 1913 was an immense protest by the Mexican people against Victoriano Huerta's usurpation, against restoring the dictatorial Porfirian regime, and against the crimes of February 1913 which involved the repudiation of a legitimately elected President. In leading the Revolution of 1913, I not only affirmed the democratic conquests achieved by the Revolution of 1910, but also established once and for all the precedent that all governments in Mexico must emanate from the popular will.

Having triumphed against Huerta and against the dictatorial and militaristic Villa, we inscribed into the 1917 Constitution our economic, political and social ideals. We also adopted principles that would strengthen presidential authority. When I accepted the nomination for President in 1917, I felt this would contribute to our revolutionary activity and because the Constitutionalist Party was threatening to split into two military camps and begin a conflict that would have serious consequences at a time when the country was facing serious economic and international difficulties.

Suffice it to say that the country has gradually followed the path of improvement. The main rebel nucleus is broken and the increasingly prosperous situation has allowed us to improve public services. We all hope that Mexico will soon enjoy a completely normal and prosperous economic and social life.

Ever since I took possession of the Government as Constitutional President, it has been my intention to use every means to fulfill revolutionary principles and to transfer power through peaceful and democratic means, putting an end to the habit of seizing the Government through the endless series of shameful cuartelazos and rebellions that have marked our history from independence onward. I have never failed to express clearly and quite frankly my intention to retire at the end of my mandate, voluntarily handing power to whoever the people elect to replace me. All my efforts have been towards ensuring a peaceful transfer of power to a successor freely elected by the people.

In early 1919, less than two full years after I assumed the Presidency, premature political passions began to stir as we prepared for the elections of 1920. When I realized that the turmoil might cause serious disruptions, I appealed to all candidates, to all public employees, to the Army and to citizens in general, asking them to suspend their electoral activity so that political conflicts would be reduced to a minimum and produce the least amount of disruption. This recommendation was ignored, and some were suspicious that this was a manoeuvre on my part to continue in power. Instead of postponing their activity, they rushed to start the electoral contest.

Two candidates were contending for the Presidency: General Alvaro Obregón and General Pablo González, the two most prominent chiefs in the Constitutionalist Army.

When General Obregón announced his candidacy, he issued a manifesto in June 1919. This dealt with the general basis of his claim to the Presidency, but the policies of General Obregón were left open to speculation. The manifesto portrayed the situation in the country as negative and desperate, placing the blame on "corrupt military officials," referring implicitly to General Pablo González, then under the orders of the government.

The manifesto did not offer a concrete program or acknowledge his affiliation to any political party. It merely guaranteed Obregón's conduct on the basis of his prestige and merits. With respect to foreign interests, it said a few words promising to protect the lives and interests of foreigners and insinuating against my international policies. It can be said that from the very beginning, the electoral campaign of Obregón was based on disapproval of my administration.

Nothing would have been objectionable had the campaign of Obregón continued in this way, but his supporters did not limit their activity to electoral propaganda. Instead they began work in open political opposition, making attacks against the President. In countless rallies and propaganda tours, the speeches of the candidate and his supporters rose in pitch until it became entirely subversive. His press adopted an insulting attitude. Within Congress, Obregón had a strong majority for months, and the activities of the opposition reached a point where the Obregonistas did nothing else than obstruct the work of the President. Bit by bit, it became clear that the campaign of General Obregón, instead of intending to take power through elections, sought the Presidency through force.

General Pablo González, meanwhile, did not issue a political program until much later, for he did not retire from military service until December 31, 1919, and had not been constitutionally eligible to run as a candidate before then. To date, González has issued no propaganda, nor has he made tours or conducted any activity of a democratic nature to promote his candidacy. On the other hand, events have shown that his efforts were aimed at strengthening his support among members of the Army Chiefs of Staff, who at one time had served under him and who support his presidential ambitions.

Over time, this approach led General Obregón and his supporters to believe that General González was an official candidate, supported by the military, and that the aims of González were authorized by me, that González was counting on Government support for some kind of military imposition.

Although there were two military candidates, the supporters of Obregón accused the government of favouring the so-called military imposition of González. Meanwhile, the supporters of González saw Obregón as a competitor supported by military elements who remained loyal to their former chief and who would sooner or later resort to arms in order to achieve the victory of their candidate. By the end of 1919, the campaign was exclusively between two candidates who hoped for victory based on the support of military forces. Everyone assumed that there would be no other candidates, so that the country seemed doomed to continue the tradition of rewarding caudillos.

I began to see a clear danger of an armed conflict that would explode sooner or later and that the Government would inevitably fall into the hands of one of the military caudillos. The idea of a civilian candidate emerged as a possible compromise between the ambitions [of] the two militarists. This evolved into a clear political trend as a remedy against the threat of civil war and caudillismo. Various elements joined the Civilian Party, including civilian and military members of the Constitutionalist Party, as well as officials, civil servants and military personnel who [had] been affiliated to the military candidates.

The entirely democratic character of this Party won support from members of the Army and sympathy from civilian elements of the Public Administration. But this made the militarists view the appearance of a civilian candidate with suspicion. They began a deliberate propaganda campaign to make it appear that the Civilian Party was supported by the President, notwithstanding repeated assurances of neutrality and evidence of my impartial behaviour. From the moment of his candidacy, Ignacio Bonillas was accused by the military candidates of being "the candidate of an imposition," first as a means of discrediting him in the eyes of the public, and then as an attack on the Government itself.

We began to understand that the presidential elections and the transfer of power could present serious dangers if we did not eliminate any interference by the army and if we did not give full assurances that the popular vote would be respected. This being understood, both the Federal and State

Governments wanted to take measures to avert any serious difficulties before, during, or after the elections.

The governors of Guanajuato, Querétaro, Jalisco and San Luis Potosí, initiated and convened a meeting of the Governors of all the States where they proposed legal measures to ensure peaceful elections and a peaceful transfer of power. All Governors were invited to this meeting, but those of Sonora, Michoacán, Zacatecas and Tabasco refused—and they later took an active role in the recent rebellion. The meeting was held February 6–10, and made certain decisions with respect to upholding the law and ensuring effective suffrage. This included placing Governors in charge of monitoring the election and recommending that the army refrain from any involvement with the elections.

At that point, the presidential campaigns of Generals Obregón and González lost their electoral character, and assumed that of a provocation to revolt. General Obregón toured the Republic, ostensibly to make electoral propaganda, while his supporters and former military subordinates made constant trips to regions where they expected to find more followers. In fact, the trips of General Obregón were not made to win votes, but to prepare for an armed uprising—this from the man who, in his manifesto had criticized the immorality of the Army as an indictment against the Government. Meanwhile, he has no compunction against sowing insubordination wherever he goes, using an ostensibly electoral tour to invite and induce military chiefs to rise in arms if his candidacy fails—and as always, accusing the Government of imposing first General González and then Bonillas.

This work of corrupting the army was carried out so persistently by Obregón and his emissaries, that when the Government realised it, a substantial portion of the army was already suborned. General Obregón did not limit himself to seeking the support of the army, but also negotiated with rebels, seeking a rapprochement with the intention of using them later. Some of these rebels, on the verge of defeat, sent emissaries to Obregón and offered their services in the form of an apparently legal surrender to him. General Obregón did not notify the Government about any of these surrenders, and we remain unaware of the arrangements he made with them.

One relatively minor link in this chain of events gave rise to a judicial inquiry that involved General Obregón. The incident was the false surrender of the Felicista rebel Roberto Cejudo. This was relatively rebellion, but it allowed the Government to discover the extent to which General Obregón had prepared a future rebellion, and that this former revolutionary felt no qualms in making an alliance with rebels or in dealing with bitter enemies of the Constitutionalist Revolution and its principles. We do not know about all the deals between General Obregón and the rebels, but the Government is convinced that the General is in contact with Félix Díaz, Manuel Peláez and some forces of Villa.

The judicial inquiry by the military authority concerning the false surrender of Cejudo, did not cause any more personal inconvenience to General Obregón other than to summon him to the capital to testify. But he used the occasion to launch his rebellion, and escaped from Mexico City at the very moment that his supporters began to take up arms under various pretexts. If there had been no evidence of a rebellion by General Obregón, his escape would be a remarkable coincidence in light of other developments. These developments, disguised as a general protest against an alleged attack on General Obregón in the form of the Cejudo inquiry are, however, telling evidence that this is the work of rebellion.

At the very moment when inquiries were being made to determine the collusion between General Obregón and the Felicista rebels, the authorities of Sonora—already supporters of General Obregon—protested that Government measures to prevent disorder during the elections were prejudicial to state sovereignty. Sonoran authorities declared that the state had "resumed its sovereignty" and rebelled against the Federal Government. But Sonora failed to appeal to the Supreme Court to resolve its complaint, indicating that the insurgency of Sonora was decided beforehand and is a rebellion by the supporters of General Obregón. The tepid support for this rebellion indicates that the timing was poor, that it was hasty, premature and unjustified to take up arms against an imposition only two months before the election.

General Obregón was in Mexico City when the insurrection of Sonora occurred, but was careful not to issue an opinion for or against it. But in the early hours of April 13, he disappeared from Mexico City and for several days his whereabouts were unknown. The escape of General Obregón appears to have [been] a signal for the uprisings to begin. On April 15, the Governor of Michoacán, Colonel Pascual Ortiz Rubio, rebelled, supported by some state social defences forces and some federal forces garrisoned there. Almost simultaneously, on April 16, the Governor of Zacatecas, General Enrique Estrada, also took up arms. These uprisings are led by Governors who are among the most prominent supporters of General Obregón, a further indication of a prior agreement to take up arms. Days later, the State of Tabasco followed, but without indicating why it repudiated the Federal Government.

So this is the attitude assumed by the Governors of Sonora, Michoacán, Zacatecas and Tabasco, precisely those who refused to attend the conference of Governors that had been convened to find a peaceful and democratic result for the presidential campaign.

Meanwhile, General Obregón went to Guerrero where he was received and welcomed by the authorities. On April 20, the State Legislature seconded the autonomist movement of Sonora. That is to say, Guerrero declared its sovereignty and invited the Governors of all other States to do the same. Also on April 20, General Obregón issued a manifesto in

Chilpancingo which accused the President of an imposition, declared an armed uprising and repudiated the three branches of the Federal Government; he accused the Executive of an imposition, while it accused the Legislature and the Judiciary of complicity for tolerating the actions of the Executive. General Obregón declared himself at the orders of the Governor of Sonora, Adolfo de la Huerta, and recognized him as his Chief.

Various uprising of a similar nature have occurred elsewhere. The military risings in Zacatecas, Michoacán, Sonora, Tabasco and Guerrero, as well as Chihuahua, Puebla, Oaxaca and México, are a general rising of forces that supported General Obregón. Their numbers, their approach, and the people involved, indicate that they had prepared this rebellion in the event that their candidate did not win, but were forced to rebel ahead of time.

With regard to General Pablo Gonzalez, it is also necessary to recount what has happened. Until the appearance of the civilian candidate Bonillas, there had been an open battle between General González and General Obregón. But when Obregón fled from Mexico City, the attitude of General González and his forces changed, perhaps by virtue of a tacit agreement between the military candidates to suspend the election campaign and begin military activities.

The practical effect is that the troops of González garrisoned in Morelos allowed General Obregon to head south. And since the Obregonista uprising began, the Federal Government has not been able to rely on the forces of González to suppress it. In every instance when they were sent against the Obregonista rebels, they refused to battle. That is what has happened in Cuernavaca and Cuautla, allowing us to say that successive acts of disobedience in the command of General González indicate a premeditated program.

However, the so-called uprisings by forces in Cuernavaca and Cuautla do not have the true character of an insurrection, but resemble a sort of strike, since they refuse to fight but have not adopted an aggressive attitude against the Government. Gonzalista forces have maintained that attitude, for General González was still in Mexico City, had good relations with the Government, and was apparently working within the law for his candidacy.

When the rebellious attitude of General Obregón became clear, General González offered with his services to the Government, hinting at his desire to re-enter the Army and resume command of his former forces, believing that his mere presence in the Army would settle the conflict.

But General González is not entirely at the orders of the Government, for he sought to impose conditions that would preserve his candidacy for the Presidency.

His readmission to the Army meant that he could not continue as a presidential candidate; as a result he wanted Bonillas to also renounce his candidacy, so that both would be in a similar situation. After a meeting between the two candidates, they agreed to waive their candidacies and to place themselves at the orders of the government and to combat the Obregonista rebellion.

General Gonzalez later refused to fulfill his agreement, claiming that he already had tacitly withdrawn his candidacy by assuming command of his troops again. Instead he demanded that only Bonillas should renounce his candidacy. When the Government realized that General González wanted to attach conditions to his military service, it became suspicious, for the Chiefs of the so-called Gonzalistas continued their strike and refused to obey orders.

The Government declined to put him back in command of his old forces. General Pablo González then left the capital on May 1 to meet with his former subordinates. So far, he has not yet stated the political or legal reasons for his attitude, but it is a fact that he has now taken up arms against the government.

Between the Obregonista and Gonzalista rebellions, there is nothing more than a tacit understanding or common purpose of overthrowing the government. However, there are considerable military forces, those under Diéguez, Castro, Murguía, Aguilar, who are loyal to the government and can be counted upon to fight the rebels.

The situation of the country can be summarized thus:

Parts of the Army, who are supporters of Generals González and Obregón, have risen in arms in order to seize power and create favourable conditions for the Presidential elections. However, another part of the army is loyal to the Government, even if it is not yet possible to precisely define how many forces remain loyal.

Among the military elements, it is not yet possible to know precisely which are really in rebellion, and whether or not the officers and soldiers share the purposes of their commanders. In some cases, soldiers and officers have returned voluntarily to loyal corps. On the other hand, we cannot judge with certainty the attitude of loyalists until they begin the armed struggle; this will reveal the tendencies of the contending forces and show how many elements will sustain the President and the legitimacy of his government.

One thing I can assure, without fear of error, is that the conflict has an exclusively military character. The problem is not political, for the people themselves have not taken part. If the situation appears delicate, it is only because the President does not yet know exactly how much of the Army is prepared to sustain his authority.

Under these conditions, no one disputes the impossibility of continuing with an election, nor is it possible that presidential elections will take place at the time prescribed by the Constitution. Civilian candidate Bonillas, and his supporters, have also suspended their activity. Meanwhile the military candidates have ruled out a democratic struggle.

Given the situation, there is no doubt about my duty as President to employ all the lawful means of my office to quell the armed movement and uphold the authority of the Government. It is completely wrong to assume that I will cede to the threat of a rebellion and abandon the post that I occupy by the will of the people. I am firmly resolved to fight as long as necessary and by all means to defeat the rebellion. As the legitimately-elected leader, I must not surrender power to those who have not been legitimately appointed.

As Chief of the Party that carried out the Constitutionalist Revolution, I declare that one of the highest duties that I have is to affirm the established principle that Public Power not be a prize for military caudillos, whose revolutionary merits are not enough to excuse subsequent acts of ambition. It is essential for the independence and sovereignty of Mexico to transfer power peacefully and by democratic means, and to entirely banish the cuartelazo as a means of rising to power. We must always maintain and respect the Constitution of 1917.

I appeal to the Nation not to leave the Government to military caudillos who will continue to bloody the homeland with their internal disputes. As President, I call upon the rebellious officers and soldiers of the Army to rectify their attitude and support of the Government. I also appeal to the loyal Army to refrain from listening to those who induce rebellion. Last, I appeal to the Mexican people to respond to the need for soldiers and to support the Government, to uphold democratic principles, to prevent a repeat of Huerta, and to stop the new usurpers.

The End of the Armed Struggle in Morelos[7]

Gildardo Magaña, June 27, 1920

Born in Michoacán, Gildardo Magaña was a middle-class radical, associated with Dolores Jiménez y Muro and the Social-Political Plan in support of Francisco Madero in 1911. With Jiménez y Muro, Magaña sided with the Zapatistas when they broke with Madero. Magaña remained with the Zapatistas and became a key advisor. Following the death of Zapata, the movement entered a crisis of succession that was not resolved for six months. In September 1919, Zapatista chieftains elected Magaña as their commander in chief. Magaña advocated negotiating an end to the conflict in Morelos on the best possible terms, and found his opening when the breach opened between Obregón and Carranza. In exchange for Zapatista support during the revolt of Agua Prieta, Obregón pledged to respect Zapatista dominance in Morelos. The Zapatistas influenced Obregón's Minister of Agriculture, and convinced his government to adopt a

Zapatista agrarian reform law. The following document is a statement issued by Magaña to the inhabitants of Morelos, urging them to support the rapprochement between Obregón and the Zapatista leadership.

Representatives of various villages in Morelos have approached me to express a desire to know how matters concerning the political and administrative organization of this entity will be resolved, and to spontaneously offer their support for my candidacy for the provisional government, which is also supported by the majority of the revolutionary chiefs of the South.

This apparent support by armed and peaceful civilians alike, was manifest at the same time as intrigues swirled around my humble personality, gratuitous accounts which have until now obstructed a final settlement of the matter in Morelos, leading some to believe that I have been led by personal ambition to accept and uphold the decision of my faithful comrades in the struggle.

I do not want my sense of duty to be interpreted by others as the product of ill intentions, for it is not only as the First Magistrate of Morelos that I can work for the sake of its inhabitants, to ensure the faithful fulfillment of revolutionary promises, and actively collaborate to enhance their indisputable future progress. I am prepared therefore to frankly and voluntarily decline the undeserved and honourable distinction that both the villages and Southern chiefs have bestowed upon me.

It is my duty, therefore, to address all the inhabitants of this heroic State, to let them know that with Carranza removed from national politics, and with the unification of the Mexican revolution, the primary duty of those who have fought for true ideals, is to ensure that the blood shed during the long years of struggle does not fall on sterile ground and that the aspirations of Mexicans are justly satisfied.

Just as in the past, when we shared the sacrifices of the revolutionary camp, so it will be today and tomorrow, as we achieve the pacification of Morelos within a broad range of activities. In this sense, I feel satisfied with placing myself at the service of this progressive State and for the benefit of its inhabitants to whom I am humbly bound with sacred and well-meaning commitments.

With the end of the armed struggle there is an urgent need to restore the sources of wealth that lie in the rich soil of the south. It is therefore imperative that all its inhabitants have the most extensive safeguards, the most comprehensive certainty that they will not be harmed in the least by the arbitrariness of those elements of disorder who sometimes appear after a revolutionary period.

The selfless and long-suffering people of Morelos, who have all made such titanic effort and so many sacrifices, must rest assured that we will strive to bring them complete justice and that their old and faithful comrades will always be vigilant in meeting the aspirations of the revolution led by the unforgettable martyr of Chinameca, Emiliano Zapata.

The Surrender of Francisco Villa

The Revolt of Agua Prieta also cleared the way for Villa's surrender, but Obregón and his Sonoran allies were not as ready to make terms as they had been with Magaña, for the history of relations between them and Villa were far more hostile. When talks began in early July 1919, Villa insisted on a hacienda for him and his men, recognition of his rank as a general, the right to retain his corps of bodyguards, and a payout for his remaining troops. General Plutarco Elías Calles, then the war minister in De la Huerta's interim government, refused and instead demanded Villa's unconditional surrender. When Calles sent troops to compel Villa's surrender, the guerrilla chieftain promptly captured the town of Sabinas, Coahuila, and its garrison as a stern reminder that he still retained a fighting capacity. Villa then demanded and obtained direct negotiations with De la Huerta's government and received the terms he had originally demanded. The corrido below celebrates Villa's surrender.

Corrido of the Surrender of Villa[8]

Eduardo Guerrero

God up in heaven protect me! I am so happy now,
for Mexico is at peace and Pancho Villa is no longer fighting.

He followed his love for our cherished homeland
and surrendered with his men after changing his ways.

Near Nieves is the hacienda of Canutillo;
That's where the famous Pancho Villa retired to.

He was a great patriot who remained in rebellion;
but given guarantees, he disarmed forever.

This modern Cincinnatus,[9] left his command and his honours
to ask Mother Earth to reward all his labours.

He proved his love for the Mexican homeland
by helping to make peace a reality.

In the hacienda of Tlahualillo, very close to Torreón,
the Villistas surrendered their arms to Obregón.

The government paid a year of their wages
and they were content to find new pleasures.

Chihuahua stayed calm and is going to prosper,
for peace now prevails and a new era begins.

The whole northern border is working and tranquil;
it is marching in the vanguard for a happier life.

Blessed Mother Guadalupe, we fall to our knees
to give you our thanks for the surrender of Villa.

He has a big heart, this famous guerrilla,
and the northerners love him and care for him dearly.

He protected the poor and the elderly too;
whoever needs help, can count on him.

When Madero rebelled, Villa formed a guerrilla
and gave the federal army a very good beating.

Villa was at the triumph of Juárez, in Chihuahua
and so was the rebel Orozco who fought with great courage.

But Huerta never liked him and tried to arrest him,
and would have shot him down if he had not escaped.

After the vile cuartelazo, Villa fought the usurper
and the whole northern region witnessed his courage.

He took back Chihuahua, Torreón, and Zacatecas,
and was everywhere famous for his deeds in the war.

When Carranza took the capital, he rewarded Villa badly,
becoming his enemy, so Villa never forgave him.

At the thrust of his sword, Carranza withdrew
and entering the capital, Villa formed a new government.

The war lasted two years, until Villa was defeated;
he retreated to the North so he would not be disturbed.

But the Yankees mistreated him whenever they wished;
but after Carrizal and Columbus he made them afraid.

With the defeat of Carranza, the right time had arrived,
so Villa agreed to surrender with honour.

Our worthy President accepted with joy and sent
General Martínez to meet him next day.

An embrace sealed the pact and, showing great wisdom,
Villa remained in surrender, in Sabinas de Angostura.

With fifty faithful men, they are sowing the land
on the Canutillo hacienda, for they don't want more war.

We give thanks to God and to Mary Guadalupe;
There is no fighting between brothers in the Mexican nation.

END MATTER

MEXICAN REVOLUTION TIMELINE: (1910–1923)

1876–1911   Porfirian Mexico. Porfirio Díaz controls politics in Mexico and is continuously president except for one term, in 1880–1884.

1876

March–November   Revolution of Tuxtepec. Porfirio Díaz rebels against Sebastian Lerdo Tejada and enters Mexico City to take power on November 1.

1883   Porfirian government passes the Law of Vacant Lands.

1892   Village of Tomóchic rebels against the Mexican government, December 1891–October 1892. The Mexican Army crushes the revolt, killing all inhabitants.

Emiliano Zapata conscripted into the Mexican Army as punishment for protesting land expropriations in Morelos.

1893   Heriberto Frías begins to anonymously publish his account of the events at Tomóchic in the newspaper *El Demócrata*.

1894   Doroteo Arango begins his bandit career as Francisco (Pancho) Villa in Durango and Chihuahua.

1900   Ricardo Flores Magón founds the radical newspaper *Regeneración*.

1901   Founding of feminist newspaper *Vesper* by Juana Belén Gutiérrez de Mendoza.

1904   Founding of feminist newspaper *La Mujer Mexicana* by Dolores Correa Zapata, Laura Méndez de Cuenca, and Mateana Murguía.

1905   Ricardo and Enrique Flores Magón help to found the Mexican Liberal Party (PLM).

1906   Mexican miners strike against the Consolidated Copper Company at Cananea, Sonora.

1907   Mexican textile workers strike in Veracruz, Puebla, and Tlaxcala.

1908   James Creelman interview with Porfirio Díaz.

1909   Francisco Madero publishes *The Presidential Succession of 1910*.

Founding of the Friends of the People Women's Club by Gutiérrez de Mendoza and Dolores Jiménez y Muro, and the Daughters of Cuauhtémoc.

1910   John Kenneth Turner publishes *Barbarous Mexico*, a scathing expose of Porfirian Mexico.

Francisco Madero helps found the Anti-Reelectionist Party, which nominates him to run for president of Mexico against Porfirio Díaz. Francisco Vázquez Gómez is Madero's candidate for vice president.

June	Porfirio Díaz bans the Anti-Reelectionist Party, places Madero under house arrest, and is reelected president of Mexico. Madero flees to San Antonio, Texas, after his release from house arrest.
October	Madero issues the *Plan of San Luis Potosí*, calling for the armed overthrow of Díaz, setting the date of rebellion for November 20.
November 19	Ricardo Flores Magón and the PLM called for armed rebellion again Díaz.
November 20	Rebellion against Díaz begins.

1911

March 18	Feminist Dolores Jiménez y Muro co-authors the revolutionary Social-Political Plan.
May 10	Pascual Orozco and Pancho Villa capture Ciudad Juárez, Chihuahua, leading to the Treaty of Juárez on May 21.
May 25	Porfirio Díaz resigns as president and goes into exile. Vice President Francisco De la Barra becomes interim president.
May 27	Ricardo Flores Magón and the PLM denounced the Treaty of Juárez.
August–October	Francisco De la Barra sends General Victoriano Huerta to Morelos to crush the Zapatistas; Madero intervenes.
October 1	Madero is elected president and is inaugurated on November 6.
November 25	The Zapatistas in Morelos issue the Plan of Ayala, denouncing Madero and calling for land reform.
December	Francisco and Emilio Vázquez Gómez rebel against Madero; they are defeated in February. Porfirian General Bernardo Reyes also rebels against Madero, is defeated by Christmas, and is imprisoned in Mexico City.

1912

March 3	Pascual Orozco rebels against Madero in Chihuahua after defeating the Vázquez Gómez revolt.
March–June	Pancho Villa and General Huerta suppress Orozco's rebellion.
June 3	Madero intervenes to prevent Huerta from executing Villa for insubordination. Villa is sent to prison in Mexico City and later escapes to the Texas.
September	Foundation of the radical labor movement, Casa del Obrero Mundial, in Mexico City.
October 12	General Félix Díaz, nephew of Porfirio Díaz, leads failed revolt against Madero in Veracruz and is imprisoned in Mexico City.
November	Woodrow Wilson elected president of the United States.

1913

February 9–18	The Ten Tragic Days. Generals Bernardo Reyes, Félix Díaz, and Victoriano Huerta rebel against Madero. Huerta arrests

	Madero and Vice President José María Pino Suárez on February 18.
February 18	Pact of the Embassy; power-sharing agreement between Huerta and Félix Díaz signed at the U.S. Embassy in Mexico City.
February 22	Assassination of Madero and Pino Suarez outside Lecumberri prison, Mexico City.
February	Zapatistas reject legitimacy of Huerta's government. Pascual Orozco supports Huerta.
March 4	Woodrow Wilson inaugurated as president of the United States.
March 7	Assassination of Chihuahua Governor Abraham González.
March 12	U.S. Ambassador Henry Lane Wilson denies responsibility for the assassination of Madero.
March 23	Governor of Coahuila Venustiano Carranza proclaims the Plan of Guadalupe, declares himself first chief of the Constitutionalist Army, and renounces Huerta.
April	Villa returns to Mexico to raise an army and fight against Huerta.
August 27	U.S. President Wilson announces policy of "watchful waiting" and withholds recognition of Huerta.
September 23	Mexican Senator Belisario Domínguez publicly denounces Huerta. Domínguez is assassinated two weeks later.
October 10	Huerta carries out his second coup, arresting 85 members of congress.
October 17	Carranza sets up a provisional government in Hermosillo, Sonora.
December 8	Villa captures Chihuahua City.

1914

February 3	U.S. President Wilson lifts the arms embargo against Carranza.
March	Beginning of open split between Villa and Carranza.
April 10	Tampico Affair involving arrest of crew from the USS *Dolphin* by Huertista officer.
April 20	U.S. President Wilson asks Congress to authorize intervention at Veracruz.
April 21	U.S. Admiral Frank Fletcher lands sailors and marines at Veracruz. Villa supports the intervention; Carranza and Zapata oppose it.
June 23	Villa captures Zacatecas. Carranza withholds ammunition and coal from Villa to slow his advance on Mexico City.
July 8	Pact of Torreón temporarily resolves conflict between Villa and Carranza.
July 20	Huerta resigns and goes into exile.

August 15	Carranza's top general, Alvaro Obregón, captures Mexico City.
October 12–November 12	Revolutionary Military Convention at Aguascalientes. General Eulalio Gutiérrez elected president.
November 23	U.S. forces leave Veracruz. Generals Alvaro Obregón and Pablo Gonzalez repudiate the Convention and rejoin Carranza in Veracruz. Villa and Zapata support the Convention and occupy Mexico City.
December 4	Pact of Xochimilco. First meeting between Villa and Zapata.
1915	
January 15	Conventionist President Eulalio Gutiérrez breaks with Villa and Zapata and flees Mexico City. Armed conflict begins between Carranza's Constitutionalists and the allied forces of Villa and Zapata.
February 17	Pact between the Casa del Obrero Mundial and the Constitutionalists, forming the Red Battalions.
April 6–15	Obregón defeats Villa at Celaya.
June–September	Obregón defeats Villa again at León; Villa retreats to Chihuahua.
October 19	The United States recognizes Carranza's government.
November 1	Carrancista forces defeat Villa at Agua Prieta, opposite Douglas, Arizona.
1916	
January 11	Villistas raid a train in Chihuahua and kill 16 U.S. engineers.
March 9	Villistas raid Columbus, New Mexico, killing 19 Americans.
March 15	Brigadier General John J. Pershing begins pursuit of Villa in Mexico, eventually with 10,000 troops. The Expedition remained in Mexico for 11 months, but failed to capture Villa.
June 21	Battle of Carrizal between U.S. troops and Carrancista forces.
October	Constitutional convention meets at Querétaro.
1917	
January 31	Querétaro Convention adopts the Constitution of 1917.
February 5	Pershing's Punitive Expedition returns to the United States.
March 11	Venustiano Carranza elected president.
March 13	President Woodrow Wilson establishes full diplomatic relations with Carranza.
May 1	Carranza inaugurated as president of Mexico.
1919	
April 10	Emiliano Zapata assassinated at Chinameca on orders of Carranza.
June 1	Alvaro Obregón declares candidacy in presidential election of 1920. Carranza endorses Ignacio Bonillas.

1920

April 2   Carranza summons Obregón to Mexico City to face charges of treason. Obregón escapes through Morelos with Zapatista help.

April 20   Obregón manifesto against Carranza.

April 22   Revolt of Agua Prieta launched by Governor of Sonora, Adolfo de la Huerta.

April 30   General Pablo González pronounces against Carranza.

May 7   Carranza flees for Veracruz.

May 21   Carranza assassinated in Tlaxcalantongo, Puebla.

June 1   Adolfo De la Huerta inaugurated as provisional president.

September 5   Obregón elected president, inaugurated on November 30.

1923

July 20   Pancho Villa assassinated in Parral, Chihuahua.

THE STATES OF MEXICO

BAJA CALIFORNIA (NORTE)

BAJA CALIFORNIA (SUR)

SONORA

CHIHUAHUA

SINALOA

DURANGO

COAHUILA

NUEVO LEON

ZACATECAS

AGUASCALIENTES

NAVARIT

JALISCO

COLIMA

MICHOACAN

GUERRERO

TAMAULIPAS

SAN LUIS POTOSI

GUANAJUATO

QUERETARIO

HIDALGO

MEXICO

FEDERAL DISTRICT

TLAXCALA

MORELOS

PUEBLA

VERACRUZ

OAXACA

TABASCO

CHIAPAS

YUCATAN

QUINTANA ROO

CAMPECHE

Courtesy of Geoffrey Clive Frazer.

SOURCES AND
COPYRIGHT HOLDERS

Chapter One: Porfirian Mexico

1. **Avitia Hernández, Antonio.** "Corrido de Tomochic," in Antonio Avitia Hernández, editor, *Corrido histórico mexicano*, volume I (Mexico: Editorial Porrúa, 1997), pp. 211–212. [289 pp.] 327 words in Spanish.
2. **Frías, Heriberto.** Heriberto Frías, *The Battle of Tomochic* (Oxford: Oxford University, 2006), pp. 9; 24; 148–149. [208 pp.] 588 words in English.
3. **King, Rosa.** Rosa King, *Tempest Over Mexico* (Boston: Little, Brown, and Company, 1935), pp. 39–44; 60–61. [319 pp.] 1,438 words in English.
4. **Madero, Francisco.** Francisco Madero, *La sucesión presidencial 1910*, 2nd ed. (San Pedro, Coahuila: n.p., 1908), pp. 14–25. 965 words in English.
5. **Manero, Antonio.** Antonio Manero, *El antiguo régimen y la Revolución* (Mexico: Tipografia y Litografia La Europe, 1911), pp. 191–195. 460 words in English.
6. *El País.* "The Strike Continues at Rio Blanco." *El País*, 1907. 272 words in English.
7. *Pearson's Magazine.* James Creelman, "Porfirio Díaz," *Pearson's Magazine*, 1908. 1197 words in English.
8. *Regeneracion.* Ricardo Flores Magon, "La Revolucion," *Regeneracion*, November 19, 1910, no. 12. 915 words in English.
9. **Sierra, Justo.** Justo Sierra, *México, su evolución social*, vol. 2 (Mèxico: J. Ballescá y Compañía, 1904), pp. 436–439. 942 words in English.
10. **Turner, John Kenneth.** John Kenneth Turner, *Barbarous Mexico* (Chicago: Charles H. Kerr and Company, 1910), pp. 120–137. 1068 words in English.

Chapter Two: Madero's Revolution

1. **Altamirano, Graziella, and Guadalupe Villa.** Luis Cabrera, "Open Letter to Francisco Madero, April 27, 1911," in Graziella Altamirano and Guadalupe Villa, editors, *La Revolución Mexicana: Textos de su Historia*, volume III (Mexico: Secretaría de Educación Pública, Instituto de Investigaciones Dr. José María Luis Mora, 1985), p. 95. [492 pp.] 4,100 words in Spanish; 1,408 in English.
2. **Bulnes, Francisco.** Francisco Bulnes, *The Whole Truth About Mexico* (New York: M. Bulnes Book Company, 1916), pp. 156–158. 715 words in English.
3. **King, Rosa.** Rosa King, *Tempest Over Mexico* (Boston: Little, Brown, and Company, 1935), pp. 39–44; 60–61. [319 pp.] 1,438 words in English.
4. **Madero, Francisco.** Francisco Madero, *Plan de San Luis Potosí*, Archivo General de la Nación, Archivo de Genevevo de la O: box 19, folder 2, sheets 1–4. 1,373 words in English.
5. **María y Campos, Armando de.** *Triumphant Entry of the Caudillo of the Revolution*, in Armando de María y Campos, editor, *La revolución mexicana a traves de los corridos populares*, volume I (Mexico: Biblioteca del Instituto Nacional de Estudios Historicos de la Revolución Mexicana, 1962), pp. 164. [408 pp.] 288 words in Spanish.
6. *Regeneración.* Ricardo Flores Magón, "Manifesto to Maderista Soldiers and Mexicans," *Regeneración*, no. 39, May 27, 1911. 1,037 words in English.
7. **U.S. Department of State.** *An Efficacious Remedy for Revolution and Banditry.* U.S. Department of State, *Papers Relating to the Foreign Relations of the United States, 1911*

(Washington: U.S. Government Printing Office, 1912), pp. 445–447. 894 words in English.

8. **Wilson, Henry Lane**. Henry Lane Wilson, *Diplomatic Episodes in Mexico* (New York: Doubleday, Page and Company, 1927), pp. 205–207. [399 pp.] 782 words in English.

Chapter Three: The Apostle of Democracy

1. **Bulnes, Francisco**. Francisco Bulnes, *The Whole Truth About Mexico* (New York: M. Bulnes Book Company, 1916), pp. 175–179. 766 words in English.
2. **King, Rosa**. Rosa King, *Tempest Over Mexico* (Boston: Little, Brown, and Company, 1935), pp. 77–78; 88–94. [319 pp.] 874 words in English.
3. **Madero, Francisco**. Francisco Madero, "Letter to General Victoriano Huerta," Archivo General de la Nación, Serie Revolución y Régimen Maderista: box 1, folder 9, sheet 217. 648 words in English.
4. **Madero, Francisco**. Francisco Madero, "Manifesto to Mexicans, March 3, 1912," Archivo General de la Nación: Cuartel del Sur: box 1, folder 3, sheets 7–9. 1,071 words in English.
5. **Magaña, Gildardo**. "General Victoriana Huerta's Letter to Francisco Madero," in Gildardo Magaña, editor, *Emiliano Zapata y el agrarismo en Morelos*, volume II (Mexico: Instituto Nacional de Estudios Históricos de la Revolución Mexicana, 1937), pp. 55–56. 368 words in English.
6. **María y Campos, Armando de**. *Corrido of the Meeting between Zapata and Madero*, in Armando de María y Campos, editor, *La revolución mexicana a traves de los corridos populares*, volume I (Mexico: Biblioteca del Instituto Nacional de Estudios Historicos de la Revolución Mexicana, 1962), pp. 228–229. [408 pp.] 480 words in Spanish.
7. **Popoca y Palacios, Lamberto**. Lamberto Popoca y Palacios, *Historia del bandalismo en el estado de Morelos* (Puebla: Tipografia Guadalupana, 1912), pp. 92–99. 1,385 words in English.
8. **U.S. Department of State**. *Will the Army Remain Loyal to Madero*. U.S. Department of State, *Papers Relating to the Foreign Relations of the United States, 1912*, pp. 850–852. 443 words in English.
9. **Zapata, Emiliano**. "Plan de Ayala," November 28, 1911. Colección Cuartel del Sur, AGN: box 1, folder 3, sheets 3–6; Archivo de Genevevo de la O: box 19, folder 1, sheet 11. 1,080 words in English.

Chapter Four: The Ten Tragic Days and the Murder of Madero

1. **Anonymous**. Luis Manuel Rojas, "Yo Acuso," in *De como vino Huerta y cómo se fué*, volume II (Mexico: Librería General, 1914), pp. 212–214. 632 words in English.
2. **Figueroa Domenich, J.** *Remove Power from Madero*. J. Figueroa Domenech, *Veinte meses de anarquía* (Mexico: n.p.), pp. 195–198. 752 words in English.
3. **Figueroa Domenich, J.** *Twenty Months of Anarchy*. J. Figueroa Domenech, *Veinte meses de anarquía* (Mexico: n.p.), pp. 16–20; 130–131; 264–271. 962 words in English.
4. **Reed, John**. John Reed, *Insurgent Mexico* (New York: D. Appleton and Company, 1914), pp. 38–39. 221 words.
5. **Sterling, Márquez**. Márquez Sterling, *Los últimos días del Presidente Madero* (Havana: El Siglo XX, 1917), pp. 356–363; 380–384. 1,219 words in English.
6. **U.S. Department of State**. *A Diplomatic Diary*. U.S. Department of State, *Papers Relating to the Foreign Relations of the United States, 1913*, pp. 706–742. 1,713 words in English.

7. **U.S. Department of State**. *Everything Was Done to Save Madero*. U.S. Department of State, *Papers Relating to the Foreign Relations of the United States, 1913*, pp. 770–772. 640 words in English.

8. **Zayas Enríquez, Rafael de**. Rafael de Zayas Enríquez, *The Case of Mexico* (New York: Albert and Charles Boni, 1914), pp. 50–51; 56–59; 75–100; 132–133. 1,149 words in English.

9. **Zayas Enríquez, Rafael de**. Rafael de Zayas Enríquez, *The Case of Mexico* (New York: Albert and Charles Boni, 1914), pp. 124–31. 861 words in English.

Chapter Five: For and Against Huerta

1. **Anonymous**. Luis Manuel Rojas, "Yo Acuso," in *De como vino Huerta y cómo se fué*, volume II (Mexico: Librería General, 1914), pp. 238–241. 646 words in English.

2. **Anonymous**. Luis Manuel Rojas, "Yo Acuso," in *De como vino Huerta y cómo se fué*, volume II (Mexico: Librería General, 1914), pp. 348–355. 663 words in English.

3. **Carranza, Venustiano**. Venustiano Carranza, "Plan de Guadalupe, March 26, 1913," in Estado de Sonora, *Ley que ratifica la adhesion del Estado al Plan de Guadalupe, agosto 20, 1913*, Archivo General de la Nación, Colección Revolución, Régimen Constitucionalista: box 3, folder 68, sheet 1. 138 words in English.

4. **Reed, John**. John Reed, *Insurgent Mexico* (New York: D. Appleton and Company, 1914), pp. 119–121, 137–146. 1,110 words.

5. **Salazar, Rosendo, and Jose G. Escobedo**. Rosendo Salazar and Jose G. Escobedo, *Las pugnas de la gleba* (Mexico: Editorial Avante, 1923), pp. 64–70. 934 words in English.

6. **U.S. Department of State**. *Carranza's Resistance and the Plan of Guadalupe*. U.S. Department of State, *Papers Relating to the Foreign Relations of the United States, 1913*, pp. 763–768. 677 words in English.

7. **U.S. Department of State**. *The Choice Is Huerta or Anarchy*. U.S. Department of State, *Papers Relating to the Foreign Relations of the United States, 1913*, pp. 772–776. 478 words in English.

8. **U.S. Department of State**. *Zapatistas Welcome Non-recognition*. U.S. Department of State, *Papers Relating to the Foreign Relations of the United States, 1913*, pp. 816–817. 260 words in English.

9. **U.S. Department of State**. *The United States Will Not Recognize Huerta*. U.S. Department of State, *Papers Relating to the Foreign Relations of the United States, 1913*, pp. 820–823. 775 words in English.

10. **U.S. Department of State**. *President Woodrow Wilson Is Deluded*. U.S. Department of State, *Papers Relating to the Foreign Relations of the United States, 1913*, pp. 823–827. 1,058 words in English.

11. **Zapata, Emiliano**. "Emiliano Zapata to Genevevo de la O, February 22–28, 1913," Archivo General de la Nación, Archivo de Genevevo de la O: box 11, folder. 10, sheets 31–35. 403 words.

12. **Zayas Enríquez, Rafael de**. Rafael de Zayas Enríquez, *The Case of Mexico* (New York: Albert and Charles Boni, 1914), pp. 148–155; 163–164. 595 words in English.

Chapter Six: The Victory Over Huerta and the Social Revolution

1. **Bulnes, Francisco**. Francisco Bulnes, *The Whole Truth About Mexico* (New York: M. Bulnes Book Company, 1916), pp. 271–297. 641 words in English.

2. **Guzmán, Martín Luis**. Martín Luis Guzmán, *The Eagle and the Serpent* (New York: Doubleday, 1965), pp. 177–78. 449 words in English.

3. **Guzmán, Martín Luis**. Martín Luis Guzmán, *Memoirs of Pancho Villa* (Austin: University of Texas Press, 1966), pp. 304–306. 682 words in English.

4. **U.S. Department of State**. *Watchful Waiting*. U.S. Department of State, *Papers Relating to the Foreign Relations of the United States, 1913*, pp. x–xi. 416 words in English.

5. **U.S. Department of State**. *Tampico Affair and Huerta's Protocol*. U.S. Department of State, *Papers Relating to the Foreign Relations of the United States, 1914*, pp. 448–476. 2,064 words English.

6. **U.S. Department of State**. *Situation in our Dealings with General Huerta*. U.S. Department of State, *Papers Relating to the Foreign Relations of the United States, 1914*, pp. 483–484. 638 words in English.

7. **U.S. Department of State**. *Intervention Violates Mexican Sovereignty*. U.S. Department of State, *Papers Relating to the Foreign Relations of the United States, 1914*, pp. 485–488. 1,004 words in English.

8. **U.S. Department of State**. *Pact of Torreón*. U.S. Department of State, *Papers Relating to the Foreign Relations of the United States, 1914*, pp. 559–561. 556 words in English.

9. **Vélez, Gilberto**. Gilberto Vélez, editor, *Corridos mexicanos* (Mexico: Editores Mexicanos Unidos, 1990), pp. 20–21. 299 words in English.

10. **Zapata, Emiliano** . Emiliano Zapata, "Letter to U.S. President Woodrow Wilson, August 23, 1914," Archivo General de la Nación, Archivo de Genevevo de lo O: box 17, folder 3, sheets 93–97. 1,305 words English.

Chapter Seven: Women, Gender, and Revolution

1. **Henestrosa, Andrés**. "La Soldadera," in Andrés Henestrosa, editor, *Espuma y flor de corridos mexicanos* (Mexico: Editorial Porrúa, 1977), 44–45 [234 pp. 200 words.] 185 words in English.

2. **Magaña, Gildardo**. Dolores Jiménez y Muro, "Plan Político-Social," in Gildardo Magaña, editor, *Emiliano Zapata y el Agrarismo en México*, Volume I (Mexico: Instituto Nacional de Estudios Históricos de la Revolución Mexicana, 1937), pp. 121–124. 630 words in English.

3. **Magaña, Gildardo**. Dolores Jiménez y Muro, "Letter to Aureliano Blanquet," in Gildardo Magaña, editor, *Emiliano Zapata y el Agrarismo en México*, Volume III (Mexico: Instituto Nacional de Estudios Históricos de la Revolución Mexicana, 1937), pp. 396–401. 1,813 words in English.

4. **Nueva Era**. *Nueva Era. The Feminist Creed*, February 17, 1912. 806 words in English.

5. **O'Shaughnessy, Edith**. Edith O'Shaughnessy, *Diplomatic Days* (New York: Harper and Brothers, 1917), pp. 27–29, 55, 101–102, 149–150, 204, 258–259; 1,226 words in English.

6. **O'Shaughnessy, Edith**. *A Diplomat's Wife in Mexico* (New York: Harper and Brothers, 1916), pp. 8, 90, 124–125, 144–145. 623 words in English.

7. **Reed, John**. John Reed, *Insurgent Mexico* (New York: D. Appleton and Company, 1914), pp. 103–109; 130–132. 1,840 words.

8. *Regeneración*. Ricardo Flores Magón, "To Women," *Regeneracion*, September 24, 1910. 1,111 words English.

9. **Vazquez Santa Ana, Higinio**. "La Soldadera," in Higinio Vazquez Santa Ana, editor, *Canciones, Cantares y Corridos Mexicanos* (Mexico: Imprenta León Sánchez, 1925), p. 113. 170 words in English.

Chapter Eight: The Revolutionary Civil War

1. **Carranza, Venustiano**. Venustiano Carranza, *Additions to the Plan of Guadalupe*, December 12, 1914. Archivo General de la Nación, Colección Revolución, Régimen Constitucionalista: box 3, file 68, sheets 5–8. 1,165 words in English.

2. **Iglesias González, Román**. *Manifesto Dismissing Villa, Zapata, and Carranza*. Román Iglesias González, editor, *Planes políticos, proclamas, manifiestos y otros documentos de la Independencia al México moderno, 1812–1940* (Mexico: Universidad Nacional Autónoma de México, 1998), pp. 744–751. [992 pp.] 1,793 words in English.

3. **Mexico, DF**. Government of the Federal District, *Pact of Xochimilco. Emiliano Zapata and Francisco Villa, 64th Anniversary Commemorative Edition* (Mexico: Department of the Federal District, General Directorate of Social and Cultural Action, 1978). 15 pp. 1,697 words in English.

4. **Salazar, Rosendo, and Jose G. Escobedo**. Rosendo Salazar and Jose G. Escobedo, *Las pugnas de la gleba* (Mexico: Editorial Avante, 1923), pp. 98–101. 1,095 words in English.

5. **Sánchez Martínez, Felipe**. "To the Armed Serfs," Archivo General de la Nación, Colección Revolución, Régimen Constitucionalista: box 3, folder 66, sheets 6–7. 803 words in English.

6. **Villegas Moreno, Gloria, y Miguel Angel Porrúa Venero**. "Speech by Citizen President of the Convention Antonio I. Villarreal," in Gloria Villegas Moreno y Miguel Angel Porrúa Venero, editors, *De la crisis del modelo borbónico al establecimiento de la República Federal*, Volume III (Mexico: Enciclopedia Parlamentaria de México, del Instituto de Investigaciones Legislativas de la Cámara de Diputados, LVI Legislatura, 1997), p. 292. 1,440 words in English.

Chapter Nine: Villa and the Punitive Expedition

1. **Avitia Hernández, Antonio**. "El corrido de Columbus," in Antonio Avitia Hernández, editor, *Corrido histórico mexicana*, Volume II (Mexico: Editorial Porrúa, 1997), pp. 236 [257 pp.] 164 words in Spanish. 183 words in English.

2. **Avitia Hernández, Antonio**. "La Persecución de Villa," in Antonio Avitia Hernández, editor, *Corrido histórico mexicana*, Volume III (Mexico: Editorial Porrúa, 1998), pp. 5–6 [270 pp.] 375 words in Spanish. 344 words in English.

3. **Calero, Manuel**. Manuel Calero, *The Mexican Policy of President Woodrow Wilson* (New York: Smith and Thomson, 1916), pp. 32–59. 2,339 words in English.

4. **U.S. Department of State**. *Withdraw U.S. Troops from Mexican Territory*. United States, Department of State, *Papers Relating to the Foreign Relations of the United States, 1916*, pp. 552–563. 2,549 words in English.

5. **U.S. Department of State**. *The Bandits Have Been Protected by Carranza*. United States, Department of State, *Papers Relating to the Foreign Relations of the United States, 1916*, pp. 581–592. 1,631 words in English.

6. **U.S. Department of State**. *Mexico for the Mexicans*. United States, Department of State, *Papers Relating to the Foreign Relations of the United States, 1916*, pp. 619–622. 1,603 words in English.

Chapter Ten: The End of the Revolution?

1. **Avitia Hernández, Antonio.** "La rendición de Villa," in Antonio Avitia Hernández, editor, *Corrido histórico mexicana*, Volume III (Mexico: Editorial Porrúa, 1998), pp.162–164. [270 pp.] 488 words in Spanish. 469 words in English.

2. **Iglesias González, Román.** *Why It Is Necessary to Take Up Arms.* Román Iglesias González, editor, *Planes políticos, proclamas, manifiestos y otros documentos de la Independencia al México moderno, 1812–1940* (Mexico: Universidad Nacional Autónoma de México, 1998), pp. 880–881. [992 pp.] 664 words in English.

3. **Iglesias González, Román.** *The Subversive Activities of Obregon and Gonzalez.* Román Iglesias González, editor, *Planes políticos, proclamas, manifiestos y otros documentos de la Independencia al México moderno, 1812–1940* (Mexico: Universidad Nacional Autónoma de México, 1998), pp. 883–896. [992 pp.] 3,494 words in English.

4. **López González, Valentín.** Jesús M. Guajardo, "Parte Oficial del asesinato de Zapata," in Valentín López González, editor, *Diccionario Histórico y Biográfico de la Revolución Mexicana, Volume IV* (México: Instituto Nacional de Estudios Históricos de la Revolución Mexicana, 1991). 679 words in English

5. **Magaña, Gildardo.** Gildardo Magaña, "End of the Armed Struggle," Archivo General de la Nación, Archivo de Genovevo de la O: box 19, file 9, sheet 63. 465 words in English.

6. **Puente, Ramón.** Ramón Puente. *El Heraldo de México*, May 19, 1919, Los Angeles, California, Archivo General de la Nación, Colección cuartel del sur: box 1, folder 1, sheet 6. 438 words in English.

7. **Reyes Avilés, Salvador.** Salvador Reyes Avilés, April 10, 1919. "Zapata was Treacherously Murdered," Archivo General de la Nación, Colección Cuartel del Sur: box 1, folder 3, sheets 145–147. 965 words in English.

8. **Zapata, Emiliano.** "The Criminal Ambition of Venustiano Carranza," Archivo General de la Nación, Colección Cuartel del Sur: box 1, folder 3, sheets 119–122. 1,253 words in English.

NOTES

Introduction

1. PRI was founded in 1929 as the *Partido Revolucionario Nacional* (PNR), or National Revolutionary Party, under the leadership of Plutarco Elias Calles. During the presidency of Lázaro Cárdenas (1934–1940), the party was reorganized and renamed the *Partido Mexicano Revolucionario* (PMR), or Mexican Revolutionary Party. Its final incarnation as the PRI occurred in 1946.
2. Alan Knight, "Interpreting the Mexican Revolution," *Texas Papers on Mexico: Pre-publication working papers of the Mexican Center, Institute for Latin American Studies* (Austin: University of Texas), p. 9.
3. E. Bradford Burns, *Latin America: A Concise Interpretive History*, 6th ed. (Englewood Cliffs, NJ: Prentice-Hall, 1994), p. 1296.
4. Alan Knight, "Interpreting the Mexican Revolution," *Texas Papers on Mexico: Pre-publication working papers of the Mexican Center, Institute for Latin American Studies*, pp. 10–11. For more discussion of the historiography, see also Thomas Benjamin, "The Leviathan on the Zocalo: Recent Historiography of the Post-Revolutionary Mexican State," *Latin American Research Review* 20, no. 3 (1995): 195–217; Eric Van Young, "Making Leviathan Sneeze: Recent Works on Mexico and the Mexican Revolution," *Latin American Research Review* 34, no. 3 (1999): 143–165; John Foran, "Reinventing the Mexican Revolution: The Competing Paradigms of Alan Knight and John Mason Hart," *Latin American Perspectives* 23, no. 4 (1996): 115–131; and Luis F. Ruíz, "Where Have All the Marxists Gone? Marxism and the Historiography of the Mexican Revolution," *A Contra Corriente* 5, no. 2 (2008): 196–219.

Chapter One: Porfirian Mexico

1. Lesley Byrd Simpson, *Many Mexicos* (Berkeley: University of California Press, 1962), p. 258.
2. Heriberto Frías, *The Battle of Tomochic* (Oxford: Oxford University, 2006), pp. 9; 24; 148–149.
3. Antonio Avitia Hernández, editor, *Corrido histórico mexicano*, volume 1 (Mexico: Editorial Porrúa, 1997), pp. 211–212. Translated by Chris Frazer.
4. Mexicans often referred to soldiers as "pelones," meaning bald-heads, a reference to the shaved scalps of soldiers.
5. Rosa King, *Tempest Over Mexico* (Boston: Little, Brown, and Company, 1935), pp. 33–39.
6. "Porfirito" is a diminutive form of "Porfirio," indicating familiarity and affection.
7. *El País*, January 1, 1907. Translated by Chris Frazer.
8. Antonio Manero, *El antiguo régimen y la Revolución* (Mexico: Tipografia y Litografia La Europe, 1911), pp. 191–195. Translated by Chris Frazer.
9. Justo Sierra, *México, su evolución social, vol. 2* (Mèxico: J. Ballescá y Compañía, 1904), pp. 436–439. Translated by Chris Frazer.
10. Paul Garner, *Porfirio Díaz* (London: Pearson Education Limited, 2001), pp. 207–208.
11. *Pearson's Magazine*, 1908.
12. John Kenneth Turner, *Barbarous Mexico* (Chicago: Charles H. Kerr and Company, 1910), pp. 120–137. "Plunderbind" is now an archaic term, but was then common in radical circles, literally meaning an "association of plunder."
13. Francisco Madero, *La sucesión presidencial 1910*, 2nd ed. (San Pedro, Coahuila: n.p., 1908), pp. 14–25. Translated by Chris Frazer.
14. *Regeneración*, November 19, 1910, no. 12. Translated by Chris Frazer.

Chapter Two: Madero's Revolution

1. Leslie Bethell, editor, *Mexico Since Independence* (New York: Cambridge University Press, 1991), p. 132.
2. Ibid.
3. "Plan de San Luis Potosí," Archivo General de la Nación, Archivo de Genevevo de la O: box 19, folder 2, pages 1–4. Translated by Chris Frazer.
4. Paul Garner, *Porfirio Díaz* (London: Pearson Education Limited, 2001), p. 218.
5. Rosa King, *Tempest Over Mexico*, pp. 39–44; 60–61.
6. U.S. Department of State, *Papers Relating to the Foreign Relations of the United States, 1911* (Washington: U.S. Government Printing Office, 1912), pp. 445–447.
7. Graziella Altamirano and Guadalupe Vill, editors, *La Revolución Mexicana: Textos de su Historia*, volume III (Mexico: Secretaría de Educación Pública, Instituto de Investigaciones Dr. José María Luis Mora, 1985), p. 95. Translated by Chris Frazer.
8. *Regeneración*, no. 39, May 27, 1911. Translated by Chris Frazer.
9. Ramón Eduardo Ruíz, *The Great Rebellion* (New York: W. W. Norton, 1980), p. 149.
10. Francisco Bulnes, *The Whole Truth About Mexico* (New York: M. Bulnes Book Company, 1916), pp. 156–158.
11. Henry Lane Wilson, *Diplomatic Episodes in Mexico* (New York: Doubleday, Page and Company, 1927), pp. 205–207.
12. Armando de María y Campos, editor, *La revolución mexicana a traves de los corridos populares*, volume I (Mexico: Biblioteca del Instituto Nacional de Estudios Historicos de la Revolución Mexicana, 1962), p. 164. Translated by Chris Frazer.

Chapter Three: The Apostle of Democracy

1. Ibid., pp. 229–229. Translated by Chris Frazer.
2. The author confused this meeting in Mexico City with a second one in Cuautla at the end of August 1911.
3. The term "ranchero" is not analogous to "rancher." In Central Mexico, a ranchero was a small farmer.
4. "Campesino" is a general term for "peasant."
5. In Central Mexico, a rancho was a small farm; a ranchito was a very small farm.
6. "Peón" means an agricultural worker on an estate or plantation, normally a landless peasant.
7. Gildardo Magaña, *Emiliano Zapata y el agrarismo en Morelos*, volume II (Mexico: Instituto Nacional de Estudios Históricos de la Revolución Mexicana, 1937), pp. 55–56; Francisco Madero, "Letter to General Victoriano Huerta," Archivo General de la Nación, Serie Revolución y Régimen Maderista: box 1, folder 9, page 217. Translated by Chris Frazer.
8. Emilio Vázquez Gómez was interior minister, while Francisco was education minister.
9. "Plan de Ayala," Colección Cuartel del Sur, AGN: box 1, folder 3, pages 3–6; Archivo de Genevevo de la O: box 19, folder 1, page 11. Translated by Chris Frazer.
10. "Cacique" is an indigenous term from the Caribbean that originally meant "chief," but came to mean "political boss" in nineteenth- and twentieth-century Mexico.
11. "Personalistas" are those who are followers of an individual rather than a particular ideal or principle.
12. Lamberto Popoca y Palacios, *Historia del bandalismo en el estado de Morelos* (Puebla: Tipografia Guadalupana, 1912), pp. 92–99. Translated by Chris Frazer.
13. "Plateados" literally means "the silvered ones," a reference to the silver used to adorn their clothing.

14. John Womack, *Zapata and the Mexican Revolution* (New York: Vintage Books, 1970), p. 142.

15. Popoca y Palacio is incorrect. José (Ché) Gómez was the mayor of Juchitán in the state of Oaxaca who led a rebellion against the state governor over the issue of municipal autonomy at the end of 1911. Oaxaca state forces assassinated Gómez while he was on his way to meet Madero in an effort to resolve the dispute.

16. Rosa King, *Tempest Over Mexico*, pp. 77–78; 88–94.

17. Archivo General de la Nación, Cuartel del Sur: box 1, folder 3, pages 7–9. Translated by Chris Frazer.

18. U.S. Department of State, *Papers Relating to the Foreign Relations of the United States, 1912*, pp. 850–852.

19. Francisco Bulnes, *The Whole Truth About Mexico*, pp. 175–179.

Chapter Four: The Ten Tragic Days and the Murder of Madero

1. J. Figueroa Domenich, *Veinte meses de anarquía* (Mexico: n.p., 1913), pp. 195–198. Translated by Chris Frazer.

2. Ibid., pp. 16–20; 130–131; 264–271. Translated by Chris Frazer.

3. Rafael de Zayas Enríquez, *The Case of Mexico* (New York: Albert and Charles Boni, 1914), pp. 50–51; 56–59; 75–100; 132–133.

4. Márquez Sterling, *Los últimos días del Presidente Madero* (Havana: El Siglo XX, 1917), pp. 356–363; 380–384. Translated by Chris Frazer.

5. U.S. Department of State, *Papers Relating to the Foreign Relations of the United States, 1913*, pp. 706–742.

6. This is a euphemism for the summary execution of prisoners without trial. Gustavo Madero was captured, tortured, and then shot.

7. Rafael de Zayas Enríquez, *The Case of Mexico*, pp. 124–131.

8. Anonymous, *De como vino Huerta y cómo se fué*, volume II (Mexico: Librería General, 1914), pp. 212–214. Translated by Chris Frazer.

9. U.S. Department of State, *Papers Relating to the Foreign Relations of the United States, 1913*, pp. 770–772.

10. John Reed, *Insurgent Mexico* (New York: D. Appleton and Company, 1914), pp. 38–39.

Chapter Five: For and Against Huerta

1. U.S. Department of State, *Papers Relating to the Foreign Relations of the United States, 1913*, pp. 772–776.

2. Archivo General de la Nación, Archivo de Genevevo de la O: box 11, folder 10, pages 31–35. Anonymous, *De cómo vino Huerta y cómo se fue*, pp. 238–241. Translated by Chris Frazer.

3. U.S. Department of State, *Papers Relating to the Foreign Relations of the United States, 1913*, pp. 763–768.

4. Estado de Sonora, *Ley que ratifica la adhesion del Estado al Plan de Guadalupe, agosto 20, 1913*, Archivo General de la Nación, Colección Revolución, Régimen Constitucionalista: box 3, folder 68, page 1. Translated by Chris Frazer.

5. John Reed, *Insurgent Mexico*, pp. 119–121; 137–145; 145–146.

6. Friedrich Katz, *The Life and Times of Pancho Villa* (Stanford, CA: Stanford University Press, 1998), p. 162.

7. "Pelado" literally means "peeled" or "skinned." It is a colloquial term for poor people in Mexico, and was particularly common in the nineteenth and early twentieth centuries.

8. In this sense, "compañeros" translates as "comrades."

9. U.S. Department of State, *Papers Relating to the Foreign Relations of the United States,* *1913,* pp. 820–823.

10. John S. D. Eisenhower, *Intervention!* (New York: W. W. Norton, 1993), p. 33.

11. U.S. Department of State, *Papers Relating to the Foreign Relations of the United States,* *1913,* pp. 823–827.

12. Ibid., pp. 816–817.

13. Rosendo Salazar and Jose G. Escobedo, *Las pugnas de la gleba* (Mexico: Editorial Avante, 1923), pp. 64–70. Translated by Chris Frazer.

14. Anonymous, *De cómo vino Huerta y cómo se fue,* pp. 348–355. Translated by Chris Frazer.

15. Rafael de Zayas Enríquez, *The Case of Mexico,* pp. 148–155; 163–164.

16. Alan Knight, *The Mexican Revolution,* Volume II (Lincoln: University of Nebraska Press, 1990), p. 91.

Chapter Six: The Victory Over Huerta and the Social Revolution

1. U.S. Department of State, *Papers Relating to the Foreign Relations of the United States,* *1913,* pp. x–xi.

2. U.S. Department of State, *Papers Relating to the Foreign Relations of the United States,* *1914,* pp. 448–476.

3. Ibid.

4. Ibid., pp. 483–484.

5. Ibid., pp. 485–488.

6. Martín Luis Guzmán, *The Eagle and the Serpent* (New York: Doubleday, 1965), pp. 177–178.

7. U.S. Department of State, *Papers Relating to the Foreign Relations of the United States,* *1914,* pp. 559–561.

8. Gilberto Vélez, editor, *Corridos mexicanos* (Mexico: Editores Mexicanos Unidos, 1990), pp. 20–21. Translated by Chris Frazer.

9. Archivo General de la Nación, Archivo de Genevevo de lo O: box 17, folder 3, pages 93–97. Translated by Chris Frazer.

10. Martín Luis Guzmán, *Memoirs of Pancho Villa* (Austin: University of Texas Press, 1966), pp. 304–306.

11. Francisco Bulnes, *The Whole Truth About Mexico,* pp. 271–297.

Chapter Seven: Women, Gender, and Revolution

1. Julia Tuñón Pablos, *Women in Mexico: A Past Unveiled* (Austin: University of Texas Press, 1999), p. 77.

2. Ibid., pp. 81, 91–92.

3. Ibid., pp. 94–95.

4. Ibid., p. 96.

5. Ibid., p. 86.

6. Elena Poniatowska, *Las Soldaderas: Women of the Mexican Revolution* (El Paso: Cinco Punto Press, 2006), p. 26.

7. Ibid., pp. 19–21.

8. *Regeneración,* September 24, 1910. Translated by Chris Frazer.

9. Julia Tuñón Pablos, *Women in Mexico: A Past Unveiled,* pp. 81–82.

10. Gildardo Magaña, *Emiliano Zapata y el Agrarismo en México,* Volume I (Mexico: Instituto Nacional de Estudios Históricos de la Revolución Mexicana, 1937),

pp. 121–124. Translated by Chris Frazer. The other signatories were the following: Joaquín Miranda Sr. and Joaquín Miranda Jr. from Guerrero; Carlos B. Múgica, Antonio Navarrete, Rodolfo and Gildardo Magaña from Michoacán; Gabriel Hernández from Tlaxcala; José Pinelo from Campeche; Francisco and Felipe Fierro from Puebla; and Francisco Maya, Miguel Frías, and Felipe Sánchez from the Federal District.

11. Francisco Bulnes, *The Whole Truth About Mexico*, Volume III (New York: M. Bulnes Book Company, 1916), pp. 396–401. Translated by Chris Frazer.

12. *Nueva Era*, February 17, 1912. Translated by Chris Frazer.

13. John Reed, *Insurgent Mexico*, pp. 130–132.

14. Ibid., pp. 103–109.

15. In this context "compadres" means "pals" or "friends."

16. "Vieja" literally means "old woman."

17. "Let's go!"

18. "Colorados" means "red-flaggers," the name adopted by the troops of Pascual Orozco.

19. "Ready."

20. "Luego" means "later."

21. "Of course."

22. Edith O'Shaughnessy, *Diplomatic Days* (New York: Harper and Brothers, 1917), pp. 27–29, 55, 101–102, 149–150, 204, 258–259; *A Diplomat's Wife in Mexico* (New York: Harper and Brothers, 1916), pp. 8, 90, 124–125, 144–145.

23. Higinio Vazquez Santa Ana, editor, *Canciones, Cantares y Corridos Mexicanos* (Mexico: Imprenta León Sánchez, 1925), p. 113. Translated by Chris Frazer.

24. Andrés Henestrosa, editor, *Espuma y flor de corridos mexicanos* (Mexico: Editorial Porrúa, 1977). Translated by Chris Frazer.

Chapter Eight: The Revolutionary Civil War

1. Martín Luis Guzmán, *The Eagle and the Serpent* (New York: Doubleday, 1965), pp. 340–342.

2. Gloria Villegas Moreno y Miguel Angel Porrúa Venero, editors, *De la crisis del modelo borbónico al establecimiento de la República Federal*, Volume III (Mexico: Enciclopedia Parlamentaria de México, del Instituto de Investigaciones Legislativas de la Cámara de Diputados, LVI Legislatura, 1997), p. 292. Translated by Chris Frazer.

3. Adolfo Gilly, *The Mexican Revolution* (New York: The New Press, 2005), p. 139.

4. The Zapatista delegates were instructed not to recognize the authority of the Convention until it adopted the Plan of Ayala.

5. Villareal is referring to the armed conflict in Sonora between pro-Villista Governor José María Maytorena and Carrancista General Benjamín Hill.

6. Government of the Federal District, *Pact of Xochimilco. Emiliano Zapata and Francisco Villa, 64th Anniversary Commemorative Edition* (Mexico: Department of the Federal District, General Directorate of Social and Cultural Action, 1978).

7. Archivo General de la Nación, Colección Revolución, Régimen Constitucionalista: box 3, folder 68, pages 5–8.

8. Román Iglesias González, editor, *Planes políticos, proclamas, manifiestos y otros documentos de la Independencia al México moderno, 1812–1940* (Mexico: Universidad Nacional Autónoma de México, 1998), pp. 744–751. Translated by Chris Frazer.

9. Rosendo Salazar and José G. Escobedo, *Las Pugnas de la glebe*, volume I, pp. 98–101. Translated by Chris Frazer.

10. Archivo General de la Nación, Colección Revolución, Régimen Constitucionalista: box 3, folder 66, pages 6–7.

Chapter Nine: Villa and the Punitive Expedition

1. There are two forms of interstate recognition. The first and most common form is recognition of a "de jure," or legally constituted, government and usually involves two states signing a mutual treaty that specifies their respective obligations and duties toward each other; recognition of a "de facto" government, or government "in fact," is normally extended to a government that has not come to power through legal and accepted constitutional means, but which nevertheless has an informal political relationship with the other government.
2. Manuel Calero, *The Mexican Policy of President Woodrow Wilson* (New York: Smith and Thomson, 1916), pp. 32–59.
3. United States, Department of State, *Papers Relating to the Foreign Relations of the United States, 1916*, pp. 552–563.
4. Ibid., pp. 581–592.
5. Ibid., pp. 619–622.
6. Antonio Avitia Hernández, editor, *Corrido histórico mexicana*, Volume II (Mexico: Editorial Porrúa, 1997), p. 236. Translated by Chris Frazer.
7. Ibid., Volume III, pp. 5–6. Translated by Chris Frazer.
8. This is a reference to then-contemporary interventions by the U.S. military in Nicaragua.

Chapter Ten: The End of the Revolution?

1. Archivo General de la Nación, Colección Cuartel del Sur: box 1, folder 3, pages 119–122. Translated by Chris Frazer.
2. Ibid.: box 1, folder 3, pages 145–147. Translated by Chris Frazer.
3. Valentín López González, editor, *Diccionario Histórico y Biográfico de la Revolución Mexicana, Volume IV* (México: Instituto Nacional de Estudios Históricos de la Revolución Mexicana, 1991). Translated by Chris Frazer.
4. *El Heraldo de México*, May 19, 1919, Los Angeles, California, Archivo General de la Nación, Colección Cuartel del Sur: box 1, folder 1, page 6. Translated by Chris Frazer.
5. Román Iglesias González, editor, *Planes políticos, proclamas, manifiestos y otros documentos de la Independencia al México moderno, 1812–1940*, pp. 880–881. Translated by Chris Frazer.
6. Ibid., pp. 883–896. Translated by Chris Frazer.
7. Archivo General de la Nación, Archivo de Genovevo de la O: box 19, folder 9, page 63. Translated by Chris Frazer.
8. Antonio Avitia Hernández, *Corrido histórico mexicana*, Volume III, pp. 162–164. Translated by Chris Frazer.
9. This is a reference to the famous general Cincinnatus of ancient Rome, credited with saving Rome from an invading army, who then retired to his farm.

BIBLIOGRAPHY

Archives and Collections

Mexico. Archivo General de la Nación.
Austin, Texas. Nettie Lee Benson Latin American Collection. University of Texas.

Newspapers and Periodicals

El Heraldo de México. Los Angeles, United States.
Nueva Era. Mexico.
El País. Mexico.
Pearson's Magazine. United States.
Regeneración. Los Angeles, United States.

Books

Altamirano, Graziella, and Guadalupe Villa, editors. *La Revolución Mexicana: Textos de su Historia*, volume III. Mexico: Secretaría de Educación Pública, Instituto de Investigaciones Dr. José María Luis Mora, 1985.

Anonymous. *De como vino Huerta y cómo se fué*, volume II. Mexico: Librería General, 1914.

Avitia Hernández, Antonio, editor. *Corrido histórico mexicano*, volumes I–III. Mexico: Editorial Porrúa, 1997.

Benjamin, Thomas. "The Leviathan on the Zocalo: Recent Historiography of the Post-Revolutionary Mexican State." *Latin American Research Review* 20, no. 3 (1995): 195–217.

Bethell, Leslie, editor. *Mexico Since Independence.* New York: Cambridge University Press, 1991.

Bulnes, Francisco. *The Whole Truth About Mexico.* New York: M. Bulnes Book Company, 1916.

Burns, E. Bradford. *Latin America: A Concise Interpretive History*, 6th ed. Englewood Cliffs, NJ: Prentice-Hall, 1994.

Calero, Manuel. *The Mexican Policy of President Woodrow Wilson.* New York: Smith and Thomson, 1916.

Domenich, J. Figueroa. *Veinte meses de anarquía.* Mexico: n.p., 1913.

Eisenhower, John S. D. *Intervention!* New York: W. W. Norton, 1993.

Foran, John. "Reinventing the Mexican Revolution: The Competing Paradigms of Alan Knight and John Mason Hart." *Latin American Perspectives* 23, no. 4 (1996): 115–131.

Frías, Heriberto. *The Battle of Tomochic.* Oxford: Oxford University, 2006.

Garner, Paul. *Porfirio Díaz.* London: Pearson Education Limited, 2001.

Gilly, Adolfo. *The Mexican Revolution.* New York: The New Press, 2005.

Guzmán, Martín Luis. *The Eagle and the Serpent.* New York: Doubleday, 1965.

———. *Memoirs of Pancho Villa.* Austin: University of Texas Press, 1966.

Henestrosa, Andrés, editor. *Espuma y flor de corridos mexicanos.* Mexico: Editorial Porrúa, 1977.

Iglesias González, Román, editor. *Planes políticos, proclamas, manifiestos y otros documentos de la Independencia al México moderno, 1812–1940.* Mexico: Universidad Nacional Autónoma de México, 1998.

Katz, Friedrich. *The Life and Times of Pancho Villa.* Stanford: Stanford University Press, 1998.

King, Rosa. *Tempest Over Mexico.* Boston: Little, Brown, and Company, 1935.

Knight, Alan. *The Mexican Revolution*, volume II. Lincoln: University of Nebraska Press, 1990.

———. "Interpreting the Mexican Revolution." *Texas Papers on Mexico: Pre-publication working papers of the Mexican Center, Institute for Latin American Studies.* Austin: University of Texas, 1988.

López González, Valentín, editor. *Diccionario Histórico y Biográfico de la Revolución Mexicana, Volume IV.* México: Instituto Nacional de Estudios Históricos de la Revolución Mexicana, 1991.

Madero, Francisco. *La sucesión presidencial 1910*, 2nd ed. San Pedro, Coahuila: n.p., 1908.

Magaña, Gildardo. *Emiliano Zapata y el agrarismo en Morelos*, volumes I–III. Mexico: Instituto Nacional de Estudios Históricos de la Revolución Mexicana, 1937.

Manero, Antonio. *El antiguo régimen y la Revolución.* Mexico: Tipografia y Litografia La Europe, 1911.

María y Campos, Armando de, editor. *La revolución mexicana a traves de los corridos populares*, volume I. Mexico: Biblioteca del Instituto Nacional de Estudios Historicos de la Revolución Mexicana, 1962.

Mexico. Government of the Federal District. *Pact of Xochimilco. Emiliano Zapata and Francisco Villa, 64th Anniversary Commemorative Edition.* Mexico: Department of the Federal District, General Directorate of Social and Cultural Action, 1978.

O'Shaughnessy, Edith. *Diplomatic Days.* New York: Harper and Brothers, 1917.

———. *A Diplomat's Wife in Mexico.* New York: Harper and Brothers, 1916.

Poniatowska, Elena. *Las Soldaderas: Women of the Mexican Revolution.* El Paso: Cinco Punto Press, 2006.

Popoca y Palacios, Lamberto. *Historia del bandalismo en el estado de Morelos.* Puebla: Tipografia Guadalupana, 1912.

Reed, John. *Insurgent Mexico.* New York: D. Appleton and Company, 1914.

Ruíz, Luis F. "Where Have All the Marxists Gone? Marxism and the Historiography of the Mexican Revolution." *A Contra Corriente* 5, no. 2 (2008): 196–219.

Ruíz, Ramón Eduardo. *The Great Rebellion.* New York: W. W. Norton, 1980.

Salazar, Rosendo, and Jose G. Escobedo. *Las pugnas de la gleba.* Mexico: Editorial Avante, 1923.

Sierra, Justo. *México, su evolución social, vol. 2.* Mèxico: J. Ballescá y Compañía, 1904.

Simpson, Lesley Byrd. *Many Mexicos.* Berkeley: University of California Press, 1962.

Sterling, Márquez. *Los últimos días del Presidente Madero.* Havana: El Siglo XX, 1917.

Tuñón Pablos, Julia. *Women in Mexico: A Past Unveiled.* Austin: University of Texas Press, 1999.

Turner, John Kenneth. *Barbarous Mexico.* Chicago: Charles H. Kerr and Company, 1910.

U.S. Department of State. *Papers Relating to the Foreign Relations of the United States.* Washington: U.S. Government Printing Office, 1911–1919.

Van Young, Eric. "Making Leviathan Sneeze: Recent Works on Mexico and the Mexican Revolution." *Latin American Research Review* 34, no. 3 (1999): 143–165.

Vazquez Santa Ana, Higinio, editor. *Canciones, Cantares y Corridos Mexicanos.* Mexico: Imprenta León Sánchez, 1925.

Vélez, Gilberto, editor. *Corridos mexicanos.* Mexico: Editores Mexicanos Unidos, 1990.

Villegas Moreno, Gloria, y Miguel Angel Porrúa Venero, editors. *De la crisis del modelo borbónico al establecimiento de la República Federal*, Volume III. Mexico: Enciclopedia Parlamentaria de México, del Instituto de Investigaciones Legislativas de la Cámara de Diputados, LVI Legislatura, 1997.

Wilson, Henry Lane. *Diplomatic Episodes in Mexico.* New York: Doubleday, Page and Company, 1927.

Womack, John. *Zapata and the Mexican Revolution.* New York: Vintage Books, 1970.

Zayas Enríquez, Rafael de. *The Case of Mexico.* New York: Albert and Charles Boni, 1914.

INDEX

FIGHTING WORDS

Fighting Words is an innovative and accessible new military history series, each title juxtaposing the voices of opposing combatants in a major historical conflict. Presented side by side are the testimonies of fighting men and women, the reportage of nations at war, and the immediate public responses of belligerent war leaders. Together, they offer strikingly different perspectives on the same events.

The extracts are short and snappy, complemented by brief introductions which set the scene. They vividly recreate the conflicts as they were experienced. At the same time, they open up new perspectives and challenge accepted assumptions. Readers will question the nature of primary sources, the motivations of the authors, the agendas that influence media reports and the omissions inherent in all of the sources. Ultimately, readers will be left to ponder the question: whose history is this?

Competing Voices from the Crusades
Andrew Holt and James Muldoon

Competing Voices from the Pacific War
Chris Dixon, Sean Brawley and Beatrice Trefalt

Competing Voices from Native America
Dewi Ioan Ball and Joy Porter

Competing Voices from the Russian Revolution
Michael C. Hickey

Competing Voices from World War II in Europe
Harold J. Goldberg

Competing Voices from the Mexican Revolution
Chris Frazer

Competing Voices from Revolutionary Cuba
John M. Kirk and Peter McKenna